Summary of Contents

THE CSS3 ANTHOLOGY

TAKE YOUR SITES TO NEW HEIGHTS

BY **RACHEL ANDREW**
4TH EDITION

The CSS3 Anthology: Take Your Sites to New Heights

by Rachel Andrew

Copyright © 2012 SitePoint Pty. Ltd.

Product Manager: Simon Mackie
Technical Editor: Tom Museth
Expert Reviewer: Louis Lazaris
Editor: Kelly Steele

Assistant Technical Editor: Diana MacDonald
Indexer: Michele Combes
Cover Designer: Alex Walker

Printing History:
   1st Ed. Nov. 2004, 2nd Ed. May 2007,
   3rd Ed. July 2009, 4th Ed. March 2012

Latest Update: March 2012

Notice of Rights

Notice of Liability

Trademark Notice

Published by SitePoint Pty. Ltd.

48 Cambridge Street Collingwood
VIC Australia 3066
Web: www.sitepoint.com
Email: business@sitepoint.com

ISBN 978-0-9871530-2-9 (print)

ISBN 978-0-9871530-6-7 (ebook)
Printed and bound in the United States of America

About Rachel Andrew

Rachel Andrew is a front- and back-end web developer who has written numerous books, including the first three editions of *The CSS Anthology*. Her work in her company edgeofmyseat.com (http://www.edgeofmyseat.com/) informs her writing, ensuring it remains grounded in the real world of client projects, large and small.

About Louis Lazaris

Louis Lazaris is a freelance web designer and front-end developer based in Toronto, Canada who has been involved in the web design industry since 2000. Louis has been working on websites ever since the days when table layouts and one-pixel GIFs dominated the industry. Over the past five years, he has come to embrace web standards while endeavoring to promote best practices that help developers and their clients reach practical goals for their projects. Louis writes regularly for a number of top web design blogs including his own site, Impressive Webs (http://www.impressivewebs.com/).

About SitePoint

SitePoint specializes in publishing fun, practical, and easy-to-understand content for web professionals. Visit http://www.sitepoint.com/ to access our blogs, books, newsletters, articles, and community forums.

For Bethany.

Table of Contents

Chapter 3   Images and Other Design Elements

Chapter 7 Cross-browser Techniques 267

Chapter 8 CSS Positioning Basics 301

Chapter 9   CSS for Layout 337

Index 409

Preface

When SitePoint asked me to write the fourth edition of this book, I initially thought it would take the same format of other editions—adding new techniques, removing content that had become outdated, and updating solutions to a more modern approach. As I started to work through the table of contents, however, I realized that the world of CSS had changed so much that a complete rewrite was needed.

Rather than being about cutting-edge or experimental CSS, this book demonstrates the tips, tricks, and solutions that I use every day. We'll thoroughly investigate the world of CSS3, many of the features of which are supported by the major browsers, and look at how to make these new techniques work in older browsers.

We'll also walk through the use of CSS for layout purposes. While the tools that we have for layout haven't changed much in the last two years, the types of devices that we need to design websites for have changed. Our sites are being viewed on hardware ranging from smartphones to desktop screens. Responsive design aims to tackle the challenge of designing a single site that provides a great experience for all.

This anthology contains minimal theory; instead, I've concentrated on providing solutions that will enable you to quickly get started with a technique or solve a problem. The sections in each chapter can also act as starting points for your own experimentation and creativity. Each one is framed as a specific issue or question, accompanied by a detailed explanation to help you understand the solution and point out any related challenges or alternate approaches.

This is a really exciting time for front-end development, and I hope that this book helps you start to explore some of the features of CSS3, and find answers to CSS problems that you might have.

Who Should Read This Book

This book is aimed at people who need to work with CSS: web designers and developers who've seen the cool CSS designs out there, but are short on the time to wade through masses of theory and debate in order to create a site. Each problem is solved with a working solution that can be implemented as it is or used as a springboard to creativity.

As a whole, this book isn't a tutorial. While Chapter 1 covers the very basics of CSS, and the early chapters cover simpler techniques than those that follow, you'll find the examples easier to grasp if you have a basic grounding in CSS.

What's in This Book

Chapter 1: *Making a Start with CSS*

This chapter is simply a quick CSS tutorial for anyone who needs to brush up on the basics of CSS. If you've been using CSS in your own projects, you might want to skip this chapter and refer to it on a needs basis, when you want to look into basic concepts in more detail.

Chapter 2: *Text Styling and Other Basics*

This chapter covers techniques for styling and formatting text in your documents; font sizing, colors, highlighting text, and the removal of extra whitespace around page elements are explained as the chapter progresses. Even if you're already using CSS for text styling, you'll find some useful tips here.

Chapter 3: *Images and Other Design Elements*

This chapter looks at the ways in which you can combine CSS and images to create powerful visual effects, such as placing background images on elements, applying gradients, making elements transparent, and positioning text with images, among other topics.

Chapter 4: *Navigation*

Every site requires usable navigation, and this chapter explains how to achieve it, CSS-style. We'll investigate image-based navigation, tabbed navigation, combining background images with CSS text to create attractive and accessible menus, and using lists to structure navigation in an accessible way.

Chapter 5: *Tabular Data*

The use of tables for layout hasn't been considered best practice for a long time. Tables should be used for their real purpose: the display of tabular data, such as that contained in a spreadsheet. This chapter will demonstrate techniques for the application of tables to create attractive and usable tabular data displays.

Chapter 6: *Forms and User Interfaces*

Whether you're a designer or a developer, it's likely that you'll spend a fair amount of time creating forms for data entry. CSS provides incredible support in this area; this chapter shows how we can build accessible, usable forms with that extra design oomph. We'll also take a look at some of the diverse HTML5 tools that are simplifying form configuration.

Chapter 7: *Cross-browser Techniques*

How can we make our CSS techniques work in older browsers or on alternative devices such as smartphones? These questions form the main theme of this chapter. We'll also see how to troubleshoot CSS bugs—and where to go for help—as well as looking at methods for integrating CSS3 selectors and HTML5 elements in older browsers.

Chapter 8: *CSS Positioning Basics*

Placing elements correctly on a web page can be tricky, but in this chapter we'll learn to master the art of positioning. Using floats effectively, nifty ways of adding margins and padding, implementing text wrapping, and creating thumbnail galleries—these are all great strategies for your CSS arsenal.

Chapter 9: *CSS for Layout*

In this chapter, we'll explore a range of CSS layout techniques that can be combined and extended upon to create numerous interesting page formations, including different column configurations and print-ready stylesheets. We'll also delve into the emerging sphere of responsive design, looking at both text- and image-heavy layouts that will render effectively and smoothly on a range of devices or screen sizes.

Where to Find Help

The Book's Website

Located at http://www.sitepoint.com/books/cssant4/, the website that supports this book will give you access to the following facilities.

The Code Archive

As you progress through this book, you'll note filenames above many of the code listings. These refer to files in the code archive, a downloadable ZIP file that contains all the finished examples presented in this book. Simply click the **Code Archive** link on the book's website to download it.

Updates and Errata

No book is error-free, and attentive readers will no doubt spot at least one or two mistakes in this one. The Corrections and Typos page[1] on the book's website will provide the latest information about known typographical and code errors, as well as offer necessary updates for new releases of browsers and related standards.

The SitePoint Forums

If you'd like to communicate with other designers about this book, you should join SitePoint's online community.[2] The CSS & Page Layout forum,[3] in particular, offers an abundance of information above and beyond the solutions in this book, and a lot of experienced web designers and developers hang out there. It's a good way to learn new tricks, have questions answered in a hurry, and just have a good time.

The SitePoint Newsletters

In addition to books like this one, SitePoint publishes free email newsletters such as the *SitePoint* newsletter, *PHPMaster*, *CloudSpring*, *RubySource*, *DesignFestival*, and *BuildMobile*. In them you'll read about the latest news, product releases, trends, tips, and techniques for all aspects of web development. Sign up to one or more of these newsletters at http://www.sitepoint.com/newsletter/.

The SitePoint Podcast

Join the SitePoint Podcast team for news, interviews, opinion, and fresh thinking for web developers and designers. They discuss the latest web industry topics, present guest speakers, and interview some of the best minds in the industry. You can catch up on the latest and previous podcasts[4] or subscribe via iTunes.

---

[1] http://www.sitepoint.com/books/cssant4/errata.php

[2] http://www.sitepoint.com/forums/

[3] http://www.sitepoint.com/launch/cssforum/

[4] http://www.sitepoint.com/podcast/

Your Feedback

If you're unable to find an answer through the forums, or if you wish to contact us for any other reason, the best place to write is books@sitepoint.com. We have an email support system set up to track your inquiries, and friendly support staff members who can answer your questions. Suggestions for improvements, as well as notices of any mistakes you may find, are especially welcome.

Acknowledgments

Firstly, I'd like to thank the SitePoint team for making a fourth edition of this book possible. Despite us being spread across a range of time zones, the whole process has been enjoyable and the comments from everyone have served to make this a better book than it would otherwise be.

To those people who are really breaking new ground in the world of CSS, those whose ideas are discussed throughout this book, and those who share their ideas and creativity with the wider community, thank you.

Thanks to Drew, for accepting yet another book project into our personal and professional lives, and for being part of so many discussions that have informed topics covered in this book. Finally, thanks must go to my daughter Bethany, who is understanding of the time I spend working, and makes me laugh when I am tired. You both make so many things possible; thank you.

Conventions Used in This Book

You'll notice that we've used certain typographic and layout styles throughout this book to signify different types of information. Look out for the following items.

Markup Samples

Any markup—be that HTML or CSS—will be displayed using a fixed-width font like so:

```
<h1>A perfect summer's day</h1>
<p>It was a lovely day for a walk in the park. The birds
were singing and the kids were all back at school.</p>
```

If the markup forms part of the book's code archive, the name of the file will appear at the top of the program listing, like this:

```
                                                              example.css
.footer {
  background-color: #CCC;
  border-top: 1px solid #333;
}
```

If only part of the file is displayed, this is indicated by the word *excerpt*:

```
                                                    example.css (excerpt)
border-top: 1px solid #333;
```

If additional code is to be inserted into an existing example, the new code will be displayed in bold:

```
function animate() {
  new_variable = "Hello";
}
```

Also, where existing code is required for context, rather than repeat all the code, a ⋮ will be displayed:

```
function animate() {
  ⋮
  return new_variable;
}
```

Some lines of code are intended to be entered on one line, but we've had to wrap them because of page constraints. A ➥ indicates a line break that exists for formatting purposes only, and should be ignored:

```
URL.open("http://www.sitepoint.com/blogs/2007/05/28/user-style-she
➥ets-come-of-age/");
```

Tips, Notes, and Warnings

 Hey, You!

Tips will give you helpful little pointers.

 Ahem, Excuse Me ...

Notes are useful asides that are related—but not critical—to the topic at hand. Think of them as extra tidbits of information.

 Make Sure You Always ...

... pay attention to these important points.

 Watch Out!

Warnings will highlight any gotchas that are likely to trip you up along the way.

Making a Start with CSS

A web page consists of **markup**—HTML, or XHTML, that describes the meaning of the content on the page—and CSS (Cascading Style Sheets) that tell the browser how the content should be displayed in browsers and other user agents that need to display it. CSS tells the browser everything from the layout of the page to the colors of your headings.

In this chapter, whose format differs to the rest of the book, I'll explain the basics of CSS syntax and how to apply CSS to your web pages. If you're experienced with CSS, feel free to skip this chapter and start with the solutions in Chapter 2.

This book is not a CSS tutorial; rather, it's a collection of problems and solutions to help you perform tasks in CSS. If you're unsure as to the very basics of HTML and CSS, I can recommend the SitePoint title *Build Your Own Website the Right Way Using HTML & CSS* (third edition) by Ian Lloyd as a companion to this book.[1] If you already have some understanding of HTML and CSS, however, this chapter should serve as a refresher, and can be used as a reference as we work through the solutions in the later chapters.

---

[1] http://www.sitepoint.com/books/html3/

How do I define styles with CSS?

The basic purpose of CSS is to allow the designer to define **style declarations**—formatting details such as fonts, element sizes, and colors—and then apply those styles to selected portions of HTML pages using **selectors**: references to an element or group of elements to which the style is applied.

Let's look at a basic example to see how this is done. Consider the following HTML document:

```
<!DOCTYPE html>
<html lang="en">
<head>
  <meta charset="utf-8" />
  <title>A Simple Page</title>
</head>
<body>
  <h1>First Title</h1>
  <p>A paragraph of interesting content.</p>
  <h2>Second Title</h2>
  <p>A paragraph of interesting content.</p>
  <h2>Third title</h2>
  <p>A paragraph of interesting content.</p>
</body>
</html>
```

This document contains three boldfaced headings, which have been created using h1 and h2 tags. Without CSS styling, the headings will be rendered using the browser's internal stylesheet; the h1 heading will be displayed in a large font size, and the h2 headings will be smaller than the h1, but larger than paragraph text. The document that uses these default styles will be *readable*, if a little plain. We can use some simple CSS to change the look of these elements:

```
<!DOCTYPE html>
<html lang="en">
<head>
  <meta charset="utf-8" />
  <title>A Simple Page</title>
  <style>
    h1, h2 {
      font-family: "Times New Roman", Times, serif;
```

```
        color: #3366cc;
    }
  </style>
</head>
<body>
  <h1>First Title</h1>
  <p>A paragraph of interesting content.</p>
  <h2>Second Title</h2>
  <p>A paragraph of interesting content.</p>
  <h2>Third title</h2>
  <p>A paragraph of interesting content.</p>
</body>
</html>
```

All the magic lies between the style tags in the head of the document, where we specify that a light blue, sans-serif font should be applied to all h1 and h2 elements on the page. Regarding the syntax, I'll explain it in detail shortly. By changing the style definition at the top of the page, it's unnecessary to add to the markup itself; it will affect all three headings, as well as any other headings that might be added at a later date.

HTML or XHTML?

Throughout this book, the examples will be presented with HTML5 documents using XML-style syntax, as this is my preference. All these examples, however, will work in an XHTML or HTML4 document.

Inline Styles

The simplest method of adding CSS styles to your web pages is to use **inline styles**. An inline style is applied to an HTML element via its style attribute, like this:

```
<p style="font-family: "Times New Roman", Times, serif;
  color: #3366cc;">
  Amazingly few discotheques provide jukeboxes.
</p>
```

An inline style has no selector; the style declarations are applied to the parent element. In the above example, this is the p tag.

Inline styles have one major disadvantage: it's impossible to reuse them. For example, if we wanted to apply the style above to another p element, we'd have to type it out again in that element's `style` attribute. And if the style needed changing further on, we'd have to find and edit every HTML tag where the style was copied. Additionally, because inline styles are located within the page's markup, it makes the code difficult to read and maintain.

Embedded Styles

Another approach for applying CSS styles to your web pages is to use the `style` element, as in the first example we looked at. Using this method, you can declare any number of CSS styles by placing them between the opening and closing `style` tags, as follows:

```
<style>
  : CSS styles go in here…
</style>
```

The `style` tags are placed inside the head element, and while it's nice and simple, the `style` tag has one major disadvantage: if you want to use a particular set of styles throughout your site, you'll have to repeat those style definitions within the `style` element at the top of every one of your site's pages.

A more sensible alternative is to place those definitions in a plain text file, then link your documents to that file. This external file is referred to as an external stylesheet.

External Stylesheets

An **external stylesheet** is a file (usually given a **.css** filename) that contains a website's CSS styles, keeping them separate from any one web page. Multiple pages can link to the same **.css** file, and any changes you make to the style definitions in that file will affect all the pages that link to it. This achieves the objective of creating site-wide style definitions as mentioned previously.

To link a document to an external stylesheet (say, **styles.css**), we simply place a link element within the document's head element:

```
<link rel="stylesheet" href="styles.css" />
```

Remember our original example in which three headings shared a single style rule? Let's save that rule to an external stylesheet with the filename **styles.css**, and link it to the web page like so:

```
<!DOCTYPE html>
<html lang="en">
<head>
  <meta charset="utf-8" />
  <title>A Simple Page</title>
  <link rel="stylesheet" href="styles.css" />
</head>
<body>
  <h1>First Title</h1>
  <p>A paragraph of interesting content.</p>
  <h2>Second Title</h2>
  <p>A paragraph of interesting content.</p>
  <h2>Third title</h2>
  <p>A paragraph of interesting content.</p>
</body>
</html>
```

The value of the rel attribute must be stylesheet. The href attribute indicates the location and name of the stylesheet file.

Not Your Type

You'll often see the link to the stylesheet written as: <link rel="stylesheet" type="text/css" href="styles.css" />. We've omitted the type attribute here because we're using HTML5, which, along with browsers, has no requirement for it.

The linked **styles.css** file contains the following style definition:

```
h1, h2 {
  font-family: "Times New Roman", Times, serif;
  color: #3366cc;
}
```

As with an image file, you can reuse this **styles.css** file in any page in which it's needed. It will save you from retyping the styles, as well as ensure that your headings display consistently across the entire site.

CSS Syntax

A stylesheet is a collection of style definitions. Every CSS style definition, or rule, has two main components:

- A list of one or more selectors, separated by commas, define the element or elements to which the style will be applied.

- The declaration block, separated by curly braces {...}, specifies what the rule actually does.

The declaration block contains one or more style declarations and each one sets the value of a specific **property**. Multiple declarations are separated by a semicolon (;). A property declaration is made up of the property name and a value, separated by a colon (:). You can see all of these elements labeled in Figure 1.1.

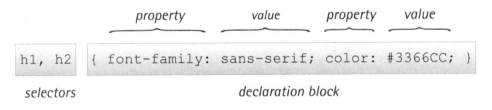

Figure 1.1. The components of a CSS rule: a list of selectors and a declaration block

The solutions throughout the book focus mainly on the different properties and the values they can take. Figure 1.1 also illustrates that a style rule can be written in a single line. Some CSS authors prefer to indent their style rules to aid readability, while others write their rules on one line to save space. The following shows the same style rule written both ways:

```
h1, h2 {
  font-family: "Times New Roman", Times, serif;
  color: #3366cc;
}

h1, h2 {
  font-family: "Times New Roman", Times, serif; color: #3366cc;
}
```

The formatting makes no difference at all; it's totally up to you how you write your stylesheet.

What are CSS selectors and how do I use them?

A selector is what we use to target the particular bit of markup on the page that we wish to style. These range from very simple (targeting a particular HTML element by name) to complex (targeting an element when it's in a certain position or state). In the following example, h1 and h2 are the selectors, which means that the rule should apply to all h1 and h2 elements:

```
h1, h2 {
   font-family: Times, "Times New Roman", serif;
   color: #3366CC;
}
```

We'll be seeing examples of CSS selectors throughout the book, so you should quickly become accustomed to the different types of selector and how they work. Below are some examples of each of the main selector types, so these should be familiar when you encounter them later.

Type Selectors

The most basic form of selector is a **type selector**, which we've already seen. By naming a particular HTML element, you can apply a style rule to every occurrence of that element in the document. Type selectors are often used to set the basic styles that appear throughout a website. For example, the following style rule might be used to set the default h1 font for a website:

```
h1 {
   font-family: Tahoma, Verdana, Arial, Helvetica, sans-serif;
   font-size: 1.2em;
   color: #000000;
}
```

Here we've set the font, size, and color for all h1 elements in the document.

Class Selectors

Assigning styles to elements is all well and good, but what happens if you want to assign different styles to identical elements that occur in various places within your document? This is where CSS **classes** come in.

Consider the following style, which colors all h2 headings blue in a document:

```
h2 {
  color: #0000ff;
}
```

That's great, but what would happen if you had a sidebar on your page with a blue background? If the text in the sidebar were to display blue as well, it would be invisible. What you need to do is define a class for your sidebar text, then assign a CSS style to that class.

First, edit your HTML to add a class to the heading:

```
<h2 class="sidebar">This text will be white, as specified by the
  CSS style definition below.</h2>
```

Now write the style for this class:

```
h2 {
  color: #0000ff;
}

.sidebar {
  color: #ffffff;
}
```

This second rule uses a class selector to indicate that the style should be applied to any element with a class value of .sidebar. The period (.) at the beginning indicates that we're naming a class instead of an HTML element.

You can add a class to as many elements in your document as you need to.

ID Selectors

In contrast with class selectors, **ID selectors** are used to select one particular element, rather than a group of elements. To use an ID selector, you first add an `id` attribute to the element you wish to style. It's important that the ID is unique within the HTML document:

```
<p id="tagline">This paragraph is uniquely identified by the ID
  "tagline".</p>
```

To reference this element by its ID selector, we precede the ID with a hash (#). For example, the following rule will make the preceding paragraph white:

```
#tagline {
  color: #ffffff;
}
```

Combinators

The next group of selectors we shall take a look at are **combinators**. The combinator refers to a character added between two simple selectors to create a selector more capable of targeting a precise part of the document.

Descendant Selectors

The descendant selector matches an element that descends from a specified element. The combinator used in this selector is a whitespace character.

You might have an h2 element on your site that's set to display as blue; however, within the sidebar of the site are some h2 elements that you want to display white in order to show up against a dark background. As we saw earlier, you could add a class to all these headings, but it would be far neater to instead target them with CSS. This is when the descendant selector is used.

Here's the new selector:

```
.sidebar h2 {
  color: #ffffff;
}
```

And here's the updated HTML:

```
<div class="sidebar">
  <h2>A heading in white</h2>
  <h2>Another heading in white</h2>
</div>
```

As you can see, a descendant selector comprises a list of selectors (separated by spaces) that match a page element (or group of elements) *from the outside in*. In this case, because our page contains a div element with a class of sidebar, the descendant selector .sidebar h2 refers to all h2 elements inside that div.

By using a descendant selector, there's no need to access your HTML to add classes directly to all elements; instead, use the main structural areas of the page—identified by classes or IDs where required—and style elements within them.

Child Selectors

Unlike the descendant selector—which matches all elements that are descendants of the parent element, including elements that are *not direct* descendants—the child selector matches all elements that are the immediate children of a specified element. The combinator used in this selector is the greater-than sign (>).

Consider the following markup:

```
<div class="sidebar">
  <p>This paragraph will be displayed in white.</p>
  <p>So will this one.</p>
  <div class="tagline">
    <p>If we use a descendant selector, this will be white too.
      But if we use a child selector, it will be blue.</p>
  </div>
</div>
```

In this example, the descendant selector we saw in the section called "Descendant Selectors", .sidebar p, would match all the paragraphs that are nested within the div element with the class sidebar, as well as those inside the div with the class tagline. But if, instead, you only wanted to style those paragraphs that were direct descendants of the sidebar div, you'd use a child selector. A child selector uses the > character to specify a direct descendant.

Here's the new selector, which sets the text color to white for those paragraphs directly inside the sidebar div (but not those within the tagline div):

```
p {
  color: #0000FF;
}

.sidebar>p {
  color: #ffffff;
}
```

Adjacent Selectors

An adjacent selector will only match an element if it's adjacent to another specified element. The combinator for this selector is the plus character (+).

Therefore, if we have HTML:

```
<h2>This is a title</h2>

<p>This paragraph will be displayed in white.</p>

<p>This paragraph will be displayed in black.</p>
```

And then use the following selector:

```
p {
  color: #000000;
}

h2+p {
  color: #FFFFFF;
}
```

Only the first paragraph will be displayed in white. The second p element is not adjacent to an h2 element, so its text will be displayed in the black we've specified for p elements in the first rule.

Pseudo-class Selectors

A pseudo-class selector acts as if an element has a class applied according to the state of that element. Pseudo-class selectors start with a colon and are usually added immediately after a type selector with no additional whitespace.

My aim here is to familiarize you with the syntax of and terminology around these selectors, so that as we meet them later, you'll have an understanding of how they work. As a result, I won't demonstrate all the selectors in this chapter, but a full list with explanations can be found online in the SitePoint CSS Reference.[2]

Links

Most of us first come across pseudo-class selectors when they're applied to links. A link has various states. It can be unvisited or visited, hovered over, or clicked. We can use CSS to target each of these states:

```css
a:link {
  color: #0000ff;
}

a:visited {
  color: #ff00ff;
}

a:hover {
  color: #00ccff;
}

a:active {
  color: #ff0000;
}
```

The first definition sets the color for the link state, which displays for links that users have visited. If they have visited the link, the second rule is used. If they hover over the link, the :hover definition is used, and when clicking or otherwise activating the link, the :active definition is used. The :hover and :active pseudo-class selectors are actually termed **dynamic pseudo-classes**, as they take effect only

---

[2] http://reference.sitepoint.com/css/selectorref

when the user interacts with the element; something has to happen before they take effect.

The order of these definitions in your document is important. The `a:active` definition needs to come last so that it overwrites the previous definitions. We'll find out why that's the case later on in this chapter, when we discuss the cascade.

First Child

The `first-child` pseudo-class selector targets an element when it's the first child of a parent element. As with all these selectors, it's far easier to understand when you can see an example.

Within your document is a set of paragraphs. These are contained inside a `div` element with a class of `article`. We can use CSS and a descendant selector to address all these paragraphs, making them larger and bold:

```
.article p {
  font-size: 1.5em;
  font-weight: bold;
}
```

If you'd just like the first paragraph to display in a larger font size and bold—by way of an introduction to the article—you can use `first-child`:

```
.article p:first-child {
  font-size: 1.5em;
  font-weight: bold;
}
```

This CSS is only applied by the browser if the paragraph is the very first p element inside an element with a class of `article`. So the `first-child` pseudo-class selector is useful for adding nice design touches, such as making the first paragraph of some text—or the first instance of a heading—slightly different.

Last Child

Just as we can use `first-child` to address the very first instance of an element inside a container, we can use `last-child` to address the last instance. The following CSS would add a bottom border to each list item in a list:

```
.navigation li {
  border-bottom: 1px solid #999999;
}
```

To prevent the border displaying on the last item, you can use the following CSS:

```
.navigation li {
  border-bottom: 1px solid #999999;
}

.navigation li:last-child {
  border-bottom: none;
}
```

Nth Child

The nth-child pseudo-class selector lets you select multiple elements according to their position in the document tree. The easiest way to see this in action is by taking a common example of striping table rows to make them easier to read.

The following CSS declaration will give a table cell a background color only if it's in an odd row of the table:

```
tr:nth-child(odd) td {
  background-color: #f0e9c5;
}
```

In addition to odd and even keywords, you can use a multiplier expression:

```
tr:nth-child(2n+1) td {
  background-color: #f0e9c5;
}
```

We'll be looking at nth-child in more depth later in the book, where I'll explain how to use these multipliers to target various parts of a data table.

Only Child

The only-child pseudo-class selector will select an element if it's the only child of its parent. For example, if I have in my markup the following two lists—the first having three list items and the second having one:

```
<ul>
  <li>Item one</li>
  <li>Item two</li>
  <li>Item three</li>
</ul>

<ul>
  <li>A single item list - not really a list at all!</li>
</ul>
```

The CSS declaration below would only match the list item in the second list, as it matches where the li is an only child of the parent ul:

```
li:only-child {
  list-style-type: none;
}
```

Pseudo-element Selectors

Pseudo-elements operate as if you've added new HTML markup into your page and then styled that markup. In the CSS3 specification, pseudo-elements are denoted with a double colon; for example, p::first-letter.

However, for pseudo-elements that existed in CSS2 (such as ::first-letter, ::first-line, ::before, and ::after), browser manufacturers are asked to maintain support for the single colon syntax that these selectors used in the past. If you're utilizing the above selectors, at the time of writing a single colon has better browser support, so I'd suggest employing this. The exception is ::selection, which was added in the CSS3 specification.

First Letter

The first-letter pseudo-element selector acts as if you've wrapped a span around the first letter of the content inside your parent element and are then styling it. For example, if we used a span within the markup we might have:

```
<div class="wrapper">
  <p><span class="firstletter">T</span>his is some text within a div
    with a class of wrapper.</p>
</div>
```

And in the CSS:

```
.wrapper .firstletter {
  font-size: 200%;
  font-weight: bold;
}
```

Or we could remove the span from the markup and target the first letter in the same way using the first-letter pseudo-element selector:

```
.wrapper:first-letter {
  font-size: 200%;
  font-weight: bold;
}
```

First Line

In the same way first-letter selects the first letter within a container, first-line selects the first line:

```
.wrapper:first-line {
  font-size: 200%;
  font-weight: bold;
}
```

The first-line selector is far more flexible than actually wrapping the first-line of text in a span and styling that. When wrapping content in a span, it's not known whether the length of the first line may change (due to the user's text size, for example, or a change in the text added by a content management system). The first-line pseudo-class selector will always format the first line of text as displayed in the browser.

Before

The before pseudo-element is used along with the content property to specify where generated content should be rendered. Generated content is content that's rendered in your document from CSS. This can be useful for a variety of reasons, which we'll look at later in the book. For now, here's the HTML for a simple example:

```
<div class="article">
  <p>Hello World!</p>
</div>
```

And the CSS:

```
.article:before {
  content: "Start here";
}
```

When viewed in a browser, this will render the words "Start here" just inside the opening div element—that's before the first p.

After

The after pseudo-element works in the same way as before, but it renders the content at the end of the parent element; that's just before the closing div in our aforementioned HTML example:

```
.article:after {
  content: "End here";
}
```

Given the same markup used for the previous before example, the previous CSS would render "End here" just before the closing div, after the closing p tag.

Attribute Selectors

Attribute selectors let you target an element based on an attribute. As an example of an attribute on an HTML element, we can look at the a element, which creates a link. Attributes on the following link are href and title:

```
<a href="http://google.com" title="Visit Google">Google</a>
```

With an attribute selector, we can check what the value of an attribute is, and show CSS based on it. As a simple example, if we take a form input field, it has a type attribute explaining what kind of field it is. Valid values for the type attribute include text, radio, and checkbox. If we try and style a checkbox in the same way as a text input field, we'll end up with a very strange result, so we can use an attribute selector to create a definition only for input fields with a type of text. For example, here is a form field:

```
<input type="text" name="name" id="fName" />
```

The CSS to target this field is as follows:

```
form input[type="text"] {
  background-color: #ffffff;
  color: #333333;
}
```

In Chapter 6, we'll be looking at more examples of using attribute selectors.

What about older browsers?

You're probably already aware that not all browsers are equal in their support of CSS, and that's before you take into consideration that some users may well have old versions of browsers on their desktop. The examples in this book should all work as described in the current versions of the main browsers; in fact, most will work on previous versions of these browsers as well. Where a certain feature is unavailable in older versions of, say, Internet Explorer, I'll indicate this fact.

In Chapter 7, I'll explain a number of ways to get older browsers up to speed with the latest CSS, such as using JavaScript to add support for CSS3 selectors in older versions of Internet Explorer. If you know that a project you're working on will have a large share of its users using old versions of IE, for example, it's advisable to turn to that chapter to plan your support strategy from the outset.

Vendor-specific Extensions

As you move through the solutions in the next few chapters, you'll see examples of one way that browsers are coping with the introduction of CSS3. The CSS3 specification is different from earlier specifications in that it is modular. The spec is broken down into modules that can each reach completion—in W3C terms this is known as a W3C Recommendation—at different times. The stages a module moves through are as follows:

1. Working Draft: the module has been published for review by the community

2. Candidate Recommendation: implementation experience is gathered during this phase

3. Proposed Recommendation: the module is sent to the W3C Advisory Committee for final endorsement

4. W3C Recommendation: the module is now endorsed by the W3C and should be widely adopted

While a module is moving through the various stages, browser manufacturers often start implementing the module at Working Draft stage. This is good, because it helps to provide implementation experience in terms of how the specification works when used; however, it is possible that implementation details could change from the initial proposal.

For example, if you had used a CSS3 property that subsequently changed, a site built a year ago might suddenly look very odd indeed in a new browser that changed the implementation to the new, correct way of doing it.

To avoid this issue, browser manufacturers often use a vendor prefix when doing their early stage implementations to create a vendor-specific implementation of the property. For example, we use border-radius to create rounded corners like so:

```
border-radius: 10px;
```

However, for rounded corners to work in earlier versions of Firefox and Safari, you'd also need to add the vendor-prefixed versions:

```
-webkit-border-radius: 10px;
-moz-border-radius: 10px;
border-radius: 10px;
```

Once the module is unlikely to change, the browsers start supporting the real property alongside their own. Some browsers may never have a vendor-specific version and just implement the one from the specification.

You'll witness many examples of these prefixed properties throughout the book, so you should soon become comfortable using them.

How does the browser decide which styles to apply?

So how does the browser understand our intentions? When more than one rule can be applied to the same element, the browser uses **the cascade** to determine which style properties to apply.

Understanding the cascade is important when dealing with CSS, because many CSS development problems are due to styles being unintentionally applied to an element. We've already presented examples in this chapter where we've written a general style rule focused on paragraph elements, and then a more specific rule aimed at one or more particular paragraphs. Both style rules target paragraphs, *but the more specific rule overrides the general rule in the case of matching paragraphs.*

There are four factors that the browser uses to make the decision: weight, origin, specificity, and source order.

The **weight** of a particular style declaration is determined by the use of the keyword !important. When the keyword appears after a property value, that value can't be overridden by the same property in another style rule, except in very specific circumstances. Using !important in your stylesheets has a huge negative impact on maintainability, and there's often little call for it anyway. For these reasons it should be avoided, which we'll do in this book. If you'd like to know more, you can read about it in the SitePoint CSS Reference.[3]

There are three possible stylesheet **origins**: the browser, the author, and the user. In this book, we focus on what are called **author stylesheets**; that's stylesheets written by the web page creator—you! We've mentioned the browser internal stylesheet that provides the default styles for all elements, but styles in author stylesheets will always override styles in the browser default stylesheet. The only other possible origin for stylesheets are user stylesheets—custom styles written by the browser users—and even these are overridden by the author stylesheet except in rare circumstances. Again, if you'd like to know more, the SitePoint CSS Reference has a whole section on it.

---

[3] http://reference.sitepoint.com/css/importantdeclarations

The two parts of the cascade that will affect your daily CSS work the most are specificity and source order. The rule of **specificity** ensures that the style rule with the most specific selector overrides any others with less-specific selectors.

To give you an example of how this works, consider this simple snippet of HTML markup:

```
<div id="content">
 <p class="message">
   This is an important message.
 </p>
</div>
```

Now consider the following style rules that are to be applied to this HTML:

```
p { color: #000000; }
.message { color: #CCCCCC; }
p.message { color: #0000FF; }
#content p.message { color: #FF0000; }
```

These four selectors all match the paragraph element in the example HTML and set the text color. What color will be applied to the paragraph? If you guessed #FF0000, or red, you'd be right. The p type selector (any p element) has the lowest level of specificity, with .message (any element with class message) coming next. The selector p.message (any p element with class message) then has a higher level of specificity. The highest is the selector #content p.message (any p element with class message that is a child of the element with id content).

Longer selectors aren't necessarily more specific. An ID selector, for example, will always have a higher specificity than an element type or class selector. It becomes trickier the more complex your selectors are, but you should find the examples in this book simple enough. If you'd like to know the exact formula for measuring specificity, once again the SitePoint CSS Reference has all the answers.[4]

If two or more style rules are still applicable to an element, the order in which the rules appear—the **source order**—is used. The last rule to be declared is applied. This is also true if you declare more than one style rule with the same selector; for example, .message in your stylesheet. It will be the second instance of the rule that

---

[4] http://reference.sitepoint.com/css/specificity

will be applied to the element. As we'll see in later chapters, this behavior is very useful.

Will using a CSS framework make it easier to learn CSS?

Since I wrote the previous edition of this book, the use of CSS frameworks by designers to speed up the development of their CSS has grown.

My take on these frameworks is that they can be very useful, but they're no substitute for learning CSS. Once you understand CSS and are used to writing it for your projects, you may come up against workflow issues that are resolved by employing some of the available tools and frameworks. If they solve a problem you have—great! There is nothing inherently wrong with building on the work of other people. However, if your problem is that you lack a good grasp of CSS, the use of any framework is more likely to compound your confusion—adding another layer of complexity that will only make it harder to come to grips with the basics.

A Decent Selection

This chapter has given you a taste of CSS and its usage at the basic level. We've even touched on the sometimes confusing concept of the cascade. If you're a newbie to CSS but have an understanding of the concepts discussed in this chapter, you should be able to start using the examples in this book.

The examples in the early chapters are simpler than those found later on, so if you're yet to work with CSS, you might want to begin with these. They will build on the knowledge you gained in this chapter to start using and, I hope, enjoying CSS.

Chapter

Text Styling and Other Basics

This chapter will explore the application of CSS for styling text. It will cover a lot of CSS basics, as well as answer some of the more frequently asked questions about these techniques. If you're new to CSS, these examples will introduce a variety of properties and their usages, and provide a solid foundation from which to start your own experiments. For those already familiar with CSS, this chapter will serve as a quick refresher for those moments when you're struggling to remember how to achieve a certain effect.

The examples I've provided here are well supported across a variety of browsers and versions, though, as always, testing your code in different browsers is important. While there may be small inconsistencies or a lack of support for these techniques in older browsers, none of the solutions presented here should cause you any serious problems. For more information on browser support, Chapter 7 is dedicated to the subject.

How do I set my text to display in a certain font?

The browser will display text in the default font used for that browser and operating system. How do you change it to the one used in your design?

Solution

Specify the typeface that your text will adopt using the font-family property:

```
p {
   font-family: Verdana;
}
```

Discussion

As well as specific fonts, such as Verdana or Times, CSS allows the specification of some more-generic family names:

- serif
- sans-serif
- monospace
- cursive
- fantasy

When you specify fonts, it's important to remember that users are unlikely to have the same fonts installed that you have on your computer. If you define a font that the user doesn't have, your text will display according to their browsers' default fonts, regardless of what you'd prefer.

To avoid this eventuality, you can simply specify generic font names and let users' systems decide which font to apply. For instance, if you want your document to appear in a sans-serif font such as Arial, you could use the following style rule:

```
p {
   font-family: sans-serif;
}
```

Now, you will probably want more control than this over the way your site displays—and you can. It's possible to specify both font names and generic fonts in the same declaration block. Take, for example, the following style rule for the p element:

```
p {
    font-family: Verdana, Geneva, Arial, Helvetica, sans-serif;
}
```

Here, we've specified that if Verdana is installed on the system, it should be used; otherwise, the browser is instructed to see if Geneva is installed; failing that, the computer will look for Arial, then Helvetica. If none of these fonts are available, the browser will then use that system's default sans-serif font.

If a font-family name contains spaces, it should be enclosed in quotation marks, like so:

```
p {
    font-family: "Courier New", "Andale Mono", monospace;
}
```

The generic font-family names should always be without quotes and appear last in the list. The list of fonts is often termed a "**font stack**," which is a good term to search on if you're looking for information on fonts to use in this way.

Fonts that you can feel fairly confident using are:

Windows   Arial, Lucida, Impact, Times New Roman, Courier New, Tahoma, Comic Sans, Verdana, Georgia, Garamond

Mac   Helvetica, Futura, Bodoni, Times, Palatino, Courier, Gill Sans, Geneva, Baskerville, Andale Mono

This list reveals the reason why we chose the fonts we specified in our style rule. We begin by specifying our first preference, a common Windows font (Verdana), then list a similar Mac font (Geneva). Then we follow up with other fonts that would be usable if neither of these fonts were available.

There is a handy article on the SitePoint website that describes some common font stacks, and these would be a good starting point if you are just beginning to explore web typography.[1]

Should I use pixels, points, ems, or another unit identifier to set font sizes?

You can size text in CSS using the font-size property, like so:

```
font-size: 12px;
```

Solution

We've used pixel sizing here, but the font-size property can take a variety of values. Before you decide which to use, you should know the relative merits of each option.

Table 2.1 identifies the units that you can use to size fonts.

Table 2.1. Units of measurement for sizing fonts

Unit Identifier	Corresponding Units
pt	points
pc	picas
px	pixels
em	ems
ex	exes
%	percentages

Points and Picas

You should avoid using **points** and **picas** to style text for display on screen. The point unit is an excellent way to set font sizes for print design, as the point measurement was created for that purpose:

---

[1] http://www.sitepoint.com/eight-definitive-font-stacks/

```
p {
  font-size: 10pt;
}
```

A point has a fixed size of 1/72nd of an inch, while a pica is one-sixth of an inch. A printed document whose fonts are specified using these units will appear exactly as you intended; after all, one-sixth of an inch is the same physical measurement whether you're printing on an A4 page or a billboard. However, computers are unable to accurately predict the physical size at which elements will appear on the monitor, so they guess—and guess badly—at the size of a point or pica, with results that vary between platforms.

If you're creating a print stylesheet (as we do in the section called "How do I create a print stylesheet?" in Chapter 9) or a document that's intended for print—rather than on screen—viewing, points and picas are the units to use. However, as a general rule of thumb we should avoid them when designing for the Web.

Pixels

Many designers like to set font sizes in **pixel** measurements:

```
p {
  font-size: 12px;
}
```

Using pixels makes it easy to achieve consistent text displays across various browsers and platforms. However, pixel measurements ignore any preferences users may have set in their own browsers; furthermore, in the case of Internet Explorer, font sizes that the designer has dictated in pixels cannot to be resized by users. This limitation presents a serious accessibility problem for users who need to make text larger in order to read it clearly.

While pixel measurements may seem like the easiest option for setting font sizes, they should be avoided if another method can be used. Even if you disregard the text resizing issue, given that many users will use page zoom rather than resize the text, using scalable font sizes will make your life far easier once you venture into modern layout techniques (we'll discuss these later in the book). If you're creating a document for print or creating a print stylesheet, you should avoid pixels entirely. Pixels have no meaning in the world of print and, like the application of points to the on-screen environment, when print applications are provided with a pixel measurement, they'll simply try to guess the size at which the font should appear on paper—with erratic results.

Ems

The **em** is a relative font measurement. The name em comes from the typographical world, where it relates to the size of the capital letter M, usually the widest character in a font. In CSS, 1em is seen to be equal to the user's default font size, or the font size of the parent element when it's set to a value other than the default.

If you use ems (or any other relative unit) to set your font sizes, users will be able to resize the text in old browsers. For example, IE6 users are unable to resize text set in pixels, and have no other zoom control.

Em values can be set using decimal numbers. For example, to display text at a size 10% smaller than the user's default (or the font size of its parent element), you could use this rule:

```
p {
    font-size: 0.9em;
}
```

To display the text 10% larger than the default or inherited size, you'd use this rule:

```
p {
    font-size: 1.1em;
}
```

Exes

The **ex** is a relative unit measurement that corresponds to the height of the lowercase letter x in the default font size. In theory, if you set the font size of some text to 1ex, the uppercase letters will display at the height at which the lowercase letter x would have appeared if the font size had been unspecified. Furthermore, the lowercase letters will be sized relative to those uppercase letters.

Historically, browsers lacked support for the typographical features needed to determine the precise size of an ex, making a rough guess for this measurement. For this reason, exes are rarely used at the time of writing.

Percentages

As with ems and exes, font sizes that are set in **percentages** will honor users' text size settings and can be resized by users:

```
p {
  font-size: 100%;
}
```

Setting the size of a p element to 100% will display your text at users' default font-size settings (as will setting the font size to 1 em). Decreasing the percentage will make the text smaller:

```
p {
  font-size: 90%;
}
```

Increasing the percentage will make the text larger:

```
p {
  font-size: 150%;
}
```

Sizing Fonts Using Keywords

As an alternative to using numerical values to set text sizes, you can use absolute and relative keywords.

Absolute-size Keywords

We can use any of seven absolute-size keywords to set text size in CSS:

- `xx-small`
- `x-small`
- `small`
- `medium`
- `large`
- `x-large`
- `xx-large`

These keywords are defined relative to each other, and browsers implement them in different ways. Most browsers display medium at the same size as unstyled text, with the other keywords resizing text to varying degrees, as indicated by their names.

These keyword measurements are considered absolute in that they don't inherit from any parent element. Yet, unlike the absolute values provided for height, such as pixels and points, they do allow the text to be resized in the browser, and will honor users' browser settings. The main problem with using these keywords is consistency between browsers—x-small-sized text may be perfectly readable in one browser and minuscule in another. Due to this lack of control, you rarely see these keywords in use.

Relative-size Keywords

Text sized using relative-size keywords—larger and smaller—takes its size from the parent element in the same way that text sized with em and % does. Therefore, if you set the size of your p element to small using absolute keywords and decide that you want emphasized text to display comparatively larger, you could add the following to the stylesheet:

chapter_02/relative.css

```
p {
    font-size: small;
}

em {
    font-size: larger;
}
```

The following markup would display as shown in Figure 2.1, because the text between the <em> and </em> tags will display larger than its parent, the p element:

chapter_02/relative.html (excerpt)

```
<p>Garlic may be known for being a little bit <em>stinky</em>, but
    baked it is absolutely delicious and as long as you feed it to
    all of your guests no-one will complain about the smell! Once
    baked the garlic becomes creamy and sweet making an ideal spread
    to accompany cheese.</p>
```

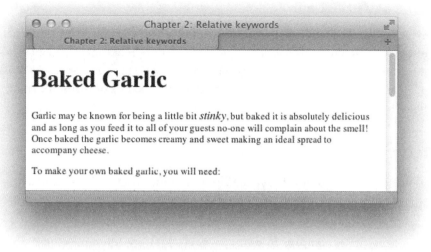

Figure 2.1. The emphasized word within the paragraph

Discussion

When you're deciding which method of text sizing to use, it's best to select one that allows all users to resize the text, as well as ensuring that the text complies with the settings users have chosen within their browsers. Relative font sizing works well as long as you're careful about the way the elements inherit sizing. In order to achieve even a basic level of accessibility, though, it's important to enable users to set fonts to a comfortable level.

Designing your layout with resizable text in mind also allows you to avoid another issue. Sometimes designers assume that setting font sizes in pixels will allow them to fix the heights of containers, or place text on top of fixed-height images. This approach will work in Internet Explorer, which doesn't resize text set in pixels; it may, however, result in a complete mess of overflowing text in Firefox (versions prior to 3, or version 3 with **Zoom** set to **zoom text only**), where the height of boxes containing text is always unknown.

I tend to use a combination of ems (to set the base size) and percentages within the document (percentages of that base size). This means that if the client decides they want the site's text to be larger or smaller, I can simply adjust the base size and all other text stays in proportion to it.

The Sky's the Limit

When designing for the Web, it's best to assume that you do not know the height of anything; it will save you a lot of grief in the future. Text resizing, people adding more text than expected via a content management system, or long words causing odd line-wrapping can all blow apart a layout that counts on elements being a fixed height.

Relative Sizing and Inheritance

When you use any kind of relative sizing, remember that the element will inherit its starting size from its parent element, then adjust its size accordingly. Be careful, though, when using a relative font size for the parent element as well; this can become problematic in complex layouts where the parent element is less obvious. Consider the following markup:

chapter_02/nesting.html (excerpt)

```
<div>
  <p>
    You'll <em>probably</em> be surprised when using
    <a href="#">a relative <code>font-size</code></a>
    and nested elements.
  </p>
</div>
```

Let's say we wanted to set the font-size of the markup text to 130% of the default size, and we made the mistake of setting it this way:

chapter_02/nesting.css

```
div, p, em, a, code {
  font-size: 130%;
}
```

The effect of this style rule is to make the font-size of the nested elements progressively bigger; that's 130% of the font-size of the parent element, which is already 130% of the font-size of its parent and so on, as demonstrated in Figure 2.2.

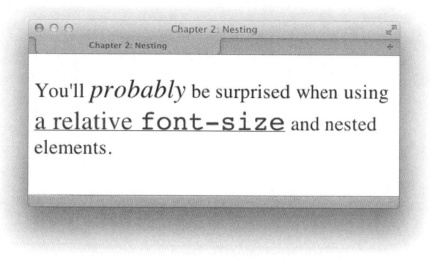

Figure 2.2. Relative font sizing

How do I remove underlines from my links?

The widely accepted default indicator that text on a web page links to another document is that it is underlined and displays in a different color from the rest of the text. However, there may be instances in which you want to remove that underline.

Solution

We use the `text-decoration` property to remove the underlines from link text. By default, the browser will set the `text-decoration` property of all elements to `underline`. To remove the underline, simply set the `text-decoration` property for the link to none:

```
text-decoration: none;
```

The CSS used to create the effect shown in Figure 2.3 is as follows:

chapter_02/textdecoration.css

```
a:link, a:visited {
  text-decoration: none;
}
```

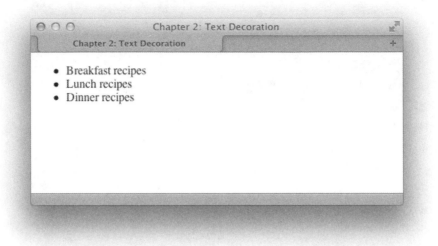

Figure 2.3. Removing underlines with `text-decoration`

Discussion

In addition to `underline` and `none`, there are other values for `text-decoration` that you can try out:

- `overline`
- `line-through`
- `blink`

It is possible to combine these values. For instance, should you wish to have an `underline` and `overline` on a particular link—as illustrated in Figure 2.4—you'd use this style rule:

```
chapter_02/textdecoration2.css
a:link, a:visited {
  text-decoration: underline overline;
}
```

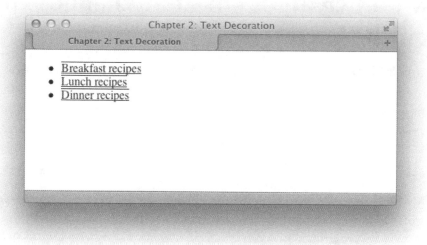

Figure 2.4. Links with `text-decoration` underline and overline set

Avoid Applying Misleading Lines

You can use the `text-decoration` property to apply underlines to any text, even if it's standard unlinked text, but be wary of doing this. The underlining of links is so widely accepted that users are inclined to think that any underlined text is a link to another document.

When is removing underlines a bad idea?

Underlining links is a standard convention followed by all web browsers, and, consequently, users expect to see links underlined. Removing the underline from links that appear within large areas of text can make it very difficult for people to realize that these words are, in fact, links, rather than just highlighted text. I'd advise against removing the underlines from links within text. There are other ways in which you can style links so that they look attractive, and removing the underline is rarely, if ever, necessary.

Links that are used as part of a menu, or appear in some other situation in which the text is quite obviously a link—for instance, where the text is styled with CSS to resemble a graphical button—are a different story. If you wish, you can remove the underline from these kinds of links, because it should be obvious from their context what they are.

How do I create a link that changes color when the cursor moves over it?

There's an attractive link effect that changes the color or otherwise alters a link's appearance when the cursor is moved across it. This effect can be applied to great advantage on navigation menus created with CSS, but it can also be used on links within regular paragraph text.

Solution

To create this effect, we need to style the :hover and :active dynamic pseudo-classes of the anchor element differently from its other pseudo-classes.

Let's look at an example. Here's a typical style rule that applies the same declarations to all of an anchor element's pseudo-classes:

chapter_02/textdecoration3.css

```
a:link, a:visited, a:hover, a:active {
  text-decoration: underline;
  color: #6A5ACD;
  background-color: transparent;
}
```

When this stylesheet is applied, our links will display in the blue color #6A5ACD with an underline, as shown in Figure 2.5.

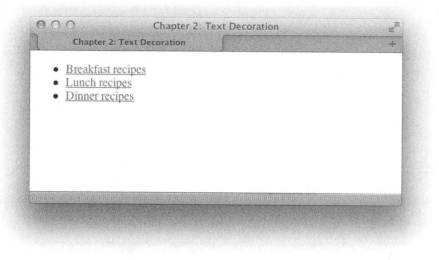

Figure 2.5. The styled links

To style our :hover and :active pseudo-classes differently, we need to remove them from the declaration with the other pseudo-classes and give them their own separate declaration. In the CSS below, I decided to remove the underline on hover. I've also set a background color and made the link's text a darker color; Figure 2.6 shows how these styles display in a browser:

```
                                           chapter_02/textdecoration4.css
a:link, a:visited {
  text-decoration: underline;
  color: #6A5ACD;
  background-color: transparent;
}

a:hover, a:active {
  text-decoration: underline overline;
  color: #191970;
  background-color: #C9C3ED;
}
```

As you've probably realized, you can style the anchor's other pseudo-classes separately, too. In particular, you might like to apply a different style to links that users have visited. To do so, you'd simply style the :visited pseudo-class separately.

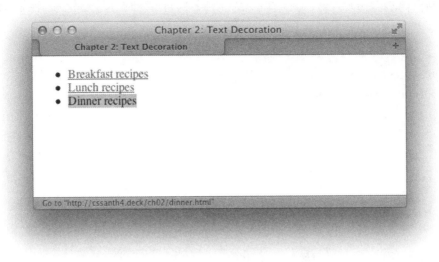

Figure 2.6. Moving the cursor over a link to which a hover style is applied

When styling pseudo-classes, take care that you leave the size or weight (or boldness) of the text unchanged. Otherwise, you'll find that your page appears to jiggle, as the surrounding content has to move to make way for the larger text to display when your cursor hovers over the link.

Ordering Pseudo-class Declarations

The anchor pseudo-classes should be declared in the following order: `:link`, `:visited`, `:hover`, `:active`, or else you may find that they work differently to how you intended. One way to remember this order is by using the mnemonic: LoVeHAte.

Fashion Police

You are limited in the styles you may apply to visited links.[2] This is because of the potential privacy implications of your browser knowing which links you have visited. If visited styles do not appear to be showing in a particular browser, it may be due to this issue.

---

[2] http://hacks.mozilla.org/2010/03/privacy-related-changes-coming-to-css-vistited/

How do I display two different styles of link on one page?

The previous solution explained how to style the different selectors of the anchor element, but what if you want to use different link styles within the same document? Perhaps you want to display links without underlines in your navigation menu, yet make sure that links within the body content are easily identifiable. Or maybe part of your document has a dark background color, so you need to use a lighter colored link style there.

Solution

To demonstrate how to create multiple styles for links displayed on one page, let's take an example in which we've already styled the regular links:

chapter_02/linktypes.css (excerpt)

```css
a:link, a:visited {
  text-decoration: underline;
  color: #6A5ACD;
  background-color: transparent;
}

a:hover, a:active {
  text-decoration: underline overline;
  color: #191970;
  background-color: #C9C3ED;
}
```

These should be taken as the default link styles: they reflect the way links will normally be styled within your documents. The first rule makes the link blue, so if an area of our page has a blue background, the links that appear in that space will be unreadable. We need to create a second set of styles for links in that area.

First, let's create a `class` or an `id` for the element that will contain the differently colored links. If the container is already styled with CSS, it may already have a `class` or `id` that we can use. Suppose that our document contains the following markup:

chapter_02/linktypes.html *(excerpt)*

```
<div class="boxout">
  <p>Visit our <a href="#store">online store</a>, for many of the
    tools you need to kit out your kitchen.</p>
</div>
```

We need to create a style rule that affects any link appearing within an element
with the class boxout:

chapter_02/linktypes.css *(excerpt)*

```
.boxout {
  color: #FFFFFF;
  background-color: #6A5ACD;
    ⋮
}

.boxout a:link, .boxout a:visited {
  text-decoration: underline;
  color: #E4E2F6;
  background-color: transparent;
}

.boxout a:hover, .boxout a:active {
  background-color: #C9C3ED;
  color: #191970;
  text-decoration: none;
}
```

As you can see in Figure 2.7, this rule will display all links in the document as per
the first style except for those that appear within the div element with the class
boxout: these links will be displayed in the lighter color.

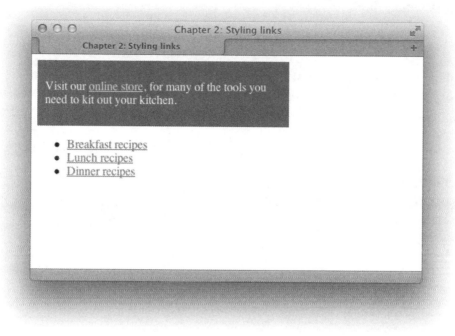

Figure 2.7. Using two link styles in one document

How do I style the first item in a list differently from the others?

Frequently, designers find that they need to style the first of a set of items—be they list items or a number of paragraphs within a container—distinct from the rest of the set. One way to achieve this is to assign a `class` to the first item, and then style that `class` uniquely from other items; however, there's a more elegant way to create this effect using the pseudo-class selector `first-child`.

Solution

Here's a simple list of items marked up as an unordered list:

```
chapter_02/firstchild.html (excerpt)

<ul>
  <li>Brie</li>
  <li>Cheddar</li>
```

```
  <li>Red Leicester</li>
  <li>Shropshire Blue</li>
</ul>
```

To change the color of the first item in the list without affecting its neighbors, we can use the `first-child` selector. This allows us to target the first element within the `ul` element, as shown in Figure 2.8:

chapter_02/firstchild.css

```
li:first-child {
  color: red;
}
```

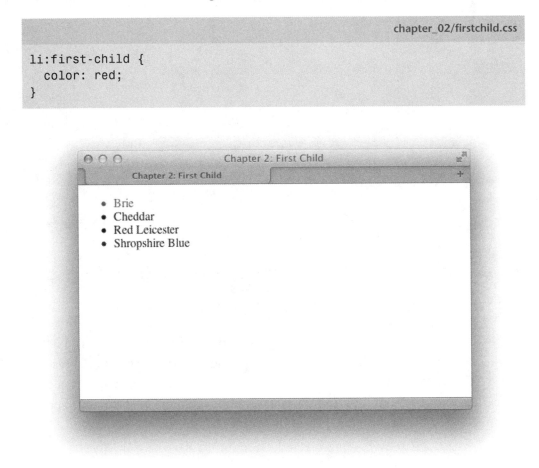

Figure 2.8. Displaying the first list item in red text

Discussion

The `first-child` pseudo-class selector is well supported in browsers as it has existed since the CSS2.1 specification. The only browser you're likely to be concerned about without support is IE6. See Chapter 7 for suggestions as to how to manage this lack of support.

How do I add a background color to a heading?

CSS allows us to add a background color to any element, including a heading.

Solution

Below is a CSS rule created for all the level-one headings in a document:

chapter_02/headingcolor.css (excerpt)

```
h1 {
  background-color: #ADD8E6;
  color: #256579;
  font: 1.6em Verdana, Geneva, Arial, Helvetica, sans-serif;
  padding: 0.2em;
}
```

The result is shown in Figure 2.9.

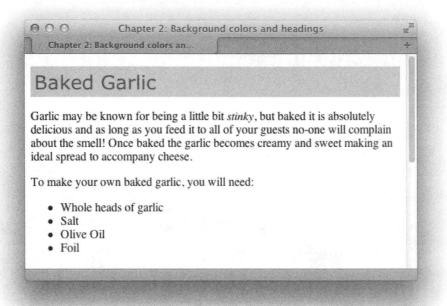

Figure 2.9. The heading with a background color

 Make Way for Color

When you add a background to a heading, you may also want to adjust the padding so that there's space between the heading text and the edge of the colored area, as I've done in the example.

How do I style headings with underlines?

Using CSS, there are two ways in which you can add an underline to your text.

Solution

The simplest way to add an underline is to use the `text-decoration` property that we encountered earlier in the section called "How do I remove underlines from my links?" This method will allow you to apply to text an underline that's the same color as the text itself, as this code and Figure 2.10, show:

chapter_02/headingunderline.css *(excerpt)*

```
h1 {
  font: 1.6em Verdana, Geneva, Arial, Helvetica, sans-serif;
  text-decoration: underline;
}
```

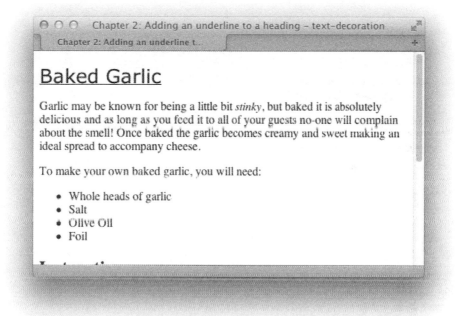

Figure 2.10. Using text-decoration to add an underline

You can also create an underline effect by adding a bottom border to the heading. This solution, which produces the result shown in Figure 2.11, is more flexible in that it allows you to separate the underline from the heading with the use of padding, and you can change the color of the underline so that it differs from that of the text.

A heading with this effect is also less likely to be confused with underlined link text than one whose underline is created using the text-decoration property. Here's the style rule you'll need:

```
h1 {
  font: 1.6em Verdana, Geneva, Arial, Helvetica, sans-serif;
  padding: 0.2em;
  border-bottom: 1px solid #AAAAAA;
}
```

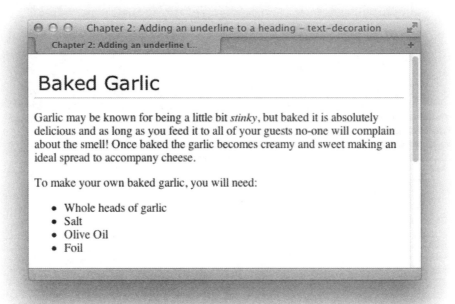

Figure 2.11. Creating an underline effect using a bottom border

How do I remove the large gap between an h1 element and the following paragraph?

By default, browsers render a gap between all heading and paragraph elements. The gap is produced by default top and bottom margins that browsers apply to these elements. The margin on the heading shown in Figure 2.12 reflects the default value. This gap can be removed using CSS.

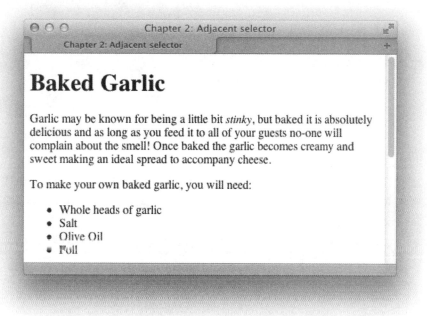

Figure 2.12. The default heading and paragraph spacing in Safari

Solution

To remove all space between a heading and the paragraph that follows it, you must remove the bottom margin from the heading as well as the top margin from the paragraph. In modern browsers—including Internet Explorer 7 and above—we can do this through CSS using an adjacent selector. To achieve the same effect in older browsers, however, we need to revert to other techniques that are better supported.

Using an Adjacent Selector

An adjacent selector lets you target an element that follows another element, as long as both share the same parent. In fact, you can use adjacent selectors to specify an element that follows several other elements instead of just one. The element to which the style is applied is always the *last element in the chain*. If you're confused, be assured that this concept will be clearer once we've seen it in action.

The following style rules remove the top margin from any paragraph that immediately follows a level-one heading. Note that the top margin is actually removed from *the paragraph* that follows the h1, rather than the level-one heading itself:

chapter_02/headingnospace.css (excerpt)

```css
h1 {
  font: 1.6em Verdana, Geneva, Arial, Helvetica, sans-serif;
  margin-bottom: 0;
}

h1+p {
  margin-top: 0;
}
```

Figure 2.13 shows the display of the original page once this rule is applied.

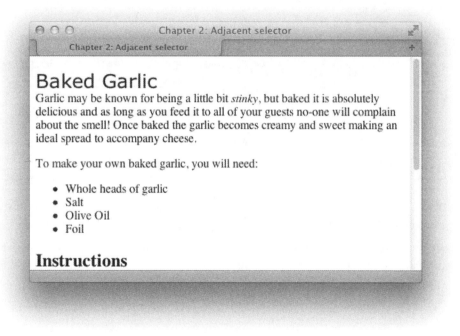

Figure 2.13. Using an adjacent selector to change the heading display

As you can see, the first paragraph that follows the h1 no longer has a top margin; all subsequent paragraphs, however, retain their top margins.

Discussion

The adjacent selector is supported in Internet Explorer 7 and above, and in all recent versions of other browsers. See Chapter 7 for details of how to manage support for IE6 if this is required.

How do I highlight text on the page?

A common feature on many websites is to highlight an important term on a page, such as the search terms visitors have used to locate our web page through a search engine. It's easy to highlight text using CSS.

Solution

If you wrap the text to be highlighted with span tags and add a class attribute, you can easily add a CSS rule for that class. For example, in the following paragraph, we've wrapped a phrase in span tags that apply the class hilite:

chapter_02/hilite.html *(excerpt)*

```
<p>Garlic may be known for being a little bit <span class="hilite">
  stinky</span>, but baked it is absolutely delicious and as long as
  you feed it to all of your guests no-one will complain about the
  smell! Once baked the garlic becomes creamy and sweet making an
  ideal spread to accompany cheese.</p>
```

The style rule for the hilite class is shown below; the highlighted section will display as seen in Figure 2.14:

chapter_02/hilite.css *(excerpt)*

```
.hilite {
  background-color: #FFFFCC;
  color: #B22222;
}
```

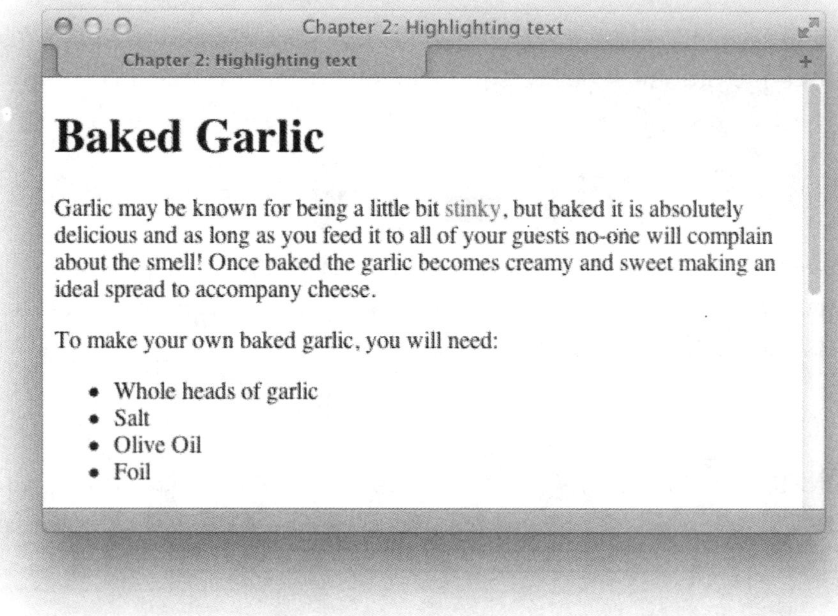

Figure 2.14. Highlighting text with a class

When It's All Done for Show

You should only highlight text in this way if the effect is purely presentational, and only relevant to those who can see the text in the browser. If the text needs to be highlighted in order to convey its meaning, consider using em (for emphasis) or strong instead, and then style the em or strong element. By using em or strong, you affect the meaning of the document. In such cases where highlighting is for looks only and no additional semantic elements are required, the technique explained here is the best one to use.

How do I alter the line height (leading) of my text?

One of the great advantages that CSS had over earlier web design methods like font tags is that it gave you far more control over the way text looked on the page. In this solution, we'll alter the leading of the text in your document.

Solution

If the default spacing between the lines of text on your page looks a little narrow, you can change it with the `line-height` property:

```
                                               chapter_02/leading.css
p {
  font: 1em Verdana, Geneva, Arial, Helvetica, sans-serif;
  line-height: 2.2;
}
```

The result is shown in Figure 2.15.

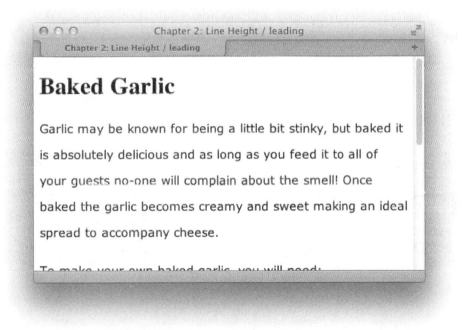

Figure 2.15. Adjusting the leading using `line-height`

Just take care not to overdo it by spacing the text out so much that it's hard to read.

For Good Measure

You'll notice that we didn't specify any unit of measurement in this example; that's because the value of 2.2 is a ratio. You can specify a value for line-height using standard CSS units of measurement, such as ems or pixels, but doing so breaks the link between the line height and the font size for child elements. For instance, if this example contained a span that set a large font-size, the line height would scale up proportionally and maintain the same ratio, because the line-height of the paragraph was set to the numerical value 2.2. If, however, the line-height was set to 2.2em or 220%, the span would inherit the actual line height instead of the ratio, and the large font size would have no effect on the line height of the span. Depending on the effect you're going for, this may actually be a desirable result.

How do I justify text?

When you justify text, you alter the spacing between the words so that both the left and right margins are aligned. You can create this effect easily using CSS.

Solution

You can justify paragraph text with the help of the text-align property, like so:

chapter_02/justify.css

```
p {
  text-align: justify;
  font: 1em Verdana, Geneva, Arial, Helvetica, sans-serif;
  line-height: 2.2;
}
```

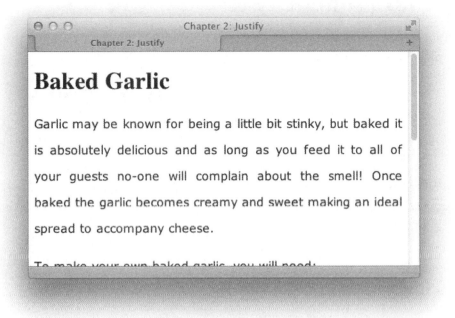

Figure 2.16. Justified text

Discussion

The other values for `text-align` are:

- `right`: aligns the text to the right of the container
- `left`: aligns the text to the left of the container
- `center`: centers the text in the container

The Language of `text-align`

The default value for `text-align` is `left` for languages that are read from left to right (such as English and French) and `right` for languages that are read right to left (Hebrew or Arabic). If no `text-align` value is set, the text will be displayed depending on the text direction of the language the site is being viewed in. If your site has to support bidirectional text flowed into the same templates, take care to test `text-align` in both language directions.

How do I indent text?

To indent text, we apply a rule to its container that sets a `padding-left` value, for example:

chapter_02/indent.html *(excerpt)*

```
<p class="indent">Garlic may be known for being a little bit
  <span class="hilite">stinky</span>, but baked it is absolutely
  delicious and as long as you feed it to all of your guests no-one
  will complain about the smell! Once baked the garlic becomes
  creamy and sweet making an ideal spread to accompany cheese.</p>
```

Here's the rule:

chapter_02/indent.css

```
.indent {
  padding-left: 1.5em;
}
```

You can see the indented paragraph in Figure 2.17.

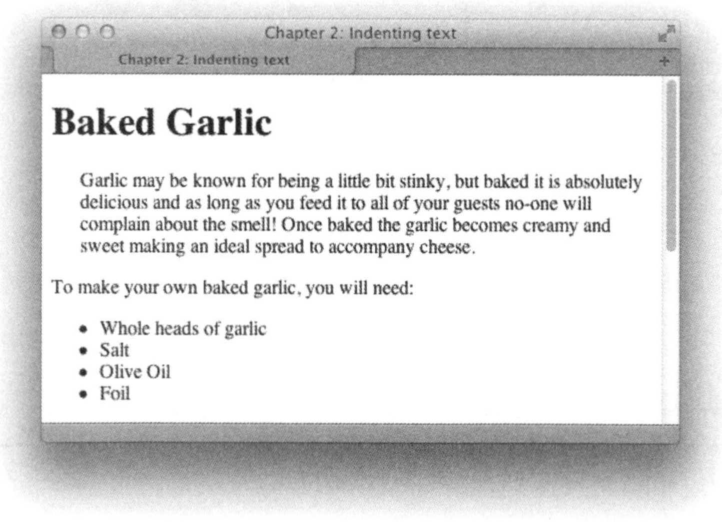

Figure 2.17. The first paragraph has been indented

Discussion

You should avoid using the HTML tag `blockquote` to indent text unless the text is actually a quote. This bad habit was a technique encouraged in the past by visual editing environments such as Dreamweaver, which played on the fact that a browser's default stylesheet usually indents a `blockquote`. Some WYSIWYG (What You See Is What You Get) editors used in content management systems also do this. If you're currently using an editor that employs `blockquote` tags to indent text, you should resist the temptation to use it for this purpose; instead, set up a CSS rule to indent the appropriate blocks as just shown.

The `blockquote` tag is designed to mark up a quote, and devices such as screen readers used by visually impaired people will read this text in a way that helps them understand that it's a quote. Hence, using `blockquote` to indent regular paragraphs will be very confusing for such users.

A One-liner

A related technique enables us to indent just the first line of each paragraph. Simply apply the CSS property `text-indent` to the paragraph—or to a `class` that's applied to the paragraphs—that you wish to display in this way:

```
                                                    chapter_02/indent2.css
p {
  text-indent: 1.5em;
}
```

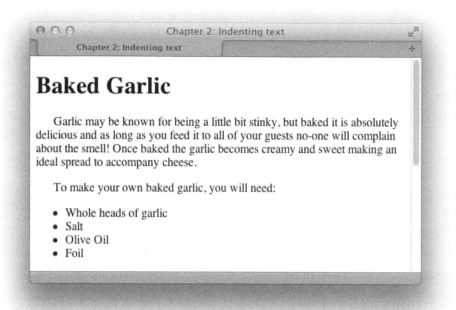

Figure 2.18. The first line of each paragraph has been indented

How do I center text?

You can center text, or any other element, using the `text-align` property.

Solution

To center a paragraph using the `text-align` property, give it a value of `center`:

```
                                    chapter_02/center.html (excerpt)

<p class="centered">Garlic may be known ...</p>
```

```
                                    chapter_02/center.css

.centered {
  text-align: center;
}
```

The result of this rule can be seen in Figure 2.19.

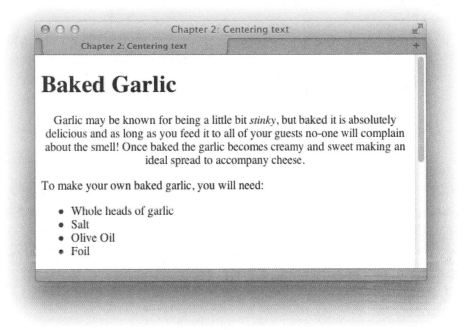

Figure 2.19. The first paragraph has been centered

How do I change text to all capitals using CSS?

Solution

You can change text to all capitals, and perform other transformations, by using the `text-transform` property:

chapter_02/uppercase.html (excerpt)

```
<p class="transform">Garlic may be known for ...</p>
```

chapter_02/uppercase.css

```
.transform {
  text-transform: uppercase;
}
```

Note the uppercase text in Figure 2.20.

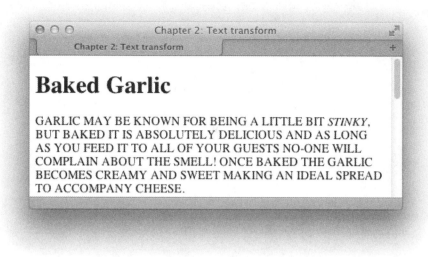

Figure 2.20. The paragraph has been transformed to uppercase

Discussion

The `text-transform` property has other useful values. The value `capitalize` will capitalize the first letter of each word, as illustrated in Figure 2.21. This is very useful for transforming headings when text is being entered via a CMS. Users are unlikely to remember to capitalize everything correctly, but with CSS you can ensure that text will display neatly, regardless of what has been entered. You should be aware, however, that words such as "a" and "the" will also be capitalized.

chapter_02/capitalize.css *(excerpt)*

```css
.transform {
  text-transform: capitalize;
}
```

Figure 2.21. The first letter of each word has been capitalized

The other values that the `text-transform` property can take are:

- `lowercase`
- `none`

How do I create a drop-caps effect?

Making the first letter in a paragraph larger—a simple drop-capitals effect—is easily achieved with CSS.

Solution

This can be achieved by using the `first-letter` pseudo-class selector:

chapter_02/dropcaps.html *(excerpt)*

```
<h1>Baked Garlic</h1>
<p>Garlic may be known for being a little bit <em>stinky</em>, but
   baked it is absolutely delicious and as long as you feed it to all
```

```
of your guests no-one will complain about the smell! Once baked
the garlic becomes creamy and sweet making an ideal spread to
accompany cheese.</p>
```

chapter_02/dropcaps.css

```
h1 + p:first-letter {
  font-size: 200%;
  font-weight: bold;
  float: left;
  width: 1em;
  line-height: 1;
}
```

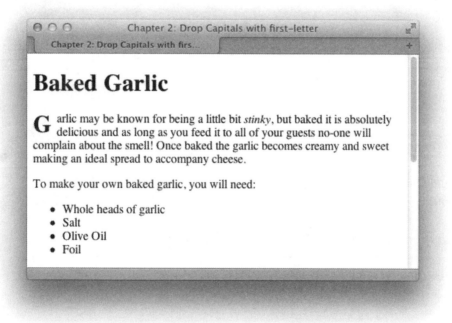

Figure 2.22. The simple drop-capitals effect

Discussion

This is a basic example demonstrating the use of the pseudo-class selector `first-letter`. I've also used an adjacent selector to only target the paragraph that comes directly after an `h1`; without this, the first letter of every paragraph would have a drop cap. Because browsers interpret line-height differently, the results can be a little inconsistent, so you'll need to experiment a little for a pleasing effect.

There is a useful article by James Edwards on the SitePoint website that discusses creating a drop-caps effect in some detail.[3]

How do I add a drop shadow to my text?

A drop shadow can be used to add a tiny shadow, whether to gently highlight some text, or allow a more dramatic shadow effect.

Solution

The text-shadow property lets you add shadows to text—from the subtle to the completely crazy:

chapter_02/textshadow.html (excerpt)

```
<h1>Baked Garlic</h1>
<p>Garlic may be known for being a little bit <em>stinky</em>, but
   baked it is absolutely delicious and as long as you feed it to all
   of your guests no-one will complain about the smell! Once baked
   the garlic becomes creamy and sweet making an ideal spread to
   accompany cheese.</p>
```

chapter_02/textshadow.css

```
h1 {
  font-size: 250%;
  color: #256579;
  text-shadow: 3px 3px 3px #999;
}
```

---

[3] http://www.sitepoint.com/a-simple-css-drop-cap/

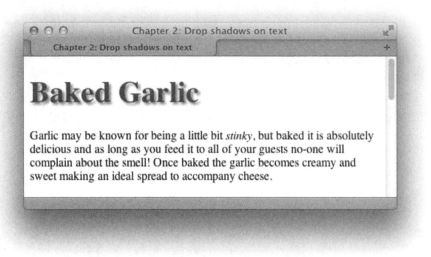

Figure 2.23. The drop shadow on a heading

Discussion

The syntax for the `text-shadow` property is straightforward:

```
text-shadow: 5px, 5px, 5px, #999;
```

The first value is the horizontal distance from the text; the second is the vertical distance; the third is the blur radius or spread of the shadow; and the final value is the color. The easiest way to see how `text-shadow` works is to create a large heading —so you can easily see your changes—and then play around with the values. You can also have a play around with `text-shadow` and many other CSS3 properties at the online CSS3 Generator[4].

Beyond a Shadow of Doubt

When adding shadows to text, make sure that your text is still legible. I find `text-shadow` most useful when adding effects to form buttons and big headings, but large quantities of body copy can be hard to read with a shadow applied. Sadly, the `text-shadow` property is unsupported in Internet Explorer (including

---

[4] http://css3generator.com/

version 9). We'll discuss this further in Chapter 7, where we'll cover ways of dealing with it.

How do I change or remove the bullets on list items?

Solution

You can change the style of bullets displayed on an unordered list by altering the `list-style-type` property. First, here's the markup for the list:

chapter_02/listtype.html (excerpt)

```
<ul>
  <li>Brie</li>
  <li>Cheddar</li>
  <li>Red Leicester</li>
  <li>Shropshire Blue</li>
</ul>
```

To display square bullets as in Figure 2.24, set the `list-style-type` property to square:

chapter_02/listtype.css

```
ul {
  list-style-type: square;
}
```

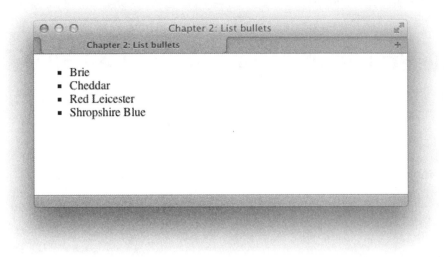

Figure 2.24. Square list bullets

Discussion

Some of the other values that the list-style-type property can take are disc, circle, decimal-leading-zero, decimal, lower-roman, upper-roman, lower-alpha, upper-alpha, and none.

You'll find that some of these values have no support in certain browsers; those browsers without support for a particular bullet type will display the default type instead. You can see the different types, and check the support your browser has for them, at the CSS Test Suite for list-style-type.[5] Setting list-style-type to none will remove bullets from the display, although the list will still be indented as if the bullets were there, as Figure 2.25 shows:

```
ul {
  list-style-type: none;
}
```

[5] http://meyerweb.com/eric/css/tests/css2/sec12-06-02a.htm

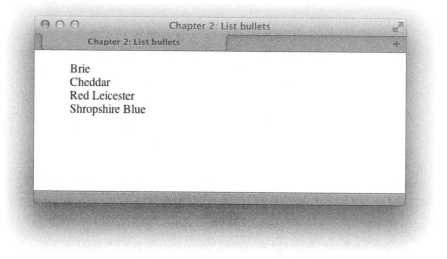

Figure 2.25. No list bullets

How do I use an image for a list-item bullet?

Solution

Create your image, then use the `list-style-image` property to set your bullets rather than `list-style-type`. This property accepts a URL, which can incorporate the path to your image file as a value:

chapter_02/listimage.css

```
ul {
  list-style-image: url(bullet.gif);
}
```

Figure 2.26 shows how this effect can be used to spruce up a list.

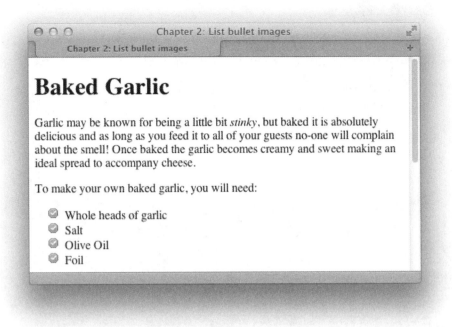

Figure 2.26. Images used for list bullets

Setting Bullets on Individual List Items

The `list-style-image` property applies to the list item (`li`) elements in the list. But if you apply `list-style-image` to the list as a whole (the `ul` or `ol` element), each individual list item will inherit it. You do, however, have the option of setting the property on individual list items by assigning a `class` or `id` to each, giving individual items their own unique bullet images.

If turning the bullet into an image is falling short of the desired result, your other option would be to use a background image, which we'll discuss in Chapter 3.

How do I remove the indented left-hand margin from a list?

If you've set `list-style-type` to `none`, you may also wish to remove or decrease the default left-hand margin that the browser sets on a list.

Solution

To remove the indentation entirely and have your list align left so that it lines up with a preceding paragraph as shown in Figure 2.27, use a style rule similar to this:

chapter_02/listnomargin.css

```css
ul {
  list-style-type: none;
  padding-left: 0;
  margin-left: 0;
}
```

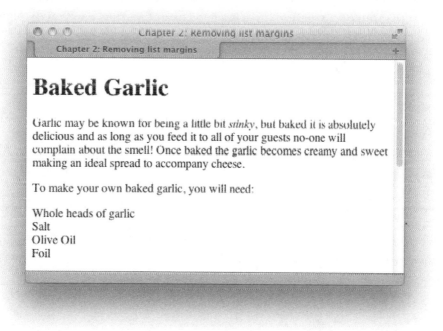

Figure 2.27. Removing the list margin and bullets

Discussion

You can apply new indentation values to the list items if you wish. To indent the content by a few pixels, try this:

chapter_02/listsmallmargin.css

```
ul {
  list-style-type: none;
  padding-left: 5px;
  margin-left: 0;
}
```

How do I display a list horizontally?

By default, list items display as block elements; therefore, each new item will display on a new line. However, there may be times when some content on your page is, structurally speaking, a list, even though you'd prefer to display it in a different way—a collection of navigation links is a good example. How can you display these list items horizontally?

Solution

You can set a list to display horizontally by altering the display property of the li element to inline, like so:

chapter_02/listinline.html *(excerpt)*

```
<ul class="nav">
  <li><a href="#breakfast">Breakfast recipes</a></li>
  <li><a href="#lunch">Lunch recipes</a></li>
  <li><a href="#dinner">Dinner recipes</a></li>
</ul>
```

chapter_02/listinline.css

```
ul.nav li {
  display: inline;
}
```

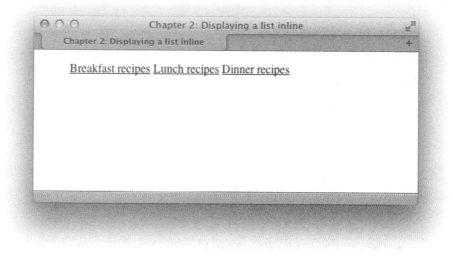

Figure 2.28. The list displayed inline

How do I remove page margins?

The default styles of most browsers add margins or padding between the browser chrome and the page content; this is so that text in an unstyled page ends before the edge of the browser window. You'll probably want to remove this gap or dictate the size of it, rather than leave it up to the browser.

Solution

To remove all margin and padding around your content, use the following style rules, which have been defined for the body element:

```
body {
  margin: 0;
  padding: 0;
}
```

The result is shown in Figure 2.29.

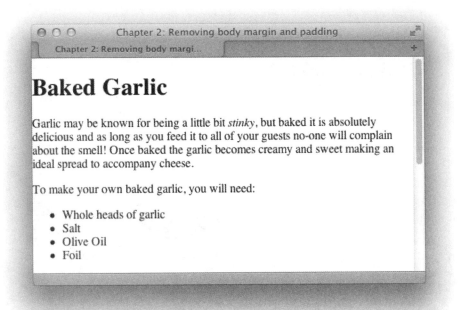

Figure 2.29. The default page padding and margins have been removed

How can I remove browsers' default padding and margins from all elements?

The display that you see in a browser when you view an unstyled document is the result of the browser's internal stylesheet. Often, the differences that arise in the way various browsers display an unstyled page occur because those browsers have slightly different internal stylesheets.

Solution

One way to solve this problem is to remove the default margins and padding from all elements before you create your styles. The following rule will set the padding and margins on all elements to zero. It will have the effect of causing every element on the page—paragraphs, headings, lists, and more—to display without leaving any space between them, as Figure 2.30 demonstrates:

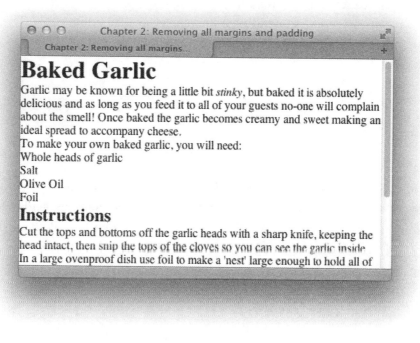

Figure 2.30. Removing padding and margins from all elements with the universal selector

chapter_02/zeropagemargin.css

```
* {
  margin: 0;
  padding: 0
}
```

Discussion

This style rule uses the universal selector—also known as the asterisk or star (*)—to remove the margins and padding from everything, a technique known as performing a **global whitespace reset**. If you're working on a particularly complex design, this may be the best way to start.

Once you've done this, though, you'll need to go back and add margins and padding to every element you use. This is particularly important for some form elements, which may be rendered unusable by this style rule.

For simpler designs, removing the whitespace from every element is usually overkill, and simply generates more work; you'll need to go back and add padding and margins to elements such as paragraphs, blockquotes, and lists. A viable alternative is to remove the margins and padding from a select set of elements only. The following style rule shows how this works, removing whitespace from heading and list elements:

```
h1, h2, h3, h4, h5, h6, ul, ol {
  margin: 0;
  padding: 0;
}
```

There has been much discussion in the web development community over whether CSS Resets are a good idea or not. Personally, I don't use them, instead preferring to perform a similar method to what we've just seen, depending on the project. If you do find them helpful, I'd suggest looking at Eric Meyer's CSS Reset[6] as a solid starting point.

How do I use fonts other than those installed on most users' computers?

When we discussed `font-family` at the beginning of this chapter, I mentioned that you have to be careful about selecting fonts, as there are only a few fonts that you can safely assume are on most users' computers. However, CSS provides a way to use other fonts, too, by loading a font file from the server.

Solution

In theory, we can import a new font using the `font-face` property:

```
@font-face {
  font-family: KaffeesatzBold;
  src: url(YanoneKaffeesatz-Bold.ttf);
}

h1 {
  font-family: KaffeesatzBold, sans-serif;
  font-weight: normal;
}
```

---

[6] http://meyerweb.com/eric/tools/css/reset/

The @font-face rule declares the name of the font, then enables you to load in a font file that's on your server with the src property. You can then just use this font in your font-family list as you would any other font.

Discussion

There are two issues with using @font-face currently. The first is that no single font format is supported across all browsers and operating systems; therefore, importing a font is a little more complicated than just loading in a single file as in the preceding example.

The second issue is licensing. Many of the fonts that you might use in Photoshop on your own computer aren't licensed to be uploaded to a web server and served in this way, as other users could download the font file itself—just as they can download an image that you're using on your website.

Browser Compatibility for Fonts You Can Upload to Your Server

If you do have a font that's licensed for use on the Web, your main issue is generating a package of fonts that will cover all browsers and operating systems. The simplest way to do this is to use one of the sites that can generate you a set of font files; I like to use Font Squirrel.[7] In addition to having a library of fonts you may use on the Web, the site has a @font-face generator that will create your set of fonts from one that you upload. Upload your font, and you can then download a package of various font types along with the CSS rules needed to include them in your site:

chapter_02/fontface.css (excerpt)

```css
@font-face {
  font-family: 'YanoneKaffeesatzBold';
  src: url('yanonekaffeesatz-bold-webfont.eot');
  src: url('yanonekaffeesatz-bold-webfont.eot?#iefix')
       format('embedded-opentype'),
     url('yanonekaffeesatz-bold-webfont.woff') format('woff'),
     url('yanonekaffeesatz-bold-webfont.ttf') format('truetype'),
     url('yanonekaffeesatz-bold-webfont.svg#YanoneKaffeesatzBold')
       format('svg');
```

---

[7] http://www.fontsquirrel.com/fontface/generator

```
    font-weight: normal;
    font-style: normal;
}
```

Add the rule to your CSS, and you can then use this font as normal. Make sure that you remember to upload the font files when deploying your site.

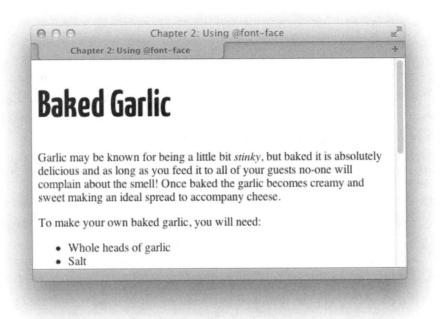

Figure 2.31. Using a custom font package generated by Font Squirrel

If Your Font is not Licensed for Web Use

If your font is without a license for such use, you can either search sites such as Font Squirrel for a similar font, or take up another option. There are a number of services now available—some from the font foundries themselves—that offer served, licensed fonts for use on websites, such as:

- Typekit[8]
- Fontdeck[9]

---

[8] https://typekit.com/
[9] http://fontdeck.com/

■ Web Fonts from Fonts.com[10]

These services host the fonts in a secure way; you sign up for an account, and can then use the fonts on your website by loading them in from the remote server. Typically, they have a tool that allows you to generate the code required for your site. Each service works in a slightly different way, but getting up and running with a font usually involves selecting it on the service and then pasting some code into your site. You can then use the fonts as normal in your CSS.

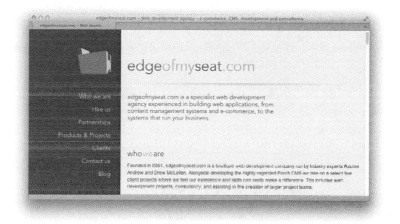

Figure 2.32. My company site, edgeofmyseat.com, uses the Avenir font hosted by webfonts.fonts.com

Each service licenses different fonts, so generally you need to select a service based on the font that you require. I think we'll see greater provision of web font services by the font foundries in the future, as designers will be selecting fonts for projects based on the availability of the web font.

Working with Style

This chapter has covered the more common questions asked by those relatively new to CSS—questions that relate to styling and manipulating text on the page. By combining these techniques, you can create attractive effects that will degrade appropriately for browsers unable to support certain aspects of CSS.

---

[10] http://webfonts.fonts.com/

Images and Other Design Elements

The Web is filled with sites featuring beautiful, rich graphic design that takes advantage of the power of CSS. In this chapter, we'll look at how to use CSS and images to create gorgeous effects. We'll be using images more in subsequent chapters, but, as with most of the solutions in this book, feel free to experiment to see what unique effects you can create.

How do I add borders to images?

Photographic images, which might be used to illustrate an article or be displayed in a photo album, look neat when they're bordered with a thin line. However, it's a time-consuming process to open each image in a graphics program in order to add borders, and if you ever need to change a given border's color or thickness, you'll be required to go through the same arduous process all over again. Fortunately, CSS makes this chore a whole lot easier.

Solution

Adding a border to an image is a simple procedure using CSS. To start, take the two images displayed in Figure 3.1.

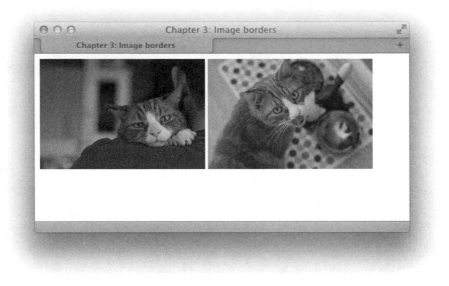

Figure 3.1. Two feline images

The following rule will add a two-pixel black border to our images:

```css
img {
  border-width: 2px;
  border-style: solid;
  border-color: #000000;
}
```

The rule could also be written in shortened form:

```css
                                          chapter_03/imageborders.css
img {
  border: 2px solid #000;
}
```

Figure 3.2 shows the effect this rule has on images.

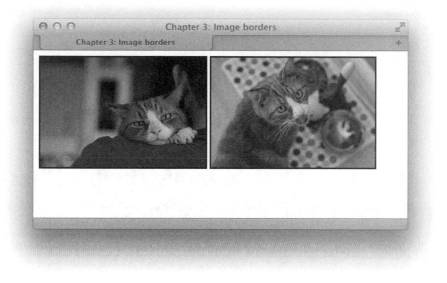

Figure 3.2. Our two images now have borders

Now this is all well and good, but your layout probably contains other images to which you don't want to apply a permanent black border. The solution is to create a CSS class for the border and apply it to selected images as required:

chapter_03/imageborders2.css

```
.imgborder {
  border: 2px solid #000;
}
```

chapter_03/imageborders2.html *(excerpt)*

```
<img src="widget1.jpg" alt="Widget the cat" class="imgborder" />
```

If you're displaying a selection of images—such as a photograph album—on the page, you could set borders on all the images within a particular container, such as an unordered list that has a class applied:

chapter_03/imageborders3.css

```
.album img {
  border: 2px solid #000;
}
```

chapter_03/imageborders3.html *(excerpt)*

```
<ul class="album">
  <li><img src="widget1.jpg" alt="Widget the cat" /></li>
  <li><img src="widget2.jpg" alt="Widget shows his tongue" /></li>
</ul>
```

This approach will save you from having to add the class to each individual image within the container.

How do I use CSS to remove the blue border around my navigation images?

If you use images in your site's navigation links, you may notice an ugly blue border in some browsers, just like the underline on text-based links. So how do you remove it using CSS?

Solution

Just as you can create a border, so you can remove one. Adding a rule with the `border` property set to `none` will remove those borders:

chapter_03/bordernone.css *(excerpt)*

```
img {
  border: none;
}
```

How do I set a background for my page using CSS?

CSS has properties that allow you to set a background color, or image, or both, on your pages.

Solution

The following rules add a background color and background image to the `body` element of the page. Then we give the `div` (which has a `class` of `wrapper`) a white background color, but no background image:

chapter_03/background.css (excerpt)

```css
body {
  background-color: #333;
  background-image: url(brushed_alu_dark.png);
  color: #fff;
  margin: 0;
  padding: 0;
  font: 0.75em/1.3 "Lucida Grande", "Lucida Sans Unicode",
    "Lucida Sans", Verdana, Tahoma, sans-serif;
}

.wrapper {
  width: 80%;
  margin: 20px auto 40px auto;
  background-color: #fff;
  color: #333;
}
```

In Figure 3.3 you can see how this looks.

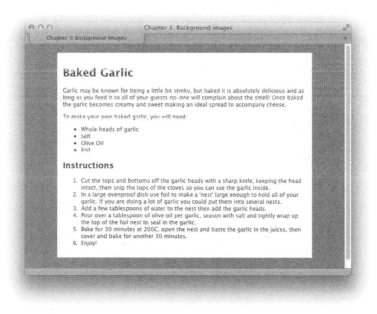

Figure 3.3. Using a background image and color

Discussion

The `background-color` property simply adds a color to the page or element to which it's applied. I've used `background-color` to set the `body` to a dark gray color (just in case the image fails to load for some reason), and then set the `wrapper div` to white. If there had been no background color of `wrapper`, the background image on the body would have showed through.

The `background-image` property allows you to specify an image to be loaded and displayed as a background image. In this case, we wanted to add it as a background image for the whole page so we used it on the `body` tag. You can use background images on most elements, as you'll see in a later example in this chapter.

By default the background will tile. In this example, I downloaded the image **brushed_alu_dark.png**, a small tile, from a site offering free patterns.[1] The browser repeats the tile to fill the available space in the element.

Figure 3.4. The background tile

---

[1] http://subtlepatterns.com

How do I control how my background image repeats?

Solution

To prevent the background from repeating at all, we'd use the keyword `no-repeat`:

```
background-repeat: no-repeat;
```

This means that the only background image we'd see would be a single square of the tile in the top-left corner, as Figure 3.5 indicates.

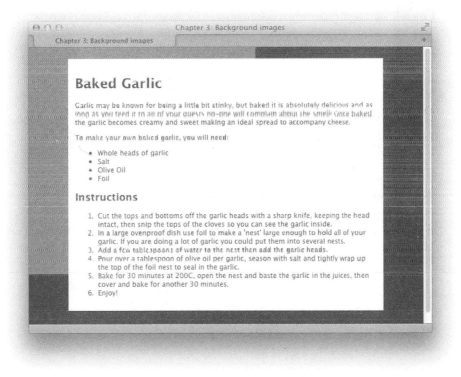

Figure 3.5. The tile is set to `no-repeat`

If we wanted to only tile along the *x* axis, as shown in Figure 3.6, we could use the following:

```
background-repeat: repeat-x;
```

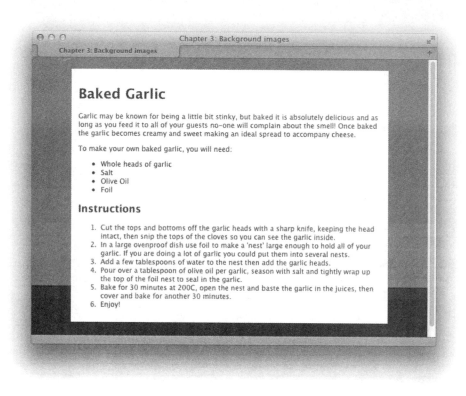

Figure 3.6. The image tiles along the *x* axis

As you've probably realized by now, we can also tile it down the *y* axis with:

```
background-repeat: repeat-y;
```

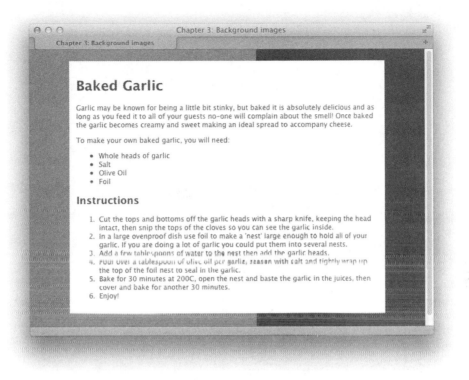

Figure 3.7. The image tiles along the y axis

How do I position my background image?

By default, if you add a single, non-repeating background image to the page, it will appear in the top-left corner of the viewport. If you've set the background to tile in any direction, the first image will appear in this location and tile from that point. However, it's possible to display the image at other locations on the page.

Solution

We use the CSS property `background-position` to position background images:

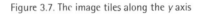

```
                                          chapter_03/backgroundposition.css

.box {
  height: 200px;
  width: 200px;
  border: 3px solid #333;
  background-image: url(gear.png);
```

```
    background-repeat: no-repeat;
    background-position: bottom right;
}
```

This rule displays a box with a gear image positioned to the bottom right of the box, as shown in Figure 3.8.

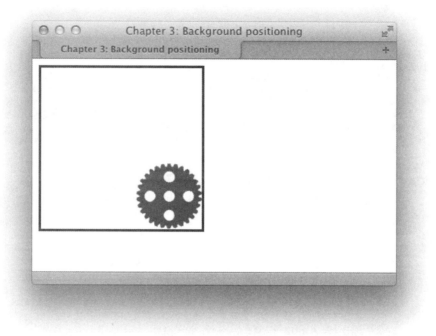

Figure 3.8. The gear image is positioned to the bottom right of the container

Discussion

The `background-position` property can take as its value keywords, percentage values, or values in units, such as pixels.

Keywords

In this example, we used keywords to specify that the background image should be displayed at the bottom right of the content `div`:

```
background-position: bottom right;
```

You can use any of these keyword combinations:

- `top left`
- `top center`
- `top right`
- `center left`
- `center center`
- `center right`
- `bottom left`
- `bottom center`
- `bottom right`

If you only specify one of the values, the other will default to `center`:

```
background-position: top;
```

This is the same as:

```
background-position: top center;
```

Percentage Values

To achieve a more accurate image placement, you can specify the values as percentages. This approach is particularly useful in a layout where other page elements are specified in percentages, so that they resize in accordance with the user's screen resolution and dimensions. This becomes particularly important when creating responsive designs, as we'll see in later chapters of this book:

```
background-position: 30% 80%;
```

The first of the percentages refers to the background's horizontal position; the second dictates its vertical position. Percentages are taken from the top-left corner of the display, with `0% 0%` placing the top-left corner of the image against the top-left corner of the browser window, and `100% 100%` placing the bottom-right corner of the image against the bottom-right corner of the window.

As with keywords, a default percentage value comes into play if you only specify one value. That default is `50%`. Take a look at the following declaration:

```
background-position: 30%;
```

This creates the same effect as:

```
background-position: 30% 50%;
```

Unit Values

You can set positioning values using any CSS unit, such as pixels or ems:

```
background-position: 20px 20px;
```

As with percentages, the first of the specified values dictates the horizontal position, while the second dictates the vertical. But unlike percentages, the measurements directly control the position of the top-left corner of the background image.

You can mix units with percentages and, if you only specify one value, the second will default to 50%.

How do I fix my background image in place while the page is scrolled?

You've probably seen sites on which the background image stays static while the content scrolls over it. This effect is achieved using the background-attachment property.

Solution

We can use the background-attachment property with a value of fixed. This will fix the background so that it remains stationary while the content moves:

chapter_03/backgroundfixed.html (excerpt)

```
body {
  background-color: #fff;
  background-image: url(gold_scale.png);
  background-attachment: fixed;
  color: #000;
  margin: 0;
  padding: 0;
```

```
    font: 0.75em/1.3 "Lucida Grande", "Lucida Sans Unicode",
        "Lucida Sans", Verdana, Tahoma, sans-serif;
}
```

This is illustrated in Figure 3.9, but to really see the effect in motion, I suggest you load up the code example in a browser.

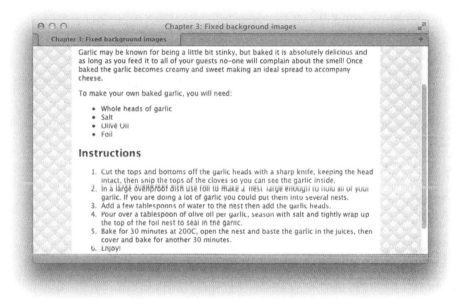

Figure 3.9. A fixed background image with the content scrolling over

Discussion

The value `fixed` for the `background-attachment` property is unsupported in Internet Explorer 6. Fortunately it degrades nicely—the background image will just scroll with the page.

In this solution, we're using several CSS properties to add our image to the background, position it, and dictate how it behaves when the document is scrolled.

Alternatively, we could use a shorthand method to supply this information—the CSS `background` property. This property allows you to declare `background-color`, `background-image`, `background-repeat`, `background-attachment`, and `background-position` in a single property declaration. Take, for example, this CSS rule:

```
body {
  background-color: #fff;
  background-image: url(gold_scale.png);
  background-attachment: fixed;
  background-repeat: repeat-x;
  background-position: 0 0;
}
```

These declarations could be written more succinctly as follows:

```
body {
  background: #fff url(gold_scale.png) repeat-x fixed 0 0;
}
```

Can I set a background image on any element?

So far in this chapter, we've looked at background images as used on the page body element; however, background images can be used on most other elements as well.

Solution

Understanding how to use images as background images is important, as you'll need to do it a lot when designing for the Web.

Figure 3.10 uses a number of background images.

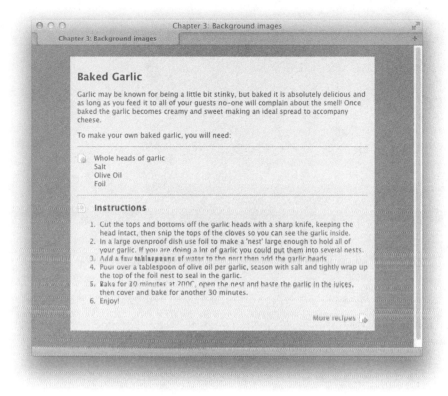

Figure 3.10. Background images applied to several elements

First, the `wrapper div` has a background image, which is a light version of the page background. This repeats along the *x* and *y* axis to cover that area:

```
                                      chapter_03/background2.css (excerpt)

.wrapper {
  width: 80%;
  margin: 20px auto 40px auto;
  background-color: #fff;
  color: #333;
  background-image: url(brushed_alu.png);
}
```

I've then added icons to both the list of ingredients and the heading of the Instructions section. For the list, we add the background image to the `ul` element:

```
                                    chapter_03/background2.css (excerpt)

ul.ingredients {
  border-top: 1px solid #999;
  border-bottom: 1px solid #999;
  list-style: none;
  margin: 1em 0 1em 0;
  padding: 1em 0 1em 30px;
  background-image: url(ingredients.png);
  background-repeat: no-repeat;
  background-position: 0 1em;
}
```

As you can see, there's a value of 1em to position the icon from the top of the container. This means that it lines up nicely with the text, as the list has a top padding of 1em applied as well. I've then added an icon to the h2 heading:

```
                                    chapter_03/background2.css (excerpt)

h2.instructions {
  background-image: url(instructions.png);
  background-repeat: no-repeat;
  background-position: left center;
  padding-left: 30px;
}
```

For both icons, I've used a left padding of 30 pixels so that the list and heading text are away from the edge of the container, and not overlapping the background image.

Finally, I've added an icon to the link at the bottom of the page in order to take the visitor to more recipes:

```
                                    chapter_03/background2.css (excerpt)

a.more:link, a.more:visited {
  display: block;
  padding: 0.3em 20px 0.3em 0;
  text-align: right;
  color: #666;
  font-weight: bold;
  background-image: url(arrow.png);
  background-position: right center;
```

```
    background-repeat: no-repeat;
    text-decoration: none;
}
```

Discussion

The use of background images is a core part of designing for the Web, but how do you know whether an image should be a background image, or if it should be part of the page as a regular image in HTML?

My rule of thumb is whether or not the image has any meaning to the rest of the document. I'd embed a photo or diagram related to the content as a regular image in the HTML document, and include the relevant `alt` text for users who are unable to see the image. Images that are added as a background image don't have `alt` text, so they'll be completely invisible to a screen reader user. Save background images for purely aesthetic design elements that would be of no interest to a user just reading the text of a page.

You might choose to omit or replace these background images when creating a mobile version of the layout, which we will discuss later in Chapter 9. Having incidental images as background images will make this task easier.

How do I create a gradient background?

It's common to require a linear gradient as the background of an entire web page or box or other element.

Solution

The CSS3 approach is to use the `background-image` property and specify a linear gradient as the value of this property:

chapter_03/gradient.css (excerpt)

```
html {
  height: 100%;
}

body {
  height: 100%;
```

```
background-attachment: fixed;
background-color: #666;
background-image: -webkit-gradient(linear, 0% 0%, 0% 100%,
  from(#000), to(#666));
background-image: -webkit-linear-gradient(top, #000, #666);
background-image: -moz-linear-gradient(top, #000, #666);
background-image: -ms-linear-gradient(top, #000, #666);
background-image: -o-linear-gradient(top, #000, #666);
background-image: linear-gradient(top, #000, #666);
color: #fff;
margin: 0;
padding: 0;
font: 0.75em/1.3 "Lucida Grande", "Lucida Sans Unicode",
  "Lucida Sans", Verdana, Tahoma, sans-serif;
}
```

This produces the effect shown in Figure 3.11.

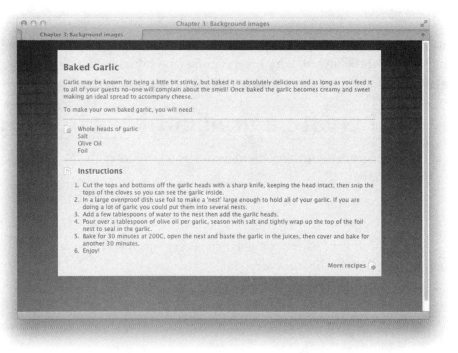

Figure 3.11. A background linear gradient using CSS3

Discussion

The value that you should be using as per the CSS3 specification is simply:

```
background-image: linear-gradient(top, #000, #666);
```

From the solution, you can see that we need to repeat this line using the different syntaxes expected by various browsers and the relevant vendor-specific extensions, as discussed in Chapter 1.

This technique works in all modern browsers except Internet Explorer. I've included it despite the lack of support in Internet Explorer because there is one environment where you're likely to find such gradients useful indeed: when you're developing for smartphones, tablets, or other mobile devices. Saving users of these devices from downloading images with large file sizes and employing CSS instead is very handy. It helps users avoid mobile limitations such as network latency, limited bandwith, and expensive data plans. We'll discuss this some more in Chapter 7.

So, what should you do if you need a gradient that works in Internet Explorer? My suggestion is to use an image. Create a one-pixel-wide image that's a gradient from black to #333333, and save it as **gradient.png**. Then use the following CSS to repeat the gradient image as a background along the *x* axis of the body element, creating a gradient background:

chapter_03/gradient2.css (excerpt)

```
body {
  background-color: #666;
  background-image: url(gradient.png);
  background-repeat: repeat-x;
  color: #fff;
  margin: 0;
  padding: 0;
  font: 0.75em/1.3 "Lucida Grande", "Lucida Sans Unicode",
    "Lucida Sans", Verdana, Tahoma, sans-serif;
}
```

Remember to set your background color to the same one that the gradient ends with, so that color continues even when the image stops.

Combining the Two Approaches

As described by Chris Coyier in his article "Speed Up with CSS Gradients,"[2] it is possible to combine the use of CSS gradients and a fallback image. Simply load the image first, then add the gradients—essentially combining the two techniques just outlined:

```
html {
  height: 100%;
}

body {
  height: 100%;
  background-attachment: fixed;
  background-color: #666;
  background-image: url(gradient.png);
  background-repeat: repeat-x;
  background-image: -webkit-gradient(linear, 0% 0%, 0% 100%,
    from(#000), to(#666));
  background-image: -webkit-linear-gradient(top, #000, #666);
  background-image: -moz-linear-gradient(top, #000, #666);
  background-image: -ms-linear-gradient(top, #000, #666);
  background-image: -o-linear-gradient(top, #000, #666);
  background-image: linear-gradient(top, #000, #666);
  color: #fff;
  margin: 0;
  padding: 0;
  font: 0.75em/1.3 "Lucida Grande", "Lucida Sans Unicode",
    "Lucida Sans", Verdana, Tahoma, sans-serif;
}
```

Because supporting browsers won't load the fallback image, this enables browsers that do support CSS3 gradients to avoid the overhead of downloading an image. This will be particularly advantageous if you use many gradients in your site, and you'll also gain the added benefit of being able to set these values as a percentage, as well as easily change the colors and settings.

---

[2] http://css-tricks.com/5700-css3-gradients/

This has been a simple introduction to gradients. To see how flexible CSS3 gradients can be—as well as learn some ready-to-use rules to paste into your CSS—try the Gradient Editor.[3]

A Final Tip on Gradients

Even if you decide that you need to create images for your gradients for better browser support, understanding CSS gradients can be really helpful while you're designing the site. Instead of creating gradients in dedicated image-editing software, saving a file, and then trying it out in the browser—simply change the values in your stylesheet. You can then create the final gradient images and add them in, saving you a whole lot of time!

Can I create a background image that scales with the browser window?

A popular effect is to use a full-size image in the background of a website that scales to the size of the browser window. How is this achieved?

Solution

To create scalable background images, you need to use the background-size property with a value of cover:

```
chapter_03/backgroundscalable.css (excerpt)

html {
  background-image: url(ballet-background.jpg);
  background-repeat: no-repeat;
  background-position: center center;
  background-attachment: fixed;
  -webkit-background-size: cover;
  -moz-background-size: cover;
  -o-background-size: cover;
  background-size: cover;
  color: #fff;
  background-color: #000;
}
```

---

[3] http://www.colorzilla.com/gradient-editor/

This will create the effect seen in Figure 3.12 and Figure 3.13, where the image still fills the entire browser window, regardless of whether the window is small or large.

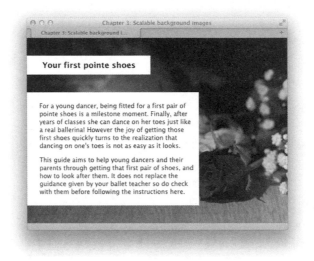

Figure 3.12. The image in a small browser window ...

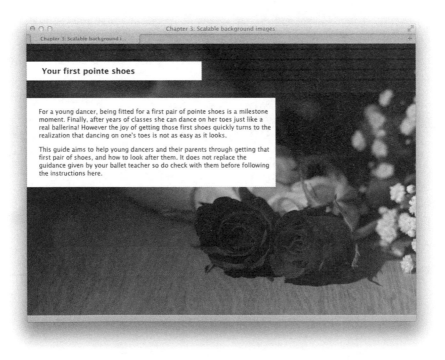

Figure 3.13. ... And in a large browser window

Discussion

This technique works in current browsers, including Internet Explorer 9. Browsers failing to support the property will display the background image centered, but not scaled down or up. Depending on your site and the image you choose, this can often be quite acceptable. For a range of more complicated methods that achieve this effect in earlier browsers, you could read Chris Coyier's article on the subject on the CSS-Tricks website.[4]

The biggest issue with scalable background images is the minimum size that it needs to be in order to render well at large sizes. Take care with your image selection and how you optimize the image so that your users avoid having to download a huge file size.

How do I add more than one background image to an element?

CSS2 only allowed for one background image to be applied to an element. In CSS3, however, you can add multiple background images.

Solution

Using the shorthand background property that we discussed earlier, we can simply add a list of background images and positioning information for the background property (each image is separated by a comma):

```
.box {
  height: 200px;
  width: 200px;
  border: 3px solid #333;
  background: url(gear.png) top right no-repeat,
  url(gear2.png) top left no-repeat,
  url(gear3.png) bottom left no-repeat,
  url(gear4.png) bottom right no-repeat;
}
```

This will display as in Figure 3.14, where each gear image is a background image.

---

[4] http://css-tricks.com/3458-perfect-full-page-background-image/

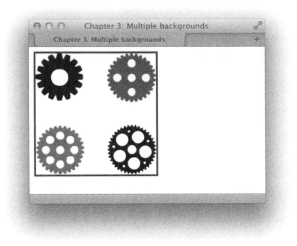

Figure 3.14. The box has four unique background images applied

Discussion

As mentioned, multiple background images are now supported in all major browsers, including Internet Explorer 9; however, be aware that in earlier browsers without support for multiple backgrounds, the browser ignores the entire rule. We'll discuss ways that you might deal with this in Chapter 7.

It's worth noting that the order of the images is important. The first image you declare will display on top of the stack, with the last being at the bottom. We can see how this works by adding a background texture to our box. If I add the background tile as the first image, it displays tiled on top of the gear images, so we're unable to see them, as Figure 3.15 reveals:

```css
.box {
  height: 200px;
  width: 200px;
  border: 3px solid #333;
  background: url(brushed_alu.png),
  url(gear.png) top right no-repeat,
  url(gear2.png) top left no-repeat,
  url(gear3.png) bottom left no-repeat,
  url(gear4.png) bottom right no-repeat;
}
```

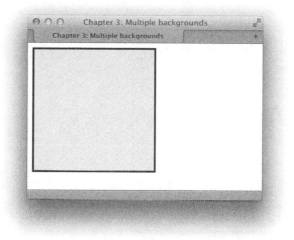

Figure 3.15. The **brushed_alu.png** image is tiled over the top of the cog images

If we were to instead make it the last image listed, it displays underneath the gear images as a background, as Figure 3.16 shows:

```
                                      chapter_03/backgroundmultiple.css
.box {
  height: 200px;
  width: 200px;
  border: 3px solid #333;
  background: url(gear.png) top right no-repeat,
  url(gear2.png) top left no-repeat,
  url(gear3.png) bottom left no-repeat,
  url(gear4.png) bottom right no-repeat,
  url(brushed_alu.png);
}
```

Figure 3.16. The background tile now displays underneath the cog images

How do I make an element transparent so that the background shows through?

The use of opacity can add subtle effects to your design. Until fairly recently, this was difficult to do across browsers and required the use of PNG images with an alpha channel—a portion of data which represents transparency information on a per-pixel basis; however, we now have ways to achieve opacity in our designs just using CSS.

Solution

I'm going to demonstrate two possible ways to make an element transparent. The first is to use the `opacity` property. This takes a value of between 0 and 1, where 0 is fully transparent and 1 is fully opaque:

```css
h1 {
  width: 40%;
  padding: 0.6em 0.6em 0.6em 2em;
  margin: 40px 0 0 0;
  font-size: 127.6%;
  background-color: #fff;
  color: #000;
  opacity: 0.5;
}

.content {
  width: 60%;
  padding: 0.6em 0.6em 0.6em 2em;
  margin: 40px 0 0 0;
  background-color: #fff;
  color: #000;
  opacity: 0.5;
}
```

The effect of using this method can be seen in Figure 3.17.

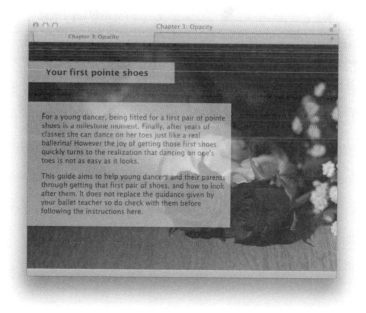

Figure 3.17. The two boxes are made transparent using opacity

The second method is to use RGBA when specifying the `background-color` value of the box. You may already be familiar with using RGB to set a color or background color. For example, to make the background white we would use:

```
background-color: rgb(255,255,255);
```

RGBA adds a fourth value to the list—the A in RGBA stands for Alpha—and controls opacity. We can use it to set the opacity level of the color, as shown in this example:

chapter_03/rgba.css (excerpt)

```
h1 {
    width: 40%;
    padding: 0.6em 0.6em 0.6em 2em;
    margin: 40px 0 0 0;
    font-size: 127.6%;
    background-color: rgba(255,255,255,0.5);
    color: #000;
}

.content {
    width: 60%;
    padding: 0.6em 0.6em 0.6em 2em;
    margin: 40px 0 0 0;
    background-color: rgba(255,255,255,0.5);
    color: #000;
}
```

The effect of the second method is shown in Figure 3.18.

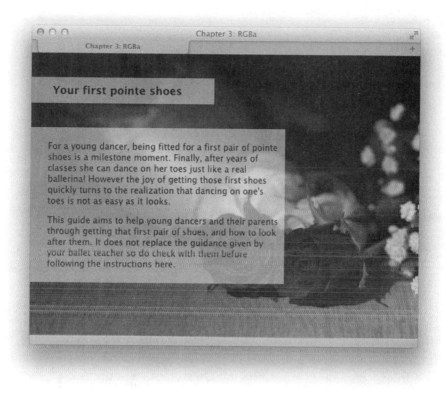

Figure 3.18. Making the background color transparent using RGBA

Discussion

While both methods are quite simple, the main difference is that when you use opacity, you make the entire box and all its content (the child elements of the element you have set `opacity` on) transparent. When using RGBA, only the color that you're specifying is affected by the rule, so the text inside our box won't inherit any transparency. As an example, I've set the foreground and background color of the heading to white in Figure 3.19. By using `opacity`, the text becomes transparent at the same time, so the background remains hidden:

```
h1 {
  width: 40%;
  padding: 0.6em 0.6em 0.6em 2em;
  margin: 40px 0 0 0;
  font-size: 127.6%;
  background-color: #fff;
```

```
  color: #fff;
  opacity: 0.3;
}
```

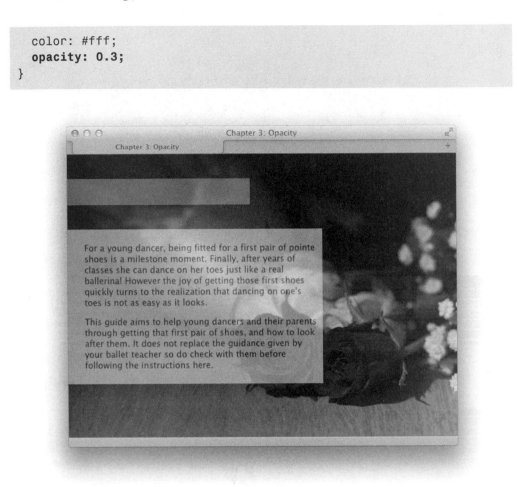

Figure 3.19. Hiding white text on a white background with `opacity`

Alternatively, using RGBA makes the background transparent, as in Figure 3.20; hence, the text appears from the background as it doesn't inherit the opacity setting:

```
h1 {
  width: 40%;
  padding: 0.6em 0.6em 0.6em 2em;
  margin: 40px 0 0 0;
  font-size: 127.6%;
  background-color: rgba(255,255,255,0.3);
  color: #fff;
}
```

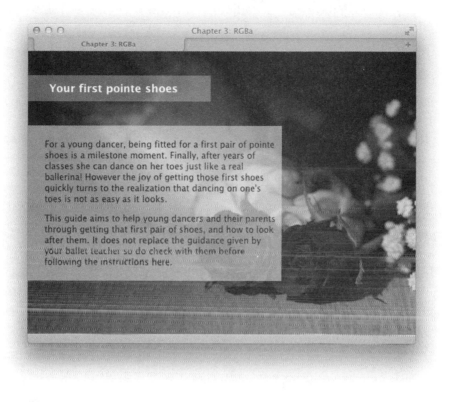

Figure 3.20. By using RGBA on the background, the text stays opaque and so is visible

The `opacity` property and RGBA are supported in all modern browsers including Internet Explorer 9. The `opacity` property will be ignored by older browsers that have no support for it. If you use RGBA, you should also provide a fallback color using RGB or hexadecimal values before the RGBA declaration. Browsers that don't understand RGBA will use the regular solid color and others will use RGBA, for example:

```
background-color: rgb(255,255,255);
background-color: rgba(255,255,255,0.3);
color: #000;
```

HSLA Color

There's a third method of using transparency when setting colors, and that's HSLA (Hue, Saturation, Lightness, and Alpha). HSLA works much like RGBA in that you set a color and then a value for the Alpha channel to control transparency. It's more uncommon, although the syntax is rather nice. If you wish to use HSLA instead of RGBA, there's a useful article on CSS-Tricks that will fill you in on the details.[5]

Being Careful with Color Contrasts

Take care when using any kind of transparency that your content will still be readable in browsers that use the solid color. It's very easy to end up with color contrasts that only work when the transparency is applied. We'll discuss these issues further in Chapter 7.

How can I add a drop shadow to an element?

In the last chapter, we looked at the text-shadow property, which allows us to add a shadow to some text. CSS3 also has a box-shadow property, which enables the adding of shadows to almost any element without having to resort to images.

Solution

Use box-shadow to create a shadow on the main container of a layout:

chapter_03/boxshadow.css *(excerpt)*

```css
.wrapper {
  width: 80%;
  margin: 20px auto 40px auto;
  background-color: #fff;
  color: #333;
  background-image: url(brushed_alu.png);
  -webkit-box-shadow: 3px 3px 10px 8px rgba(0, 0, 0, 0.4);
  -moz-box-shadow: 3px 3px 10px 8px rgba(0, 0, 0, 0.4);
  box-shadow: 3px 3px 10px 8px rgba(0, 0, 0, 0.4);
}
```

You can see the box-shadow effect applied to the wrapper div in Figure 3.21:

---

[5] http://css-tricks.com/6565-yay-for-hsla/

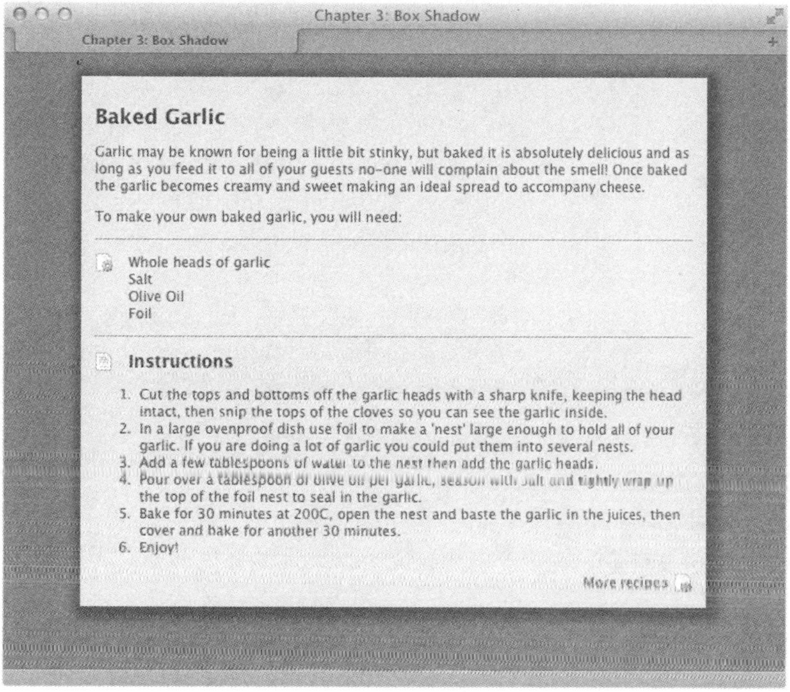

Figure 3.21. The main wrapper has a box-shadow applied

Discussion

The use of box-shadow makes adding shadows incredibly simple—far removed from the pain of creating shadow images in image-editing software and adding them as backgrounds. The official W3C syntax for box-shadow is:

```
box-shadow: 3px 3px 10px 8px rgba(0, 0, 0, 0.4);
```

The values are as follows, listed in the order shown above:

Horizontal offset value   This can be a positive or negative value. If positive, the shadow will be on the right side of the box; a negative value positions it to the left.

Vertical offset value	This can also be positive or negative, with positive placing the shadow below the box and negative above it.
Blur radius	A low value here means the shadow will be sharper, while a higher value makes it more blurred. This value must be 0 or a positive value; negative values aren't allowed.
Spread	Positive values cause the shadow shape to spread in all directions, while negative values cause the shadow to contract.
Color	This may be RGBA, as used in this example, or hex.

You can also add a keyword of `inset` at the beginning of the list of values, which will create an inner shadow:

```
box-shadow: inset 3px 3px 10px 8px rgba(0, 0, 0, 0.4);
```

Playing around with the values is the best way to get a feel for how `box-shadow` works. I often use an online `box-shadow` generator at the CSS3 Generator site[6] as it creates the syntax for me, and I can play around with values to see what effect they'll have.

The `box-shadow` property is supported by all modern browsers, including Internet Explorer 9, and will be ignored by earlier browsers without support.

How do I create rounded corners on an element?

To create rounded corners on an element, such as the wrapper in Figure 3.22, use the `border-radius` property:

---

[6] http://css3generator.com/

```
                                          chapter_03/borderradius.css (excerpt)

.wrapper {
  width: 80%;
  margin: 20px auto 40px auto;
  background-color: #fff;
  color: #333;
  background-image: url(brushed_alu.png);
  -webkit-box-shadow: 3px 3px 10px 8px rgba(0, 0, 0, 0.4);
  -moz-box-shadow: 3px 3px 10px 8px rgba(0, 0, 0, 0.4);
  box-shadow: 3px 3px 10px 8px rgba(0, 0, 0, 0.4);
  -webkit-border-radius: 10px;
  -moz-border-radius: 10px;
  border-radius: 10px;
}
```

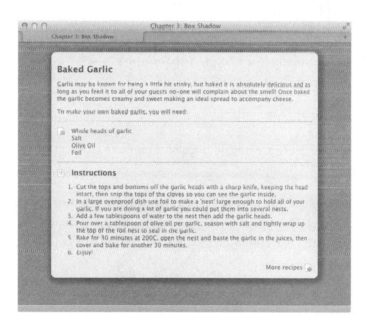

Figure 3.22. The wrapper now has rounded corners

Discussion

In this example, I've used a border-radius value of 10px to create a nicely rounded corner. You can use tiny values for a neat little edge, or substantial values to create a more rounded-box look. It's unnecessary to round all corners equally; for example, to round only the top-right corner, you could use:

```
-moz-border-radius-topright: 10px;
-webkit-border-radius: 0 10px 0 0;
border-radius: 0 10px 0 0;
```

I kept the shadow from the previous example in place on my wrapper, and you can see that after using border-radius, the shadow also curves round the corner. All current major browsers support border-radius, including Internet Explorer 9. It will be ignored by earlier browsers, which will simply display the square corners.

Can I rotate images without using image-editing software?

Another exciting feature of CSS3 is CSS transforms. It enables you to manipulate elements on the page using just CSS. In this solution, we'll use the transform property to gently rotate an image on the page.

Solution

I've included an image on my recipe page and given it a little drop shadow using box-shadow, as shown in Figure 3.23.

I'd like to slightly rotate this image. If my recipes were coming out of a content management system, I'd never expect people to open each image in image-editing software and apply the correct angle to each one before uploading them, so I'll use CSS to apply the rotation.

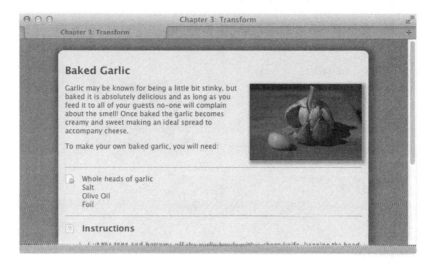

Figure 3.23. The image casts a shadow on the page

```
.recipe img {
  float: right;
  width: 200px;
  margin: 0 0 1em 1em;
  -webkit-box-shadow: 3px 3px 5px 3px rgba(0, 0, 0, 0.4);
  -moz-box-shadow: 3px 3px 5px 3px rgba(0, 0, 0, 0.4);
  box-shadow: 3px 3px 5px 3px rgba(0, 0, 0, 0.4);
  -webkit-transform: rotate(5deg);
  -moz-transform: rotate(5deg);
  -o-transform: rotate(5deg);
  -ms-transform: rotate(5deg);
  transform: rotate(5deg);
}
```

The image now displays as in Figure 3.24.

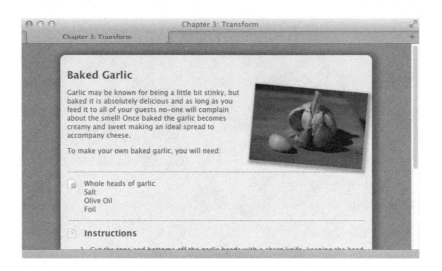

Figure 3.24. Our image is now rotated on the recipe page

Discussion

The `transform` property is one of the more fiddly properties added in the CSS specification, but it can be used to great effect in your designs, so I'd encourage you to play around with it. In addition to rotating, `transform` can be used to:

- scale an element, making it larger or smaller than it really is
- "translate" an element, which is moving it along the x and y axis
- skew an element, which skews the image and makes it slant along the x and y axis

These transformations really come into their own when applied as a user interacts with the page; for example, causing an element to grow as the user mouses over it using `scale`, or `rotate`. For more information on how to use transforms in your work, I recommend the article "A Primer on CSS3 Transforms" on the SitePoint website,[7] written by Louis Lazaris, the expert reviewer of this book.

---

[7] http://www.sitepoint.com/a-primer-on-css3-transforms/

It's important to note that when using transforms the rest of the content will not reflow to make room for the changed element. Therefore, when using rotate, you need to ensure that your rotated image won't obscure any text.

By using the vendor prefixes in the aforementioned example, you'll find that transforms are supported in all modern browsers and ignored in older browsers. Here an older browser would simply show the image in its unrotated state.

What should I be aware of in terms of accessibility when using color?

When using color and opacity in your designs, it's vital to keep in mind that not all users see color in the same way, or that some may use browsers or devices that don't support all the CSS that you've used, and so fail to load images and so on. By being careful when creating your CSS, you'll ensure that all users can read your content, even if they're unable to experience the full effect of the design.

Solution

This solution comprises a short checklist of what to think about when using color. I've already mentioned many of them while describing other solutions in this chapter, but it's worth highlighting them again here in one place.

Set Background Colors When Using Background Images

If you've used a background image in your design underneath some text—such as giving a background color to a column or box—make sure that you also add a background color. That way, if the image fails to load, the color will ensure that the text on top remains at a high enough contrast to be read.

If You Set a Foreground Color, You Need to Set a Background Color, and Vice Versa

In the interests of readability, color settings should always be considered in tandem; that is, the foreground and background colors should be chosen together so that they contrast sufficiently. If you were to only set one color, say the background, and a user's default foreground color lacks contrast with your choice of color, it may leave your text unreadable. For example, if the user has set their background color to black and foreground to white, and you then set the main text color to black, the text will seem to disappear! If you want users to be able to make their own choices as to colors, you should leave all colors unset—but very few web designers would feel able to do that!

Use Sensible Fallback Colors When Using RGBA as a Background or Foreground Color

As mentioned when we discussed setting background transparency, you should ensure that your fallback color will cause the text to be readable if the browser is without support for RGBA.

Check Color Contrasts

Take care to check the contrast of text against background colors. For users with any kind of visual impairment, a low contrast between the text and the background can make the text very hard to read. You should also consider those users with color blindness who may find certain combinations of foreground and background colors difficult to distinguish. WCAG 2.0 Success Criterion 1.4.3[8] requires that, in general, text and images of text should have a contrast ratio of at least 4.5:1. To help you assess whether your chosen colors will pass this ratio, you can use the handy Luminosity Contrast Ratio Analyzer[9] written by Gez Lemon.

You can also test your pages using the Colorblind Web Page Filter.[10] This simulates the different types of color blindness, giving you an idea of how your design might be seen by those who have some form of color blindness.

Backgrounds Should Only Be Decorative

It's so easy to use background images in CSS that we can fall into the trap of using them everywhere. It's worth remembering, however, that anyone who is unable to load images and/or CSS won't know if the image exists at all if it is set as a background image. This is acceptable if the image is purely for visual display, but if it's important to the content, it's more appropriate to put the image inline with descriptive `alt` text; that way, users who are unable to see the image understand it's there and what it represents.

---

[8] http://www.w3.org/TR/2008/REC-WCAG20-20081211/#visual-audio-contrast-contrast
[9] http://juicystudio.com/services/luminositycontrastratio.php
[10] http://colorfilter.wickline.org/

In the Picture?

With the increase in support for CSS3, we have so many more tools at our disposal than when I first started writing earlier editions of this book. Without resorting to using images, we can apply subtle and beautiful effects to our web pages and user interfaces such as rounded corners, gradients, shadows, and transforms. However, with all this new power comes the responsibility of ensuring that our finishing touches don't render our information unusable to some users.

Enjoy playing with these different effects. If you're yet to use CSS3, it can be an enjoyable exercise to take an older design and see how many of the images can be replaced by CSS. You'll see many more examples of these design elements throughout the book.

Navigation

Unless you limit yourself to one-page websites, you'll need to incorporate navigation into your design. In fact, navigation is among the most important parts of any web design, and requires a great deal of thought if visitors are to move around your site easily.

Making site navigation easy is one area in which CSS really comes into its own. While you could use images for your navigation, this practice can have considerable downsides. Navigation created from images means that it may be less accessible, as the images can't be resized easily to make the text larger. Zooming images of text can also lead to hard-to-read text. In addition, if your site is built using a CMS, when you want to add a new navigation item you'll need to create a new image, which may require the intervention of the designer. CSS allows you to create attractive navigation that is, in reality, no more than text—text that can be marked up in such a way as to ensure that it's both accessible and understandable by all, and easy to content-manage.

In this chapter, we'll look at a variety of solutions for creating CSS-based navigation and give you the skills to start creating your own navigation styles.

How do I style a structural list as a navigation menu?

Navigation is essentially a list of places to visit on your site, so marking up navigation menus as lists makes sense semantically and we can hook our CSS styles to the list elements themselves. It's important, however, to avoid having our navigation look like a standard bulleted list as rendered by the browser's internal stylesheet.

Solution

The simple navigation bar shown in Figure 4.1 is marked up as an unordered list and then styled using CSS.

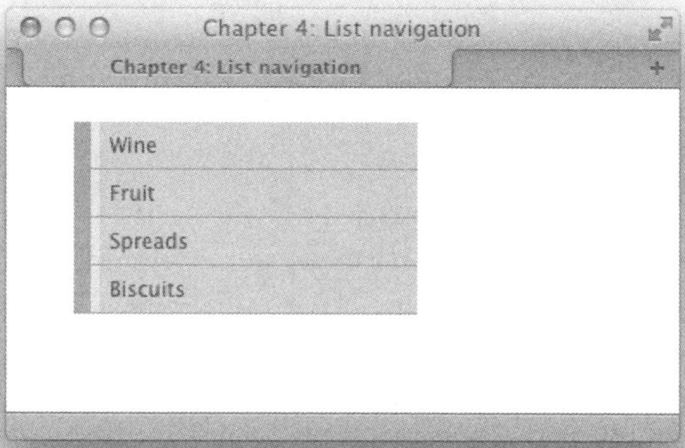

Figure 4.1. The list navigation

Here's the markup:

```
                                                chapter_04/listnav.html
<!DOCTYPE html>
<html>
<head>
  <meta charset="utf-8" />
  <title>Chapter 4: List navigation</title>
  <link rel="stylesheet" href="listnav.css" />
```

```
</head>
<body>
  <div class="wrapper">
    <ul class="nav">
      <li><a href="">Wine</a></li>
      <li><a href="">Fruit</a></li>
      <li><a href="">Spreads</a></li>
      <li><a href="">Biscuits</a></li>
    </ul>
  </div>
</body>
</html>
```

Here is the CSS used to transform this plain list into a standard-looking vertical navigation bar:

chapter_04/listnav.css *(excerpt)*

```
.nav {
  list-style: none;
  margin: 0;
  padding: 0;
  width: 200px;
}

.nav li {
  border-left: 10px solid rgb(144,154,181);
  border-bottom: 1px solid rgb(144,154,181);
}

.nav li a:link,
.nav li a:visited {
  background-color: rgb(192,202,229);
  color: rgb(49,52,61);
  padding: 0.5em;
  display: block;
  text-decoration: none;
  border-left: 5px solid rgb(239,213,252);
}
```

Discussion

To produce navigation based on an unordered list, you first have to create your list, placing each navigation link inside a li element:

chapter_04/listnav.html *(excerpt)*

```
<ul>
  <li><a href="">Wine</a></li>
  <li><a href="">Fruit</a></li>
  <li><a href="">Spreads</a></li>
  <li><a href="">Biscuits</a></li>
</ul>
```

You need to be able to identify this particular list, so either add a class or ID to the opening ul as we're doing here, or place the list inside another container:

chapter_04/listnav.html *(excerpt)*

```
<ul class="nav">
  <li><a href="">Wine</a></li>
  <li><a href="">Fruit</a></li>
  <li><a href="">Spreads</a></li>
  <li><a href="">Biscuits</a></li>
</ul>
```

As Figure 4.2 shows, this now looks like a regular list with the browser's default styles applied.

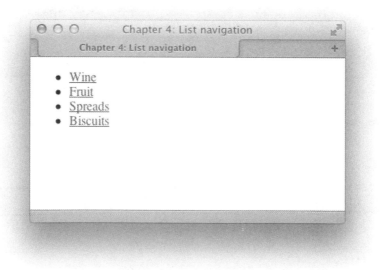

Figure 4.2. The list before styling with CSS

Our next job is to style the unordered list itself, removing list bullets, margins, and padding, and giving the list itself a width as this will become the container for the items within:

chapter_04/listnav.css *(excerpt)*

```
.nav {
  list-style-type: none;
  margin: 0;
  padding: 0;
  width: 200px;
}
```

Our list now displays as a list of text in the browser, with nothing to visually identify it as a list, as seen in Figure 4.3.

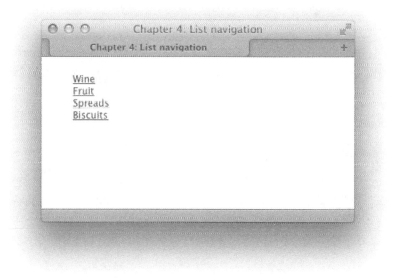

Figure 4.3. Our list after removing bullets, margins, and padding

The next task is to add some CSS to the list items themselves. All I'm doing is adding a chunky left border and thin bottom border. No padding is added to the elements themselves here, so it all looks a bit squashed up as you can see in Figure 4.4:

```
                                    chapter_04/listnav.css (excerpt)

.nav li {
  border-left: 10px solid rgb(144,154,181);
  border-bottom: 1px solid rgb(144,154,181);
}
```

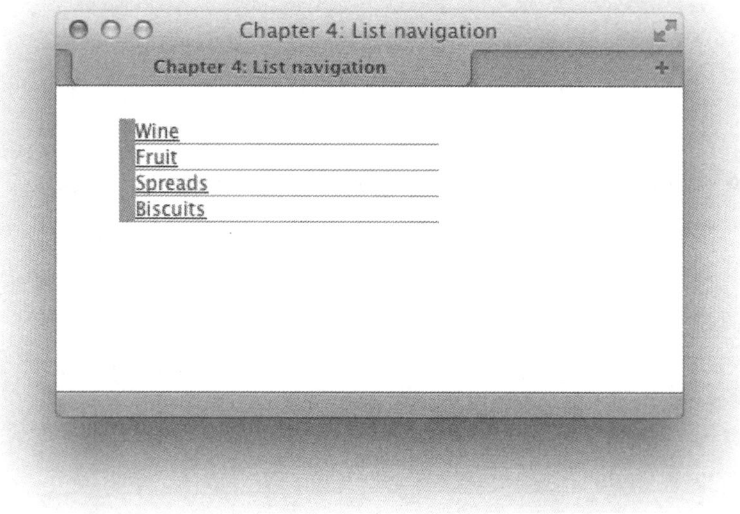

Figure 4.4. After styling the li elements

Finally, we'll add CSS to the links themselves. This is where our list really starts to look like navigation:

```
                                    chapter_04/listnav.css (excerpt)

.nav li a:link,
.nav li a:visited {
  background-color: rgb(192,202,229);
  color: rgb(49,52,61);
  padding: 0.5em;
  display: block;
  text-decoration: none;
  border-left: 5px solid rgb(239,213,252);
}
```

I have added a `background-color` and `color` using RGB color values in this case, although you could also use hex. I've also added padding to the link itself and set it to `display: block`.

This last tweak is important, because the link is an inline element and by default doesn't take up the full area of the `li`—so it's not a nice easy target to click. To make links display like block-level elements, we need to explicitly declare the value of the `display` property to be `block`. We'll discover more about this in later chapters; for now, remember that if you want your link to take up the full area of its container, it needs to be set to `display: block`.

We need to add the padding to the link, not the list item; if we added it to the list item, the padding area would be unclickable—and we want to create an area where it's easy to click the link.

I've also set `text-decoration` to be `none` so as to remove the underline that browsers apply to links, and given the link a left border, producing a double border effect as the `li` already has a border.

You should now have a navigation bar as shown in Figure 4.1. You can play around with this technique trying different colors and stylistic effects once you've mastered the basic idea.

How do I use CSS to create rollover navigation without images or JavaScript?

Site navigation often features a **rollover effect**: when a user holds the cursor over a menu button, a new button image displays, creating a highlighting effect. We can create this effect a number of ways, and we'll look at more advanced variations later in the chapter. Here, however, is a very simple method.

Solution

Using CSS to build your navigation makes the creation of attractive rollover effects far simpler than it would be if you used images. The CSS rollover is created using the `:hover` pseudo-class, which we met when discussing styling links in Chapter 2.

Let's take the previous list-navigation example and add the following rule to create a rollover effect:

```
                                    chapter_04/listnav-hover.css (excerpt)

.nav li a:hover {
  background-color: rgb(144,154,181);
  color: rgb(255,255,255);
  border-left: 5px solid rgb(250,136,234);
}
```

Figure 4.5 shows the effect seen when the cursor is positioned over the first menu item.

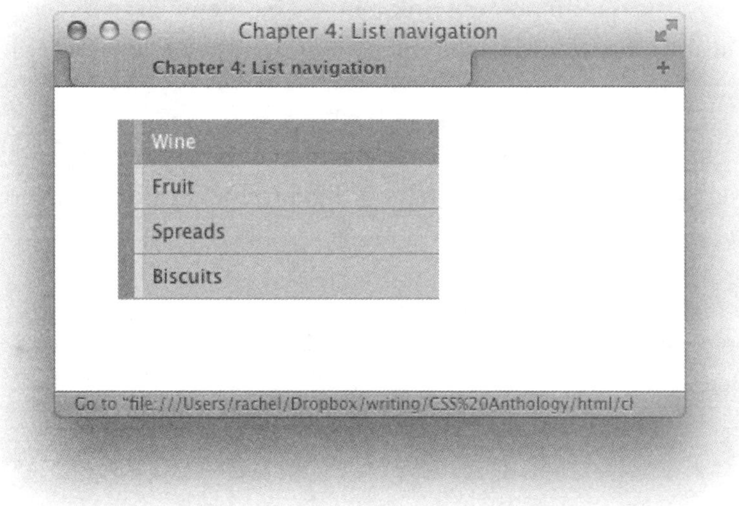

Figure 4.5. The menu showing the hover state

Discussion

Put simply, I've changed the color of three rules applied to the link: background color, color of the text, and left border. This then creates a pleasing visual effect when the link is hovered over.

Hover Gets Broad Support

In modern browsers, you can apply a :hover pseudo-class to any element you like. Internet Explorer 6 and below only allow you to apply it to links.

Can I use CSS and lists to create a navigation system with subnavigation?

So far we've only looked at one simple level of navigation. How do we include a second level of navigation within a menu?

Solution

Lists remain a perfect tool to structure navigation that contains subnavigation, as we can create a list within a list, and the two lists will be easy to understand when marked up this way. This applies even for browsers without support for CSS, or that read the contents of the navigation to a user.

To demonstrate multilevel navigation, we can edit the example used in Figure 4.5 and add a nested list:

```
chapter_04/listnav-nested.html
<!DOCTYPE html>
<html>
<head>
  <meta charset="utf-8" />
  <title>Chapter 4: List navigation</title>
  <link rel="stylesheet" href="listnav-nested.css" />
</head>
<body>
  <div class="wrapper">
    <ul class-"nav">
      <li><a href="">Wine</a>
        <ul>
          <li><a href="">Red</a></li>
          <li><a href="">White</a></li>
          <li><a href="">Ros&eacute;</a></li>
        </ul>
      </li>
      <li><a href="">Fruit</a></li>
      <li><a href="">Spreads</a></li>
      <li><a href="">Biscuits</a></li>
    </ul>
  </div>
</body>
</html>
```

```css
body {
  background-color: #fff;
  color: #000;
  margin: 0;
  padding: 0;
  font: 0.75em/1.3 "Lucida Grande", "Lucida Sans Unicode",
    "Lucida Sans", Verdana, Tahoma, sans-serif;
}

.wrapper {
  width: 80%;
  margin: 20px auto 40px auto;
}

.nav {
  list-style: none;
  margin: 0;
  padding: 0;
  width: 200px;
}

.nav li {
  border-left: 10px solid rgb(144,154,181);
  border-bottom: 1px solid rgb(144,154,181);
}

.nav li a:link,
.nav li a:visited {
  background-color: rgb(192,202,229);
  color: rgb(49,52,61);
  padding: 0.5em;
  display: block;
  text-decoration: none;
  border-left: 5px solid rgb(239,213,252);
}

.nav li a:hover {
  background-color: rgb(144,154,181);
  color: rgb(255,255,255);
  border-left: 5px solid rgb(250,136,234);
}
.nav ul {
  list-style: none;
```

```
  margin: 0;
  padding: 0;
  border: 0;
}

.nav ul li {
  border: 0;
}

.nav ul li a:link,
.nav ul li a:visited {
  background-color: rgb(237,241,252);
  color: rgb(49,52,61);
  padding: 0.5em 0.5em 0.5em 1em;
  display: block;
  text-decoration: none;
  border-left: 5px solid rgb(239,213,252);
}

.nav ul li a:hover {
  background-color: rgb(255,255,255);
  color: rgb(49,52,61);
  border-left: 5px solid rgb(250,136,234);
}
```

The result of this can be seen in Figure 4.6.

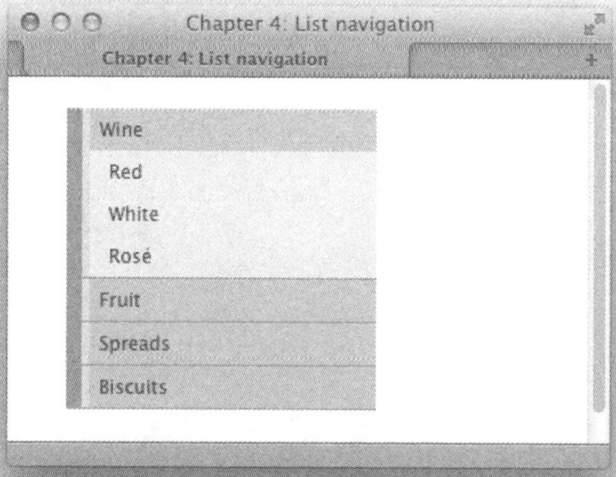

Figure 4.6. A list with subnavigation

Discussion

Nested lists are a perfect way to describe the navigation system that we're working with here. The first list contains the main sections of my site: food and drink that goes nicely with cheese. The subsections of the wine section are then nested underneath the Wine list item. Even without any CSS styling, the structure of the site is clear and intelligible, as you can see in Figure 4.7.

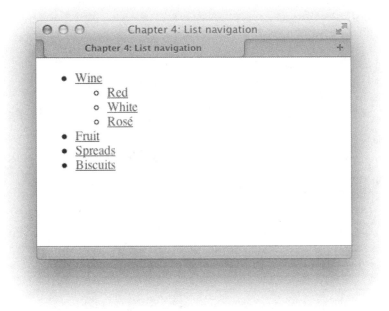

Figure 4.7. The navigation without any styling

The markup simply nests the sublist within the `li` element of the main list:

chapter_04/listnav-nested.html *(excerpt)*

```html
<ul class="nav">
  <li><a href="">Wine</a>
    <ul>
      <li><a href="">Red</a></li>
      <li><a href="">White</a></li>
      <li><a href="">Ros&eacute;</a></li>
    </ul>
  </li>
  <li><a href="">Fruit</a></li>
```

```
    <li><a href="">Spreads</a></li>
    <li><a href="">Biscuits</a></li>
  </ul>
```

If we took our example from earlier and just added the nested list markup, we'd end up with the example shown in Figure 4.8: our second list has inherited a lot of the styling of the parent list, but looks a little strange. Due to this inheritance effect, we need to overwrite values used in the first list when styling our nested list.

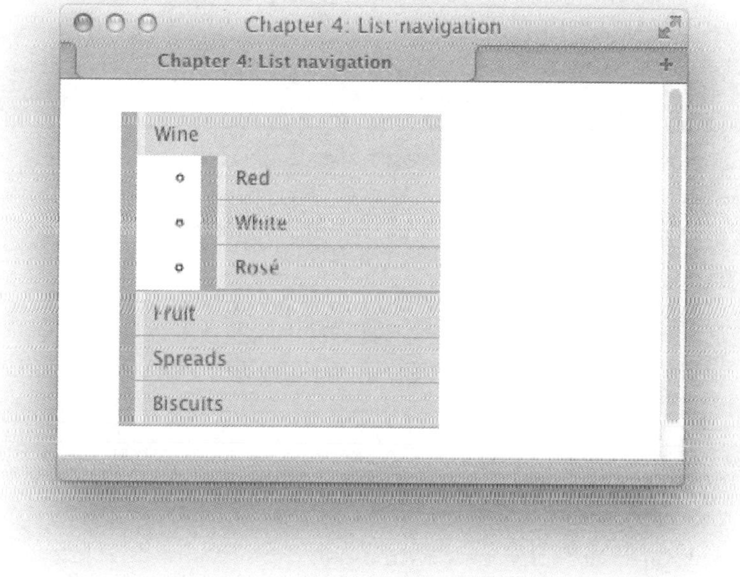

Figure 4.8. After adding the markup

First, I remove the bullets, margins, and padding from the nested list. Then I remove the decorative left-hand border from the li. The list now displays as in Figure 4.9:

chapter_04/listnav-nested.css *(excerpt)*

```css
.nav ul {
  list-style: none;
  margin: 0;
  padding: 0;
  border: 0;
}
```

```
.nav ul li {
  border: 0;
}
```

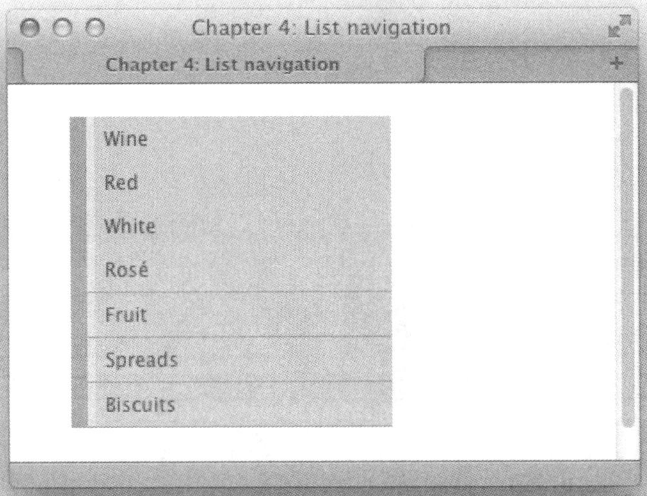

Figure 4.9. By adding a few rules, the list is pulled back into alignment

The nested links are now harder to distinguish from the top-level items, so I'll style the links within the nested list so that they're distinct from the main section links:

chapter_04/listnav-nested.css (excerpt)

```
.nav ul li a:link,
.nav ul li a:visited {
  background-color: rgb(237,241,252);
  color: rgb(49,52,61);
  padding: 0.5em 0.5em 0.5em 1em;
  display: block;
  text-decoration: none;
  border-left: 5px solid rgb(239,213,252);
}

.nav ul li a:hover {
```

```
    background-color: rgb(255,255,255);
    color: rgb(49,52,61);
    border-left: 5px solid rgb(250,136,234);
}
```

All I've done here is change the colors and padding on the links within our nested `li` to create a pleasing effect; I also added some different rules for the hover state of these subitems. Remember that here you're overwriting the values set on links for the external list, so you only need to set those you've changed.

How do I make a horizontal menu using lists and CSS?

The examples so far in this chapter have dealt with vertical navigation, usually found to the left or right of a site's main content area; however, site navigation is also commonly found as a horizontal menu close to the top of the document.

Solution

Figure 4.10 shows a horizontal navigation menu that's created using a list.

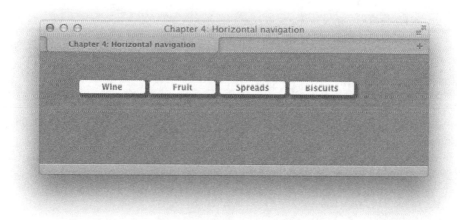

Figure 4.10. Simple horizontal navigation

Here's the HTML and CSS used to create this display:

```html
<!DOCTYPE html>
<html>
<head>
  <meta charset="utf-8" />
  <title>Chapter 4: Horizontal navigation</title>
  <link rel="stylesheet" href="horizontal.css" />
</head>
<body>
  <div class="wrapper">
    <ul class="nav">
      <li><a href="">Wine</a></li>
      <li><a href="">Fruit</a></li>
      <li><a href="">Spreads</a></li>
      <li><a href="">Biscuits</a></li>
    </ul>
  </div>
</body>
</html>
```

```css
.nav {
  list-style: none;
  margin: 0;
  padding: 0;
}

.nav li {
  float: left;
  min-width: 8em;
  margin-right: 0.5em;
  text-align: center;
}

.nav li a:link,
.nav li a:visited {
  background-color: rgb(255, 255, 255);
  color: rgb(85, 85, 102);
  display: block;
  padding: 0.2em;
  text-decoration: none;
  font-weight: bold;
  margin: 0 0 0.2em 0;
```

```
  -webkit-border-radius: 3px;
  -moz-border-radius: 3px;
  border-radius: 3px;
  -webkit-box-shadow: 3px 3px 3px 3px rgba(43, 43, 77, 0.5);
  -moz-box-shadow: 3px 3px 3px 3px rgba(43, 43, 77, 0.5);
  box-shadow: 3px 3px 3px 3px rgba(43, 43, 77, 0.5);
}

.nav li a:hover {
  background-color: rgba(255, 255, 255, 0.8);
  color: rgb(43, 43, 77);
}
```

Discussion

This navigation starts out with an identical list to the one we used earlier to create vertical navigation:

chapter_04/horizontal.html *(excerpt)*

```
<ul class="nav">
  <li><a href="">Wine</a></li>
  <li><a href="">Fruit</a></li>
  <li><a href="">Spreads</a></li>
  <li><a href="">Biscuits</a></li>
</ul>
```

I start by removing the list bullets, margins and padding:

chapter_04/horizontal.css *(excerpt)*

```
.nav {
  list-style: none;
  margin: 0;
  padding: 0;
}
```

We now want our list items to display next to each other, rather than on separate lines. There are two ways we can do this. We could set the display property of the li to inline as we discussed in Chapter 2 ; however, to make the list items easier to style, I'm going to use a different method that relies on the float property. We'll discuss `float` properly later in the book; for now, you can see how it floats items alongside each other:

```
chapter_04/horizontal.css (excerpt)

.nav li {
  float: left;
  min-width: 8em;
  margin-right: 0.5em;
  text-align: center;
}
```

Our menu displays as in Figure 4.11 .

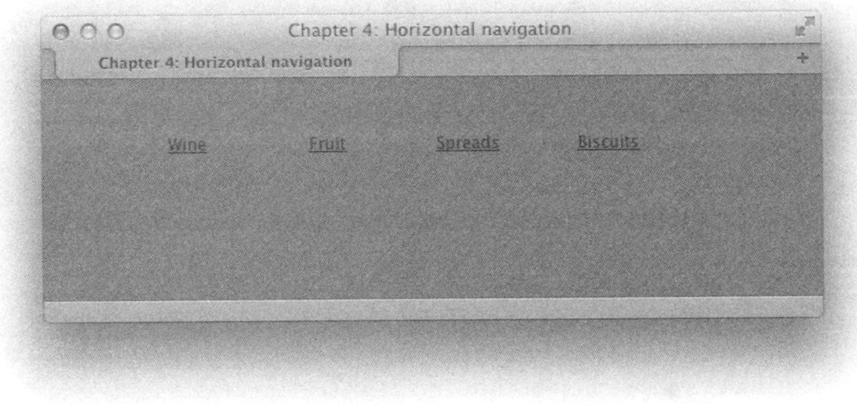

Figure 4.11. After floating the list items

With our list items in place, we just need to style the links. First, we can style these items using CSS that will work even with very old browsers:

```
chapter_04/horizontal.css (excerpt)

.nav li a:link,
.nav li a:visited {
  background-color: rgb(255, 255, 255);
  color: rgb(85, 85, 102);
  display: block;
  padding: 0.2em;
  text-decoration: none;
  font-weight: bold;
```

```
    margin: 0 0 0.2em 0;
    ⋮
}
```

This gives us little block-like navigation items. I really want them to be rounded, though, and have drop shadows, so to achieve this I use some CSS3 properties:

chapter_04/horizontal.css *(excerpt)*

```
.nav li a:link,
.nav li a:visited {
  background-color: rgb(255, 255, 255);
  color: rgb(85, 85, 102);
  display: block;
  padding: 0.2em;
  text-decoration: none;
  font-weight: bold;
  margin: 0 0 0.2em 0;
  -webkit-border-radius: 3px;
  -moz-border-radius: 3px;
  border-radius: 3px;
  -webkit-box-shadow: 3px 3px 3px 3px rgba(43, 43, 77, 0.5);
  -moz-box-shadow: 3px 3px 3px 3px rgba(43, 43, 77, 0.5);
  box-shadow: 3px 3px 3px 3px rgba(43, 43, 77, 0.5);
}
```

It's quite possible that a person is going to view the site using a browser lacking support for these properties; however, the navigation looks fine without them—I've added them as extra styling for those browsers with support. This practice is known as progressive enhancement, and we'll discuss this tactic for supporting older browsers later in the book.

Finally, I've added a hover state, tweaking the alpha value of the background color using RGBA. I could equally have just set a different color here:

chapter_04/horizontal.css *(excerpt)*

```
.nav li a:hover {
  background-color: rgba(255, 255, 255, 0.8);
  color: rgb(43, 43, 77);
}
```

If you're creating boxes around each link—as I have here—remember that in order to make more space between the text and the edge of its container, you'll need to add more left and right padding to the links. To create more space between the navigation items, add left and right margins to the links.

How do I create tabbed navigation using CSS?

Navigation that appears as tabs across the top of the page is popular. Many sites create these tabs using images; however, this can make it less accessible, and it's also problematic if your navigation is created using a Content Management System, as users of such a system are unable to add tabs or change the text in the tabs. The good news is it's possible to create a tab effect just using CSS.

Solution

The navigation in Figure 4.12 was created by styling a horizontal list with CSS.

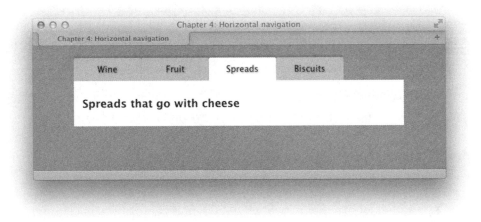

Figure 4.12. CSS tabbed navigation

And here's the markup for it:

chapter_04/tabs.html

```html
<!DOCTYPE html>
<html>
<head>
  <meta charset="utf-8" />
  <title>Chapter 4: Horizontal navigation</title>
  <link rel="stylesheet" href="tabs.css" />
</head>
<body>
  <div class="wrapper">
    <ul class="nav">
      <li><a href="">Wine</a></li>
      <li><a href="">Fruit</a></li>
      <li class="selected"><a href="">Spreads</a></li>
      <li><a href="">Biscuits</a></li>
    </ul>
    <div class="content">
      <h1>Spreads that go with cheese</h1>
    </div>
  </div>
</body>
</html>
```

chapter_04/tabs.css (excerpt)

```css
.nav {
  list-style: none;
  margin: 0;
  padding: 0;
  float: left;
  width: 100%;
}

.nav li {
  float: left;
  min-width: 8em;
  text-align: center;
}

.nav li a:link,
.nav li a:visited {
  background-color: rgba(255,255,255,0.4);
  color: rgb(0,0,0);
  text-decoration: none;
```

```
  display: block;
  padding: 0.75em;
  -moz-border-radius-topleft: 3px;
  -moz-border-radius-topright: 3px;
  -webkit-border-radius: 3px 3px 0px 0px;
  border-radius: 3px 3px 0px 0px;
  -webkit-box-shadow: 0px -3px 2px 0px rgba(0, 0, 0, 0.2);
  -moz-box-shadow: 0px -3px 2px 0px rgba(0, 0, 0, 0.2);
  box-shadow: 0px -3px 2px 0px rgba(0, 0, 0, 0.2);
  text-shadow: 1px 1px 3px rgba(0, 0, 0, 0.5);
}

.nav li.selected a:link,
.nav li.selected a:visited {
  background-color: rgb(255,255,255);
}

.nav li a:hover {
  background-color: rgba(255,255,255,0.8);
}

.content {
  clear: both;
  background-color: #fff;
  color: #000;
  padding: 1em;
}

h1 {
  font-size: 128.6%;
}
```

Discussion

This navigation started life in a similar way to the previous solution that created horizontal navigation—marked up as a list. Imagine that we're now on the main page of one of our sections, so we want to have a tab highlighted to show where we are. I've added a class of selected to one item:

chapter_04/tabs.html *(excerpt)*

```
<ul class="nav">
  <li><a href="">Wine</a></li>
  <li><a href="">Fruit</a></li>
```

```
<li class="selected"><a href="">Spreads</a></li>
<li><a href="">Biscuits</a></li>
</ul>
```

The first two CSS declarations put our list items into horizontal alignment:

chapter_04/tabs.css *(excerpt)*

```
.nav {
  list-style: none;
  margin: 0;
  padding: 0;
  float: left;
  width: 100%;
}

.nav li {
  float: left;
  min-width: 8em;
  text-align: center;
}
```

Now we can start to style the unselected tabs. I am using RGBA for the background color; this creates a semitransparent effect, letting the background show through. If you're concerned about browsers that lack RGBA support, you could use a solid color here instead:

chapter_04/tabs.css *(excerpt)*

```
.nav li a:link,
.nav li a:visited {
  background-color: rgba(255,255,255,0.4);
  color: rgb(0,0,0);
  text-decoration: none;
  display: block;
  padding: 0.75em;
  -moz-border-radius-topleft: 3px;
  -moz-border-radius-topright: 3px;
  -webkit-border-radius: 3px 3px 0px 0px;
  border-radius: 3px 3px 0px 0px;
  -webkit-box-shadow: 0px -3px 2px 0px rgba(0, 0, 0, 0.2);
  -moz-box-shadow: 0px -3px 2px 0px rgba(0, 0, 0, 0.2);
```

```
  box-shadow: 0px -3px 2px 0px rgba(0, 0, 0, 0.2);
  text-shadow: 1px 1px 3px rgba(0, 0, 0, 0.5);
}
```

This gives us a set of tabs as shown in Figure 4.13. I'm using `border-radius` to slightly curve the top corners of the tabs, `box-shadow` to create a shadow effect round the sides and top, and `text-shadow` to enhance the text.

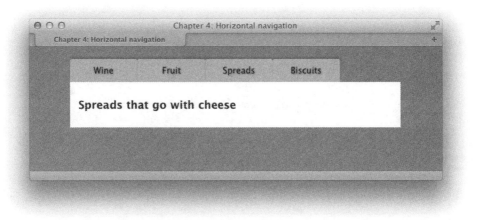

Figure 4.13. The tabs after styling the list items

I now want to make my selected tab look as if it joins onto the background color of the content area. I do this using the following declaration which targets the `li` with a `class` of `selected`. All it does is change the background color to white:

chapter_04/tabs.css *(excerpt)*

```
.nav li.selected a:link,
.nav li.selected a:visited {
  background-color: rgb(255,255,255);
}
```

A final touch is to add a hover state to the tabs. Again, I'm just tweaking the opacity using RGBA, but this could also be a solid color:

chapter_04/tabs.css *(excerpt)*

```
.nav li a:hover {
  background-color: rgba(255,255,255,0.8);
}
```

Embrace CSS3-enhanced Effects

With the use of CSS—and, in particular, the finishing touches offered by CSS3—we can easily create attractive tab effects. But this hasn't always been the case.

Previous versions of this book contained a solution that was based on the popular "sliding doors" method of using images to create flexible tabs.[1] This method uses four background images to create the rounded-corner tab effect. If you need to support ancient browsers with a full visual effect, or are tied to a look and feel that's very graphic-heavy, you may need to consider these older methods. For most sites, I'd encourage you to make clever use of CSS3 to enhance a slightly plainer view of the site for older browsers.

My navigation is in an include, so how can I indicate which is the selected tab?

The last solution added a class to the selected menu item, but if your menu is stored in a linked server-side file—say a PHP file pulled in with an `include` statement—this may not be possible. How can you indicate which menu item is selected here?

Solution

Here's a neat little trick for highlighting a menu tab. First, edit the HTML to add a class to every menu tab; I usually use the section name. Add an ID to the body element of the page that is the same as one of the classes:

chapter_04/selected.html

```
<!DOCTYPE html>
<html>
<head>
  <meta charset="utf-8" />
```

---

[1] http://www.alistapart.com/articles/slidingdoors/

```
  <title>Chapter 4: Horizontal navigation</title>
  <link rel="stylesheet" href="selected.css" />
</head>
<body id="spreads">
  <div class="wrapper">
    <ul class="nav">
      <li class="wine"><a href="">Wine</a></li>
      <li class="fruit"><a href="">Fruit</a></li>
      <li class="spreads"><a href="">Spreads</a></li>
      <li class="biscuits"><a href="">Biscuits</a></li>
    </ul>
    <div class="content">
      <h1>Spreads that go with cheese</h1>
    </div>
  </div>
</body>
</html>
```

In the CSS, we can now target the li with a class only if it's inside the body with the same id:

chapter_04/selected.css *(excerpt)*

```
.nav {
  list-style: none;
  margin: 0;
  padding: 0;
  float: left;
  width: 100%;
}

.nav li {
  float: left;
  min-width: 8em;
  text-align: center;
}

.nav li a:link,
.nav li a:visited {
  background-color: rgba(255,255,255,0.4);
  color: rgb(0,0,0);
  text-decoration: none;
  display: block;
  padding: 0.75em;
```

```
   -moz-border-radius-topleft: 3px;
   -moz-border-radius-topright: 3px;
   -webkit-border-radius: 3px 3px 0px 0px;
   border-radius: 3px 3px 0px 0px;
   -webkit-box-shadow: 0px -3px 2px 0px rgba(0, 0, 0, 0.2);
   -moz-box-shadow: 0px -3px 2px 0px rgba(0, 0, 0, 0.2);
   box-shadow: 0px -3px 2px 0px rgba(0, 0, 0, 0.2);
   text-shadow: 1px 1px 3px rgba(0, 0, 0, 0.5);
}
#spreads .nav li.spreads a:link,
#spreads .nav li.spreads a:visited,
#fruit .nav li.fruit a:link,
#fruit .nav li.fruit a:visited,
#wine .nav li.wine a:link,
#wine .nav li.wine a:visited,
#biscuits .nav li.biscuits a:link,
#biscuits .nav li.biscuits a:visited {
   background-color: rgb(255,255,255);
}

.nav li a:hover {
   background-color: rgba(255,255,255,0.8);
}
```

Discussion

If you switch the body element's ID to any of the other ID names, you will see the selected menu tab change. This works because when we use the following selector, we're saying, "target the link inside an li with a class of spreads, which is inside an element with an ID of spreads":

```
#spreads .nav li.spreads a:link
```

So a li with a class of wine fails to match, and a li with a class of spreads inside the body with an id of wine also wouldn't match. You then just need to output the section name as an id on the body tag, which you may have access to in your page, or be able to output via your CMS.

How do I put additional information in my navigation bar?

A popular style of navigation is to have the title of the section plus some descriptive text underneath. How should we create this using CSS?

Solution

Once again, we're using a list structure for our navigation, but this time adding more information to each link. This creates the navigation shown in Figure 4.14.

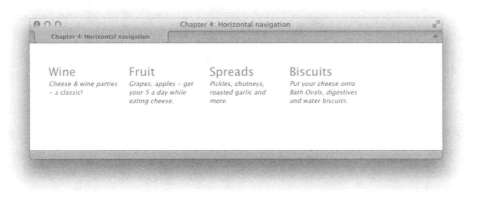

Figure 4.14. Horizontal navigation with extra text

In this example, the section titles are in the same a elements as their descriptions, but also within strong elements set to display as blocks:

```
                                                    chapter_04/horizontal2.html

<!DOCTYPE html>
<html>
<head>
  <meta charset="utf-8" />
  <title>Chapter 4: Horizontal navigation</title>
  <link rel="stylesheet" href="horizontal2.css" />
</head>
<body>
  <div class="wrapper">
    <ul class="nav">
      <li><a href=""><strong>Wine</strong>
```

```
      <small>Cheese &amp; wine parties - a classic!</small>
      </a></li>
      <li><a href=""><strong>Fruit</strong>
      <small>Grapes, apples - get your 5 a day while eating
        cheese.</small>
      </a></li>
      <li><a href=""><strong>Spreads</strong>
      <small>Pickles, chutneys, roasted garlic and more.</small>
      </a></li>
      <li><a href=""><strong>Biscuits</strong>
      <small>Put your cheese onto Bath Ovals, digestives and water
        biscuits.</small>
      </a></li>
    </ul>
  </div>
</body>
</html>
```

chapter_04/horizontal2.css *(excerpt)*

```css
.nav {
    list-style: none;
    margin: 0;
    padding: 0;
}

.nav li {
  float: left;
  width: 130px;
  margin-right: 20px;
}

.nav li a:link strong,
.nav li a:visited strong {
  font-size: 157.1%;
  display: block;
  font-weight: normal;
  color: rgb(119,126,134);
  font-style: normal;
}

.nav li a:link,
.nav li a:visited {
  text-decoration: none;
  color: rgb(93,78,72);
```

```
    font-style: italic;
}

.nav li a:hover, .nav li a:hover strong {
    color: rgb(0,0,0);
}
```

Discussion

This solution is simply an extension of the original horizontal navigation we created. You can add any elements within your list items, and style them however you like.

How can I visually indicate which links are external to my site?

It can be helpful to visitors if links that lead to another site are displayed differently from links to pages on your own site. Adding a class to every link in order to be able to select it, however, is far from practical.

Solution

If your internal links omit your site's full domain, we can use attribute selectors to target external links: icons are placed next to external links, but not internal links.

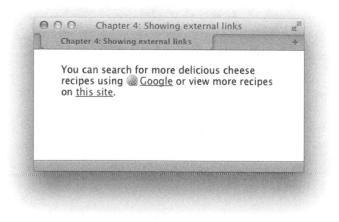

Figure 4.15. Displaying external links with an icon

chapter_04/external-links.html

```
<!DOCTYPE html>
<html>
<head>
  <meta charset="utf-8" />
  <title>Chapter 4: Showing external links</title>
  <link rel="stylesheet" href="external-links.css" />
</head>
<body>
  <div class="wrapper">
    <p>You can search for more delicious cheese recipes using
      <a href="http://google.com">Google</a> or view more recipes on
      <a href="/recipes">this site</a>.</p>
  </div>
</body>
</html>
```

We can use an attribute selector that looks for href attributes containing a value starting with http: and add a background image:

chapter_04/external-links.css *(excerpt)*

```
a[href^="http:"] {
  padding-left: 20px;
  background-image: url(icon-link-external.png);
  background-repeat: no-repeat;
}
```

Now, any links on our page that start with http: (which should be external, as we don't link to pages on our own site this way) will display with the world icon.

Mind Your Protocols

This solution relies on your internal links not having the http:// in front of them. If you're using an editor or CMS that adds the full domain of your site to internal links, this solution is unsuitable.

Discussion

The attribute selector is widely supported in modern browsers, although it will be ignored in Internet Explorer 6. In browsers that lack support for this selector, the link will just display as normal; thus, it's a nice enhancement for browsers with support while leaving the experience unchanged for those with older browsers.

Let's take a closer look at that selector:

```
a[href ^="http:"]
```

We're selecting the `href` attribute, and we want our selector to match when it finds the text `http:` at the beginning of the attribute value. The `^=` operator means "begins with." You could use a similar selector to match all email links; for example, `a[href ^="mailto:"]`.

Another useful attribute selector is to target the file extension of a link. This means that you can add a small icon to show that a document is a PDF or other document type, depending on the extension. The selector `a[href $=".pdf"]` will match any link that has a file extension of **.pdf**. The `$=` operator means "ends with," so this selector will match when an `href` attribute value ends with **.pdf**:

chapter_04/external-links2.html

```
<!DOCTYPE html>
<html>
<head>
  <meta charset="utf-8" />
  <title>Chapter 4: Using attribute selectors</title>
  <link rel="stylesheet" href="external-links2.css" />
</head>
<body>
  <div class="wrapper">
    <ul class="links">
      <li><a href="http://google.com">Go somewhere else</a></li>
      <li><a href="/files/example.pdf">Download a PDF</a></li>
      <li><a href="mailto:info@example.com">Send an email</a></li>
    </ul>
  </div>
</body>
</html>
```

chapter_04/external-links2.css *(excerpt)*

```css
a[href^="http:"] {
  padding-left: 20px;
  background-image: url(icon-link-external.png);
  background-repeat: no-repeat;
}

a[href^="mailto:"] {
  padding-left: 20px;
  background-image: url(icon-link-email.png);
  background-repeat: no-repeat;
}

a[href$=".pdf"] {
  padding-left: 20px;
  background-image: url(icon-pdf.png);
  background-repeat: no-repeat;
}
```

Figure 4.16 shows all three types in action.

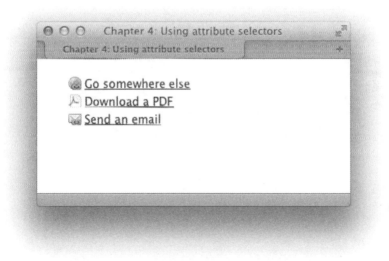

Figure 4.16. Using the attribute selector to add icons to various types of links

How do I create rollover images in my navigation without using JavaScript?

With the properties offered by CSS3, we can create many navigation effects without using images at all; however, you're likely to also want to work with images in your navigation. Combining images and text gives you many opportunities to create attractive and usable navigation.

Solution

This solution demonstrates how to use images in your navigation, including a rollover effect without JavaScript, as seen in Figure 4.17.

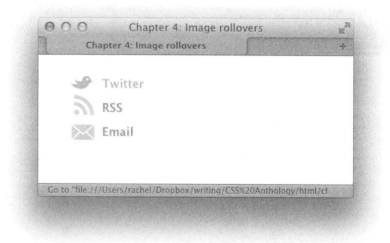

Figure 4.17. An image rollover using CSS

chapter_04/rollover-image.html

```
<!DOCTYPE html>
<html>
<head>
  <meta charset="utf-8" />
  <title>Chapter 4: Image rollovers</title>
  <link rel="stylesheet" href="rollover-image.css" />
</head>
<body>
```

```
  <div class="wrapper">
    <ul class="intouch">
      <li class="twitter"><a href="">Twitter</a></li>
      <li class="rss"><a href="">RSS</a></li>
      <li class="email"><a href="">Email</a></li>
    </ul>
  </div>
</body>
</html>
```

chapter_04/rollover-image.css *(excerpt)*

```css
.intouch {
  list-style: none;
  margin: 0;
  padding: 0;
}

.intouch li a:link, .intouch li a:visited {
  padding: 0.5em 0 0.5em 40px;
  display: block;
  font-weight: bold;
  background-repeat: no-repeat;
  background-image: url(sprite-roll.png);
  text-decoration: none;
  color: rgb(136,136,136);
}

.intouch li.twitter a:link, .intouch li.twitter a:visited {
  background-position: 0 6px;
}

.intouch li.rss a:link, .intouch li.rss a:visited {
  background-position: 0 -30px;
}

.intouch li.email a:link, .intouch li.email a:visited {
  background-position: 0 -60px;
}

.intouch li.twitter a:hover {
  background-position: 0 -90px;
  color: rgb(105,210,231);
}
```

```
.intouch li.rss a:hover {
  background-position: 0 -126px;
  color: rgb(243,134,48);
}

.intouch li.email a:hover {
  background-position: 0 -156px;
  color: rgb(56,55,54);
}
```

Discussion

This solution uses one single image file (**sprite-roll.png**, shown in Figure 4.18) that combines all the inactive and hovered states of the image. We then use this file as a background image, adjusting its location to show the default image for each link, and then the hover image on hovering the link.

Figure 4.18. The sprite combining all the different icons

Combining images in this way is known as creating an **image sprite**, and it's a highly useful technique that helps to reduce load on your server by enabling one request to be made for a file, rather than several requests for lots of small files.

The markup is just a list of links, where I've given each li a class to indicate the type of link it is:

chapter_04/rollover-image.html *(excerpt)*

```
<ul class="intouch">
  <li class="twitter"><a href="">Twitter</a></li>
  <li class="rss"><a href="">RSS</a></li>
  <li class="email"><a href="">Email</a></li>
</ul>
```

I add some basic styles to the list and each list item, and then style the links, adding the sprite as a background image set to no-repeat:

chapter_04/rollover-image.css *(excerpt)*

```css
.intouch {
  list-style: none;
  margin: 0;
  padding: 0;
}

.intouch li a:link, .intouch li a:visited {
  padding: 0.5em 0 0.5em 40px;
  display: block;
  font-weight: bold;
  background-repeat: no-repeat;
  background-image: url(sprite-roll.png);
  text-decoration: none;
  color: rgb(136,136,136);
}
```

If you look at the list now in Figure 4.19, I can see the sprite showing the same image for all items.

Figure 4.19. After adding the background image

We can now start to shift the background image into place to show the initial images (the gray icon). The first link is almost correct; I just want to tweak the position of the bird a little:

chapter_04/rollover-image.css *(excerpt)*

```
.intouch li.twitter a:link, .intouch li.twitter a:visited {
   background-position: 0 6px;
}
```

With the second link, I need to shift the background image until it shows the gray RSS icon. I then do the same for the final mail icon:

chapter_04/rollover-image.css *(excerpt)*

```
.intouch li.rss a:link, .intouch li.rss a:visited {
   background-position: 0 -30px;
}

.intouch li.email a:link, .intouch li.email a:visited {
   background-position: 0 -60px;
}
```

Our gray icons are now in place, and I can add some CSS to pull the background into position when each link is hovered over using exactly the same principle:

chapter_04/rollover-image.css *(excerpt)*

```
.intouch li.twitter a:hover {
   background-position: 0 -90px;
   color: rgb(105,210,231);
}

.intouch li.rss a:hover {
   background-position: 0 -126px;
   color: rgb(243,134,48);
}

.intouch li.email a:hover {
   background-position: 0 -156px;
   color: rgb(56,55,54);
}
```

This gives us a rollover image effect that combines a single background image and text for an accessible, search-engine-friendly navigation bar.

Using Opacity for Rollover Effects

Before finishing this solution, I want to show you an alternate method of creating a nice rollover effect using the `opacity` property.

The effect shown in Figure 4.20 is achieved with the same markup we've been using and an image sprite, but this one only has three states in it. I have then used the `opacity` property to make the image and text semitransparent.

Figure 4.20. Rollovers using opacity

On hover, I set `opacity` to 1—that's fully opaque (not transparent at all), making a simple rollover effect:

```
                                        chapter_04/rollover-opacity.css (excerpt)
.intouch li a:link, .intouch li a:visited {
  padding: 0.5em 0 0.5em 40px;
  display: block;
  font-weight: bold;
  background-repeat: no-repeat;
  background-image: url(sprite.png);
  text-decoration: none;
```

```
}

.intouch li.twitter a:link, .intouch li.twitter a:visited {
  background-position: 0 6px;
  color: rgb(105,210,231);
  opacity: 0.5;
}

.intouch li.rss a:link, .intouch li.rss a:visited {
  background-position: 0 -30px;
  color: rgb(243,134,48);
  opacity: 0.5;
}

.intouch li.email a:link, .intouch li.email a:visited {
  background-position: 0 -60px;
  color: rgb(56,55,54);
  opacity: 0.5;
}

.intouch li.twitter a:hover,
.intouch li.rss a:hover,
.intouch li.email a:hover {
  opacity: 1;
}
```

How should I style a sitemap?

A sitemap is a helpful page on your website that lists all pages in the site. It can help those who are unable to find what they're looking for in the navigation, as well as provide a quick way to see what's available and go to it with one click.

Solution

A sitemap is really a list of all the destinations on your site, so it's ideally marked up as a set of nested lists. The first list is your main navigation, with the internal navigation nested within each main navigation point. A list works even if your site structure has many levels and should be easy to generate from a content management system. Figure 4.21 displays the results of the following code:

chapter_04/sitemap.html

```html
<!DOCTYPE html>
<html>
<head>
  <meta charset="utf-8" />
  <title>Chapter 4: Sitemaps</title>
  <link rel="stylesheet" href="sitemap.css" />
</head>
<body>
  <div class="wrapper">
    <ul class="sitemap">
      <li><a href="">Home</a></li>
      <li><a href="">About us</a>
        <ul>
          <li><a href="">Directors</a></li>
          <li><a href="">History</a></li>
        </ul>
      </li>
      <li><a href="">Products</a></li>
      <li><a href="">Ordering information</a>
        <ul>
          <li><a href="">Our shops</a>
            <ul>
              <li><a href="">London</a></li>
              <li><a href="">Newcastle</a></li>
            </ul>
          </li>
          <li><a href="">Other stockists</a></li>
        </ul>
      </li>
      <li><a href="">Contact Us</a></li>
    </ul>
  </div>
</body>
</html>
```

chapter_04/sitemap.css *(excerpt)*

```css
.sitemap {
  list-style: none;
  margin: 0;
  padding: 0;
}
```

```css
.sitemap > li {
  border: 2px solid rgba(153,178,183,0.2);
  -webkit-border-radius: 10px;
  -moz-border-radius: 10px;
  border-radius: 10px;
  margin: 0 0 1em 0;
}

.sitemap > li:hover {
  border: 2px solid rgba(153,178,183,1);
}

.sitemap > li > a:link, .sitemap > li > a:visited {
  background-color: rgba(153,178,183,0.1);
  color: rgb(0,0,0);
  text-decoration: none;
  display: block;
  padding: 0.75em;
}

.sitemap > li:hover > a:link, .sitemap > li:hover > a:visited {
  background-color: rgba(153,178,183,0.5);
}

.sitemap ul {
  margin: 1em 0 1em 0;
  padding: 0;
  list-style: none;
  line-height: 1.8;
}

.sitemap ul ul {
  margin: 0.5em 0 0.5em 0;
}

.sitemap ul a:link, .sitemap ul a:visited {
  padding: 0.75em;
  text-decoration: none;
  color: rgb(69,80,83);
}

.sitemap ul ul a:link:before, .sitemap ul ul a:visited:before {
  content: "> ";
}
```

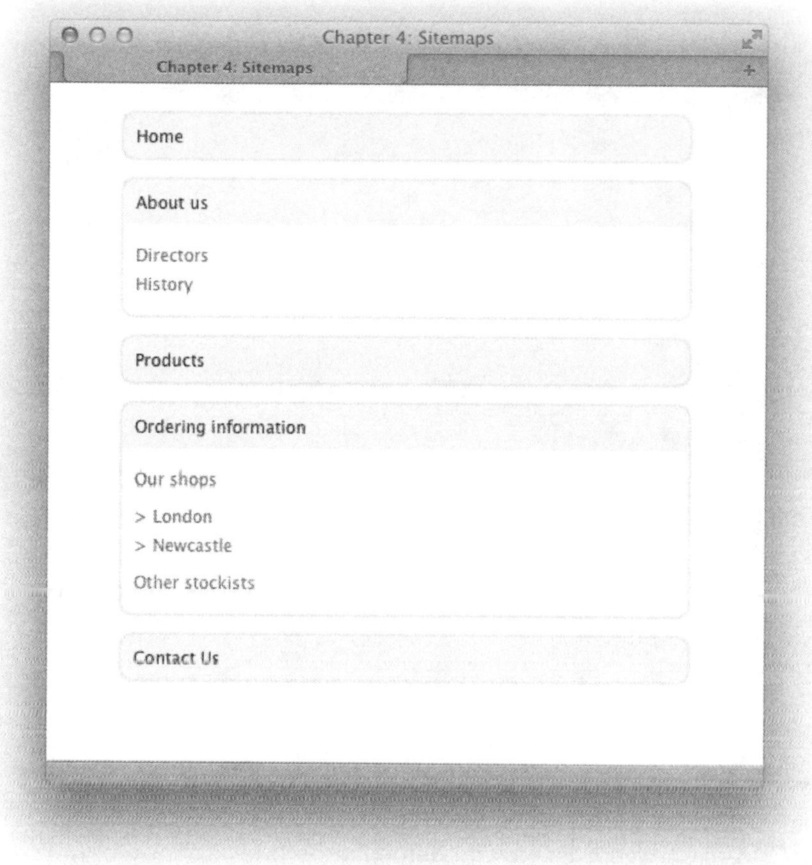

Figure 4.21. A sitemap styled using CSS

Discussion

The sitemap starts life as a list for the main navigation elements with the submenus nested inside—the same way the list with subnavigation discussed in the section called "Can I use CSS and lists to create a navigation system with subnavigation?" did. The difference with the sitemap is that *all* menus will display their subnavigation. If the sitemap becomes deeper (with further levels), you just continue nesting in the same way, with subpages being a sublist of their parent page.

Take care to nest the list items properly. The submenu needs to go before the closing li of the parent list. Without CSS, the sitemap displays as in Figure 4.22.

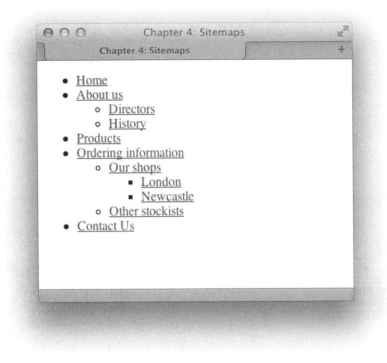

Figure 4.22. The unstyled list

I'm going to wrap each main section—that's each top-level navigation point and its subnavigation—with a border to help demonstrate it is a section of the site:

```
                                    chapter_04/sitemap.css (excerpt)
.sitemap {
  list-style: none;
  margin: 0;
  padding: 0;
}

.sitemap > li {
  border: 2px solid rgba(153,178,183,0.2);
  -webkit-border-radius: 10px;
  -moz-border-radius: 10px;
  border-radius: 10px;
  margin: 0 0 1em 0;
}
```

```
.sitemap > li:hover {
  border: 2px solid rgba(153,178,183,1);
}
```

I've used the child selector here as I only want to target the li that is a direct child of .sitemap; these will be the top-level navigation elements. This is indicated in Figure 4.23. I'm using RGBA for the border so that I can tweak the alpha value on hover of the list item; this will give a nice visual indication of the part of the map the user is in.

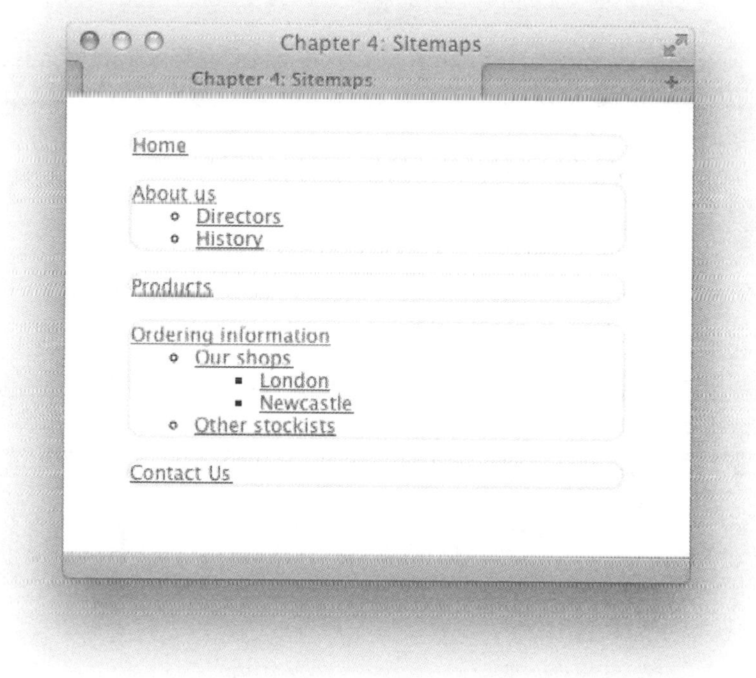

Figure 4.23. Upon styling the main list items

Now I move on to the links that are within these top-level list items, making them visually display as the main navigation item for that section:

chapter_04/sitemap.css *(excerpt)*

```css
.sitemap > li > a:link, .sitemap > li > a:visited {
  background-color: rgba(153,178,183,0.1);
  color: rgb(0,0,0);
  text-decoration: none;
  display: block;
  padding: 0.75em;
}

.sitemap > li:hover > a:link, .sitemap > li:hover > a:visited {
  background-color: rgba(153,178,183,0.5);
}
```

Note that I'm targeting the links inside li:hover so that the state change happens when any part of the li is hovered over, as in Figure 4.24.

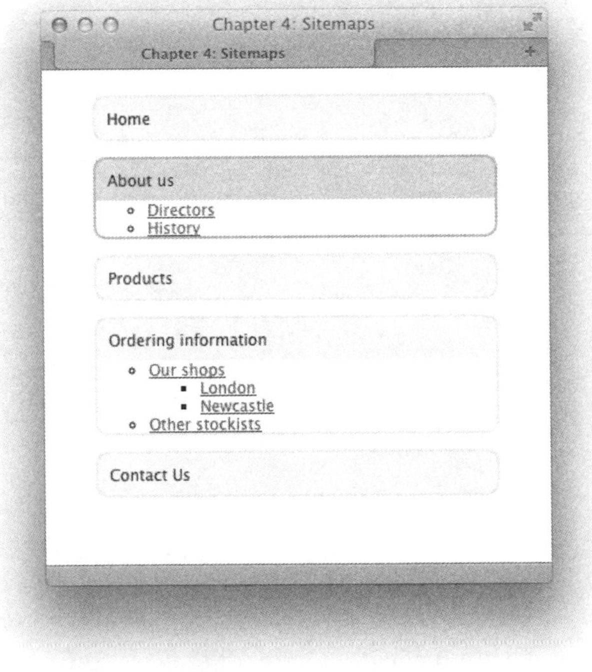

Figure 4.24. After styling the links

We can now style the items inside the section—the sublists and links:

```
                                        chapter_04/sitemap.css (excerpt)
.sitemap ul {
  margin: 1em 0 1em 0;
  padding: 0;
  list-style: none;
  line-height: 1.8;
}

.sitemap ul ul {
  margin: 0.5em 0 0.5em 0;
}

.sitemap ul a:link, .sitemap ul a:visited {
  padding: 0.75em;
  text-decoration: none;
  color: rgb(69,80,83);
}

.sitemap ul ul a:link:before, .sitemap ul ul a:visited:before {
  content: "> ";
}
```

This should all be quite familiar now if you've looked at the other examples in this chapter. I'm using descendant selectors to style the internal list and sublists, and adding a > character on the "sub sub" lists using the pseudo element :before and generated content.

How do I create a drop-down menu with CSS?

Drop-down menus have lost some of their popularity in recent years, but they can be used to give quick access to parts of your site, so you might want to know how to use them in a sensible way.

Solution

This solution creates a drop-down menu from a nested, horizontal list and uses a jQuery plugin to enhance the CSS:

```
<!DOCTYPE html>
<html>
<head>
  <meta charset="utf-8" />
  <title>Chapter 4: Dropdown navigation</title>
  <link rel="stylesheet" href="dropdown.css" />
  <script src="http://ajax.googleapis.com/ajax/libs/jquery/1.7.1/
➥jquery.min.js" type="text/javascript"></script>
  <script src="superfish.js" type="text/javascript"></script>
  <script>
    $(document).ready(function() {
      $('ul.nav').superfish({
        delay:       1000,
        animation:   {opacity:'show',height:'show'},
        speed:       'fast',
        autoArrows:  false,
        dropShadows: false
      });
    });
  </script>
</head>
<body>
  <div class="wrapper">
    <ul class="nav">
      <li><a href="">Home</a></li>
      <li><a href="">About us</a>
        <ul>
          <li><a href="">Directors</a></li>
          <li><a href="">History</a></li>
        </ul>
      </li>
      <li><a href="">Products</a></li>
      <li><a href="">Ordering</a>
        <ul>
          <li><a href="">Our shops</a></li>
          <li><a href="">Other stockists</a></li>
        </ul>
      </li>
      <li><a href="">Contact Us</a></li>
    </ul>
  </div>
</body>
</html>
```

```css
.nav {
  list-style: none;
  margin: 0;
  padding: 0;
  font-size: 114.3%;
}

.nav > li {
  float: left;
  width: 130px;
  margin-right: 20px;
  position: relative;
}

.nav li a:link, .nav li a:visited {
  display: block;
  text-decoration: none;
  color: rgb(122,106,83);
}

.nav li:hover ul, .nav li.sfHover ul {
  margin-left: 0;
}

.nav li a:hover {
  color: rgb(153,178,183);
}

.nav ul {
  position: absolute;
  background-color: rgb(213,222,217);
  border: 5px solid rgb(153,178,183);
  -webkit-border-radius: 10px;
  -moz-border-radius: 10px;
  border-radius: 10px;
  padding: 0.5em;
  margin: 0.5em 0 0 -9999px;
  -webkit-box-shadow: 2px 2px 2px 2px rgba(0,0,0,0.2));
  -moz-box-shadow: 2px 2px 2px 2px rgba(0,0,0,0.2);
  box-shadow: 2px 2px 2px 2px rgba(0,0,0,0.2));
  list-style: none;
  font-size: 85.7%;
  width: 8em;
```

```
    line-height: 1.8;
}

.nav ul li a:link, .nav ul li a:visited {
    color: rgb(0,0,0);
}

.nav ul li a:hover {
    color: rgb(122,106,83);
}
```

Figure 4.25 shows the result.

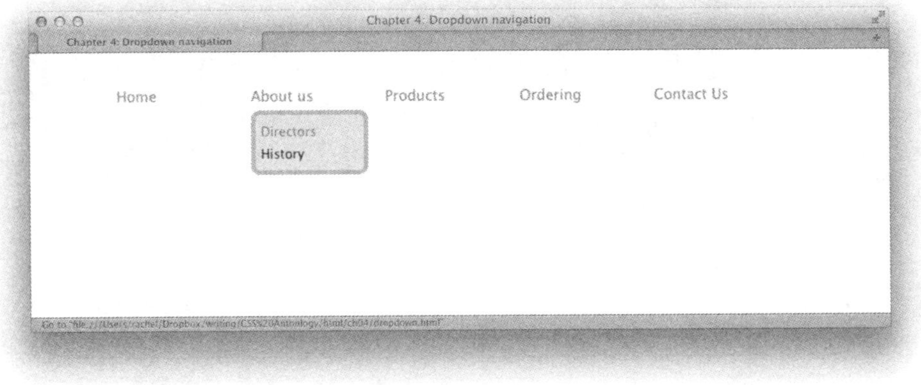

Figure 4.25. The completed menu system

Discussion

The original drop-down menus were knocked for being inaccessible and bloated. They often required JavaScript to work, leaving you without any navigation at all if you didn't have JavaScript enabled. Because of this, drop-down menus were never popular with web designers.

More recently, web developers realized that the support of the :hover dynamic pseudo-class on elements other than links would enable us to create CSS-only drop-down menus without needing JavaScript at all. Solutions such as the now-famous Suckerfish menus were developed using this technique.[2]

---

[2] http://www.alistapart.com/articles/dropdowns

The problem with CSS-only menus is that they can be very difficult to use. While there are no accessibility issues for screen-reader users in the way there were for those using old JavaScript-inserted menus (because the markup is right there on the page), the menus are generally inaccessible for those using a keyboard to navigate, and can be fiddly to click on when using a mouse, as we'll soon see. My advice is to create your menus using CSS, but then use JavaScript to enhance their usability, as I'll show you here.

We start with a set of nested lists, as seen in Figure 4.26.

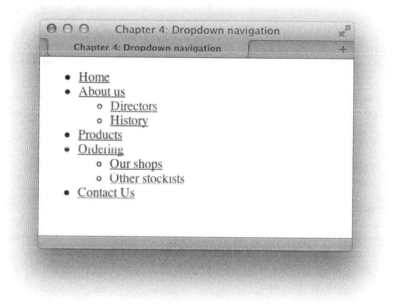

Figure 4.26. The unstyled nested lists

We can now use CSS to display this list as a horizontal menu:

chapter_04/dropdown.css *(excerpt)*

```css
.nav {
  list-style: none;
  margin: 0;
  padding: 0;
  font-size: 114.3%;
}
```

```
.nav > li {
  float: left;
  width: 130px;
  margin-right: 20px;
  position: relative;
}

.nav li a:link, .nav li a:visited {
  display: block;
  text-decoration: none;
  color: rgb(122,106,83);
}

.nav li a:hover {
  color: rgb(153,178,183);
}
```

I've added a rule here to style the links as well. If you refresh the browser, you will see that we have created a horizontal menu with the subnavigation displaying underneath the main navigation points, as indicated in Figure 4.27.

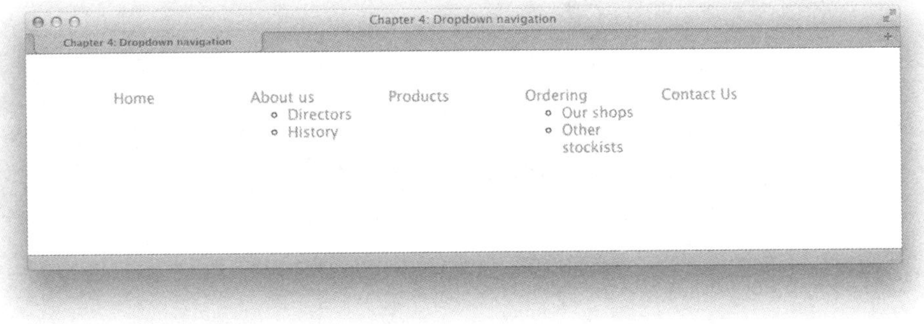

Figure 4.27. After floating the main list items

Next, we want to style our drop-downs. The drop-down part is the nested ul. I'm giving these a border and background color, and also having some fun with CSS3 properties, adding rounded corners and a box-shadow:

chapter_04/dropdown.css *(excerpt)*

```
.nav ul {
  position: absolute;
  background-color: rgb(213,222,217);
```

```
   border: 5px solid rgb(153,178,183);
   -webkit-border-radius: 10px;
   -moz-border-radius: 10px;
   border-radius: 10px;
   padding: 0.5em;
   margin: 0.5em 0 0 0;
   -webkit-box-shadow: 2px 2px 2px 2px rgba(0,0,0,0.2));
   -moz-box-shadow: 2px 2px 2px 2px rgba(0,0,0,0.2);
   box-shadow: 2px 2px 2px 2px rgba(0,0,0,0.2));
   list-style: none;
   font-size: 85.7%;
   width: 8em;
   line-height: 1.8;
}

.nav ul li a:link, .nav ul li a:visited {
   color: rgb(0,0,0);
}

.nav ul li a:hover {
   color: rgb(122,106,83);
}
```

Refreshing the browser should give you the completed effect, with both menus showing as you can see in Figure 4.28.

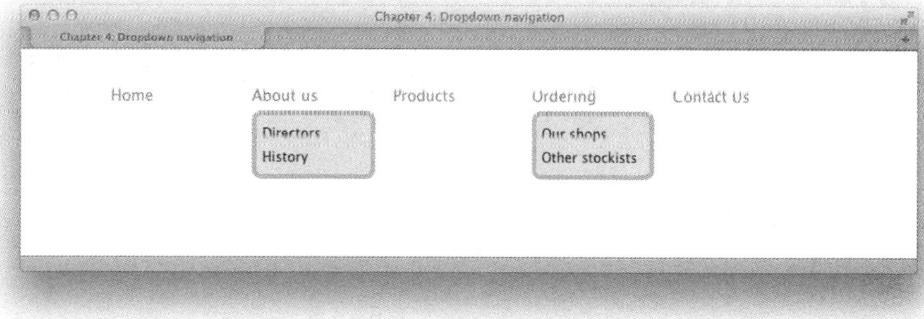

Figure 4.28. The styled menus

We hide the menus by setting the left margin on the menu ul to a large negative value, throwing it off the side of the screen:

```
.nav ul {
  position: absolute;
  background-color: rgb(213,222,217);
  border: 5px solid rgb(153,178,183);
  -webkit-border-radius: 10px;
  -moz-border-radius: 10px;
  border-radius: 10px;
  padding: 0.5em;
  margin: 0.5em 0 0 -9999px;
  -webkit-box-shadow: 2px 2px 2px 2px rgba(0,0,0,0.2));
  -moz-box-shadow: 2px 2px 2px 2px rgba(0,0,0,0.2);
  box-shadow: 2px 2px 2px 2px rgba(0,0,0,0.2));
  list-style: none;
  font-size: 85.7%;
  width: 8em;
  line-height: 1.8;
}
```

You could also set the menus to `display: none` to hide them. I'm using a negative margin rather than `display: none` because screen readers that honor CSS may read the `display: none` declaration and not give the user the opportunity to navigate to the hidden items.

The menus will now disappear when the page is reloaded. To bring them back on hover, add the following rule:

```
.nav li:hover ul {
  margin-left: 0;
}
```

When we hover over the `li`, the `ul` within that `li` will have its `margin-left` set to 0, bringing it back into view.

If you test this out, you'll see that your drop-downs work; however, you'll probably also find that being able to click a link in the drop-down is tricky. Sometimes it will disappear before you get onto it! The other issue is that if you try and tab to the links using the keyboard, you'll find that the browser does tab to the hidden items—but because they're offscreen, they're invisible to the naked eye.

To deal with this issue, we can add some JavaScript. There are a number of methods of doing this, but as an example, I'm going to use a jQuery plugin called Superfish.[3] This plugin simply enhances the CSS menu you've already built.

Introducing jQuery

jQuery[4] is a JavaScript library designed to make using JavaScript simpler and more efficient. In addition to the basic library, there is a range of plugins that can help you to achieve various tasks—such as drop-down menus.

To use a jQuery plugin, you need to include jQuery in your page and the plugin itself. The jQuery link I've used in the following markup points to a version of the library hosted on Google; you can, however, also download the latest version of jQuery from the jQuery website.

The only change you need to make is to add an extra selector to the rule where you set your margin on hover:

```
.nav li:hover ul, .nav li.sfHover ul {
  margin-left: 0;
}
```

Download Superfish, add the **superfish.js** file to your site, and then add the JavaScript to the head of your document:

chapter_04/dropdown.html *(excerpt)*

```
<head>
  <meta charset="utf-8" />
  <title>Chapter 4: Dropdown navigation</title>
  <link rel="stylesheet" href="dropdown.css" />
  <script src="http://ajax.googleapis.com/ajax/libs/
➥jquery/1.7.1/jquery.min.js" type="text/javascript"></script>
  <script src="superfish.js" type="text/javascript"></script>
  <script>
    $(document).ready(function() {
      $('ul.nav').superfish({
        delay:       1000,
        animation:   {opacity:'show',height:'show'},
```

---

[3] http://users.tpg.com.au/j_birch/plugins/superfish/

[4] http://jquery.com/

```
        speed:      'fast',
        autoArrows:  false,
        dropShadows: false
      });
    });
  </script>
</head>
```

We're including the latest jQuery and the Superfish plugin, with some configuration settings for Superfish. There are lots of ways you can customize the plugin; details are on the Superfish website.[5]

You should now find that your menus are much easier to use. Even better, when you tab to a main item, the submenu displays and you can tab to the subitems as shown in Figure 4.29. When assessing any plugin or script to create drop-down menus, this is a basic test of whether you should use it.

Figure 4.29. Tabbing to the menu items

Navigating Your Way to Success

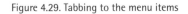

We've now looked at a whole range of navigation styles, while using many CSS properties and techniques. As you can see, even the most complicated-looking menu can be broken down into some fairly simple techniques. For navigation inspiration, I'd recommend checking out the Navigation collection on the Pattern Tap website.[6] With a solid knowledge of CSS and your own design skills, you should be able to create navigation that's both attractive and usable with CSS.

---

[5] http://users.tpg.com.au/j_birch/plugins/superfish/#options
[6] http://patterntap.com/tags/type/navigation

Tabular Data

You've probably heard the mantra "tables are for tabular data, not layout." Originally designed to display tabular data correctly in HTML documents, they were soon misappropriated as a way to lay out web pages. Back then, understanding how to create complex layouts using nested tables was a part of the standard skill set of every web designer. Yet using tables in this way requires large amounts of markup, making a website increasingly complex and difficult to maintain, as well as causing pages to load slowly. This method also creates problems for users who are trying to access content using screen readers or other text-only devices. Since then, the Web Standards movement has pushed for the replacement of tabular layouts with CSS, which is designed for the job and is, ultimately, far more flexible, as we'll discover in Chapter 9.

But, far from being evil, tables can (and should) still be used for their true purpose—that of displaying tabular data. This chapter will illustrate some common, correct uses of tables, incorporating elements and attributes that, though used infrequently, help to make your tables accessible. We'll also look at how CSS can make these tables more attractive and usable for those viewing them in a web browser.

How do I lay out spreadsheet data using CSS?

The quick answer is, you don't! Spreadsheet data is tabular by nature and, therefore, should be displayed in an HTML table. However, we can still spruce up the display of that data using CSS, as we'll see later in this chapter. And we should still be concerned about the accessibility of our tables, even when we're using them to display the right kind of content.

Discussion

Tabular data is information that's displayed in a table, and which may be logically arranged into columns and rows.

Your accounts, when stored in spreadsheet format, are a good example of tabular data. If you needed to mark up the annual accounts of an organization for which you were building a site, you might be given a spreadsheet that looked like Figure 5.1.

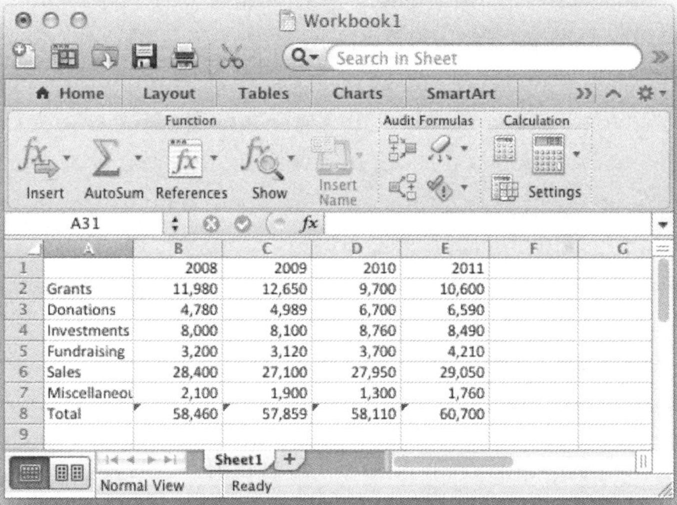

Figure 5.1. Displaying the accounts information in Excel

Obviously, this is tabular data. We see column and row headings to which the data in each cell relates. Ideally, we'd display this data in a table, as shown in Figure 5.2, complete with table headings to ensure that the data is structured logically.

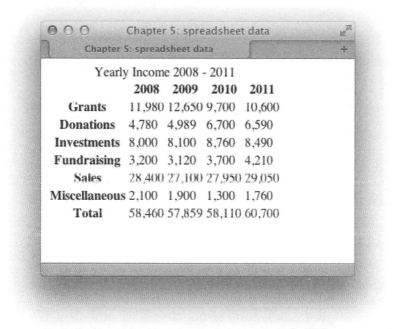

Figure 5.2. The accounts information displayed as a table using HTML

How do I make my tabular data accessible?

The HTML table specification includes elements and attributes that go beyond the basics required to achieve a certain look for tabular data. These extra parts of the table can be used to ensure that its content is clear when it's read out to visually impaired users who are unable to see the layout for themselves. They're also easy to implement, though they're often omitted by web developers. Take a look at this example:

chapter_05/table.html *(excerpt)*

```
<table class="datatable">
  <caption>
    Yearly Income 2008 - 2011
  </caption>
```

```
<tr>
  <th></th>
  <th scope="col">2008</th>
  <th scope="col">2009</th>
  <th scope="col">2010</th>
  <th scope="col">2011</th>
</tr>
<tr>
  <th scope="row">Grants</th>
  <td>11,980</td>
  <td>12,650</td>
  <td>9,700</td>
  <td>10,600</td>
</tr>
<tr>
  <th scope="row">Donations</th>
  <td>4,780</td>
  <td>4,989</td>
  <td>6,700</td>
  <td>6,590</td>
</tr>
<tr>
  <th scope="row">Investments</th>
  <td>8,000</td>
  <td>8,100</td>
  <td>8,760</td>
  <td>8,490</td>
</tr>
<tr>
  <th scope="row">Fundraising</th>
  <td>3,200</td>
  <td>3,120</td>
  <td>3,700</td>
  <td>4,210</td>
</tr>
<tr>
  <th scope="row">Sales</th>
  <td>28,400</td>
  <td>27,100</td>
  <td>27,950</td>
  <td>29,050</td>
</tr>
<tr>
  <th scope="row">Miscellaneous</th>
  <td>2,100</td>
```

```
    <td>1,900</td>
    <td>1,300</td>
    <td>1,760</td>
  </tr>
  <tr>
    <th scope="row">Total</th>
    <td>58,460</td>
    <td>57,859</td>
    <td>58,110</td>
    <td>60,700</td>
  </tr>
</table>
```

Discussion

This markup creates a table that uses elements and attributes to clearly explain the contents of each cell. Let's discuss the value that each of these elements and attributes adds.

The `caption` element

chapter_05/table.html *(excerpt)*

```
<caption>
  Yearly Income 2008 - 2011
</caption>
```

The caption element adds a caption to the table. By default, browsers generally display the caption above the table, however, you can manually set the position of the caption in relation to the table using the caption side CSS property:

```
table {
  caption-side: bottom;
}
```

Why might you want to use a caption instead of just adding a heading or paragraph text for display with the table? By using a caption, you can ensure that the text is tied to the table, and that it's recognized as the table's caption; there's no chance that the screen reader could interpret it as a separate element. If you want your table captions to display as paragraph text or level-three headings in a graphical browser, no problem! You can create CSS rules for captions just as you would for any other element.

The th element

```
<th scope="col">2011</th>
```

The th element identifies data that's a row or column heading. The example markup contains both row and column headings and, to ensure that this is clear, we use the scope attribute of the th tag. The scope attribute shows whether a given heading is applied to the column (col) or row (row).

Before you begin to style your tables to complement the look and feel of the site, it is good practice to ensure the accessibility of those tables to users of devices such as screen readers. Accessibility is one of those concerns that many developers brush off, saying, "I'll check it when I'm finished." But if you leave accessibility checks until the end of development, you may never actually deal with them; the problems they identify may well require time-consuming fixes, particularly in complex applications. Once you make a habit of keeping accessibility in mind as you design, you'll find that it becomes second nature and adds very little to a project's development time.

CSS attributes make the styling of data tables simple and quick. For instance, when I begin a new site on which I know I'll have to use a lot of data tables, I create a style rule with the class selector .datatable; this contains the basic styles that I want to affect all data tables, and can easily be applied to the table tag of each. I then create style rules for .datatable th (the heading cells), .datatable td (the regular cells), and .datatable caption (the table captions).

From that point, adding a new table is easy. All the styles are there—I just need to apply the datatable class. If I decide to change the styles after I've created all the tables in my site, I simply edit my stylesheet.

How do I add a border to a table?

You can add borders to tables just as you can with other HTML elements. Borders are particularly useful for tables, as they help to make the data understandable:

```
                                              chapter_05/table.css (excerpt)

.datatable {
  border: 1px solid #338ba6;
}
```

This style rule will display a one-pixel, light-blue border around your table, as in Figure 5.3.

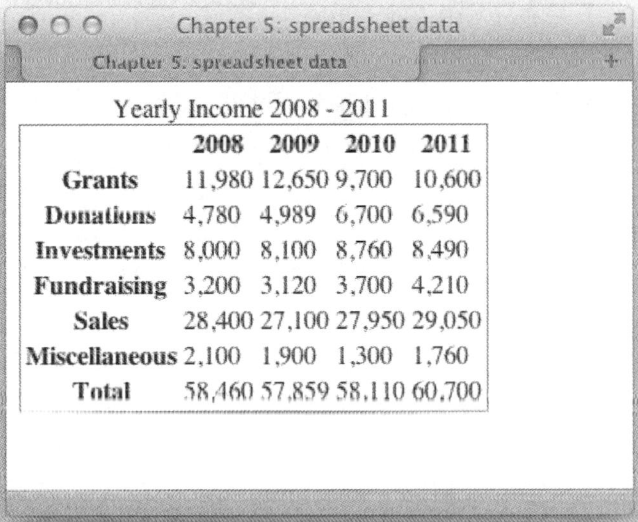

Figure 5.3. Applying a border to the `table` element

You can also add borders to individual cells:

```
.datatable td, .datatable th {
  border: 1px solid #73c0d4;
}
```

This style rule renders a slightly lighter border around `td` and `th` table cells that have a class of `datatable`, as Figure 5.4 shows.

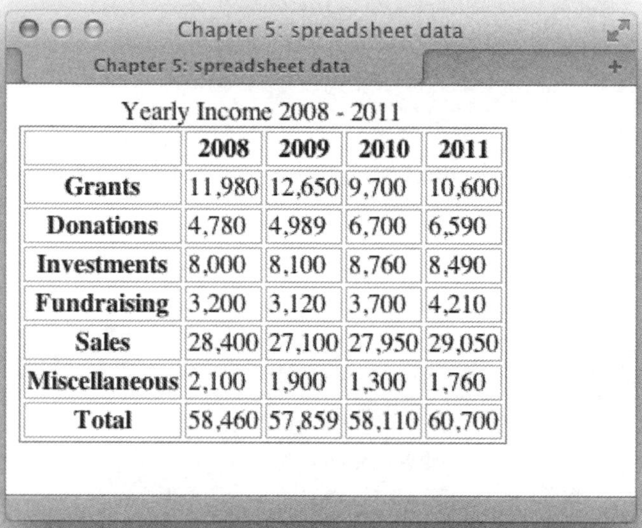

Yearly Income 2008 - 2011

	2008	2009	2010	2011
Grants	11,980	12,650	9,700	10,600
Donations	4,780	4,989	6,700	6,590
Investments	8,000	8,100	8,760	8,490
Fundraising	3,200	3,120	3,700	4,210
Sales	28,400	27,100	27,950	29,050
Miscellaneous	2,100	1,900	1,300	1,760
Total	58,460	57,859	58,110	60,700

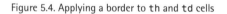

Figure 5.4. Applying a border to `th` and `td` cells

Discussion

By experimenting with CSS borders on your tables, you can create many appealing effects—even if the data contained within is dull! You can use differently colored borders for table headings and table cells, and apply various thicknesses and styles of border to table cells. You might even try out such tricks as using one shade for top and left borders, and another for bottom and right borders, to create an indented effect.

We can apply a range of values to the CSS `border-style` property. We've already met `solid`, which displays a solid line as the border, and this is shown along with the other available options in Figure 5.5.

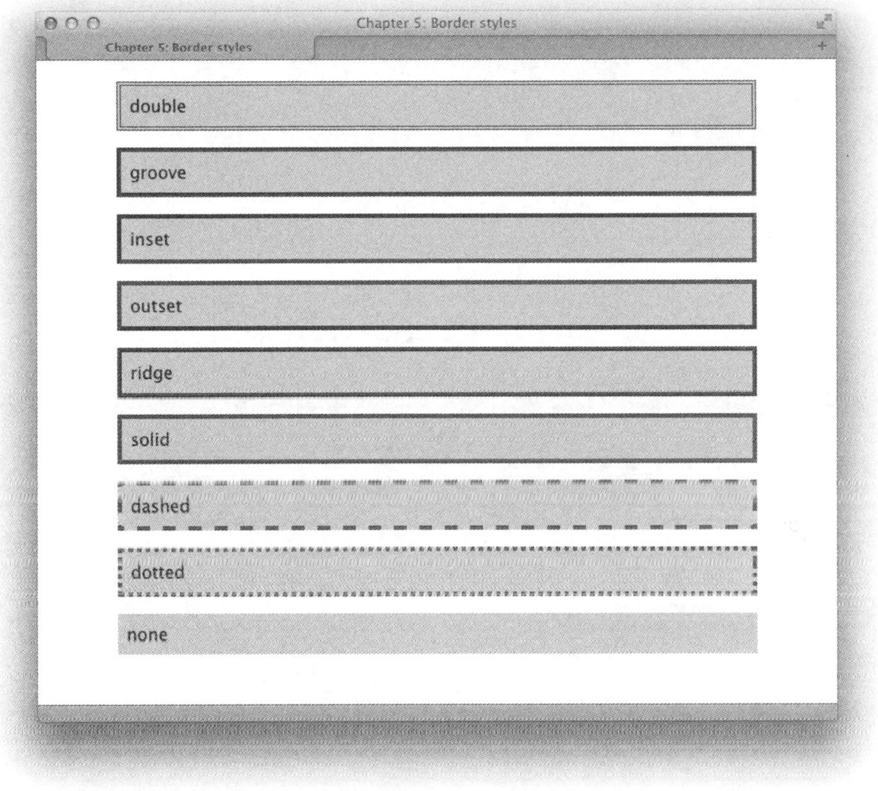

Figure 5.5. Border styles all using a four-pixel red border

Here's the markup that will produce the preceding range of border styles:

```
                                            chapter_05/borderstyles.html
<!DOCTYPE html>
<html>
<head>
  <meta charset="utf-8" />
<title>Chapter 5: Border styles</title>
  <link rel="stylesheet" href="borderstyles.css" />
</head>
<body>
  <div class="wrapper">
  <div class="double">double</div>
  <div class="groove">groove</div>
  <div class="inset">inset</div>
  <div class="outset">outset</div>
```

```
  <div class="ridge">ridge</div>
  <div class="solid">solid</div>
  <div class="dashed">dashed</div>
  <div class="dotted">dotted</div>
  <div class="none">none</div>
</div>
</body>
</html>
```

chapter_05/borderstyles.html

```
body {
  background-color: #fff;
  color: #111;
  margin: 0;
  padding: 0;
  font: 1em/1.4 "Lucida Grande", "Lucida Sans Unicode",
    "Lucida Sans", Verdana, Tahoma, sans-serif;
}

.wrapper {
  width: 80%;
  margin: 20px auto 40px auto;
}

.wrapper div {
  background-color: #ccc;
  padding: 0.5em;
  margin: 0 0 1em 0;
}

.double {
  border: 4px double red
}

.groove {
  border: 4px groove red;
}

.inset {
  border: 4px inset red;
}

.outset {
  border: 4px outset red;
```

```
}

.ridge {
  border: 4px ridge red;
}

.solid {
  border: 4px solid red;
}

.dashed{
  border: 4px dashed red;
}

.dotted {
  border: 4px dotted red;
}

.none {
  border: none;
}
```

How do I stop spaces appearing between the cells of my tables when I've added borders using CSS?

In the previous solution, after adding a border to the th and td elements, you can see in Figure 5.4 that there are gaps between the borders applied to each cell. Simply setting margin or padding to 0 won't remove this space.

Solution

You can remove the spaces between the cells by setting the value of the border-collapse property to collapse:

chapter_05/table.css

```
.datatable {
  border: 1px solid #338ba6;
  border-collapse: collapse;
}
```

```
.datatable td, .datatable th {
  border: 1px solid #73c0d4;
}
```

Figure 5.6 shows the effect this has on the example seen in Figure 5.4.

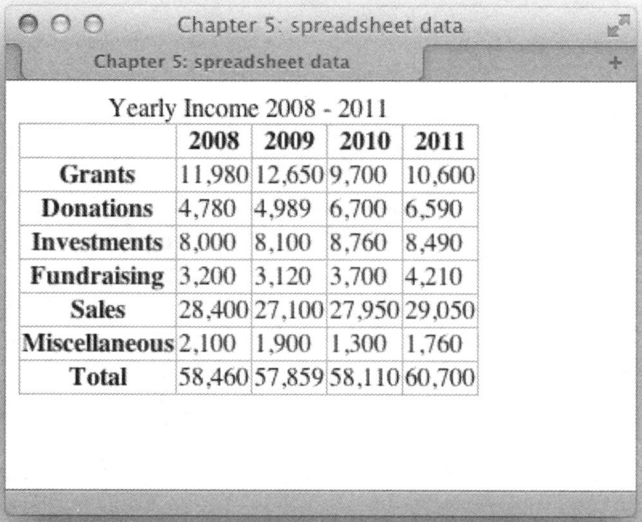

Figure 5.6. Using border-collapse to remove spacing between cells

How do I display spreadsheet data in an attractive and usable way?

The HTML table is the best way to structure spreadsheet data, even though its default appearance is unattractive. Luckily, we can style the table using CSS, which keeps markup to a minimum and allows us to control our data table's appearance using the stylesheet.

Solution

The data we saw displayed as an HTML table earlier in this chapter is an example of spreadsheet data. That markup, which is shown unstyled in Figure 5.7, forms the basis for the following example.

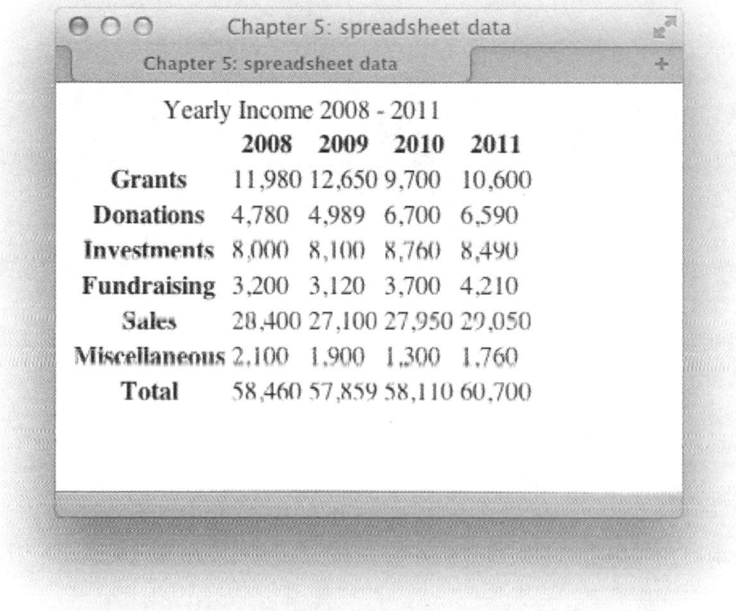

Figure 5.7. The unstyled table

Let's apply the following stylesheet to that table:

```
                                    chapter_05/spreadsheet.css (excerpt)
body {
  background-color: #fff;
  color: #111;
  margin: 0;
  padding: 0;
  font: 0.75em/1.3 "Lucida Grande", "Lucida Sans Unicode",
    "Lucida Sans", Verdana, Tahoma, sans-serif;
}

.wrapper {
```

```
   width: 80%;
   margin: 20px auto 40px auto;
}

.datatable {
   border: 1px solid #d6dde6;
   border-collapse: collapse;
}

.datatable td {
   border: 1px solid #d6dde6;
   text-align: right;
   padding: 0.2em;
}

.datatable th {
   border: 1px solid #828282;
   background-color: #bcbcbc;
   font-weight: bold;
   text-align: left;
   padding: 0.2em;
}

.datatable caption {
   font-size: 116.7%;
   font-weight: bold;
   background-color: #b0c4de;
   color: #111;
   padding: 0.4em 0 0.3em 0;
   border: 1px solid #789ac6;
}
```

Discussion

In this solution, I aimed to display the table in a way that's similar to the appearance of a desktop spreadsheet.

First I styled the table as a whole, setting the borders to `collapse`:

chapter_05/spreadsheet.css *(excerpt)*

```css
.datatable {
  border: 1px solid #d6dde6;
  border-collapse: collapse;
}
```

As we've already seen, `border` displays a border around the outside of the table, while `border-collapse` removes spaces between the table's cells.

Next, I turned my attention to the table cells:

chapter_05/spreadsheet.css *(excerpt)*

```css
.datatable td {
  border: 1px solid #d6dde6;
  text-align: right;
  padding: 0.2em;
}
```

Here, I added a border to the table cells and used `text-align` to right-align their contents for that "spreadsheety" look. If you preview the document at this point, you'll see a border around each cell in the table (except the header cells), as shown in Figure 5.8.

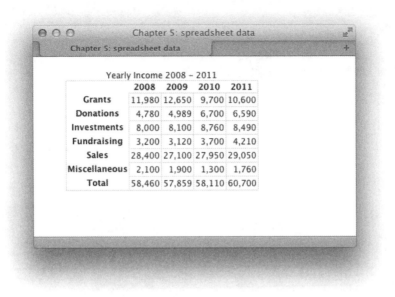

Figure 5.8. Styling the `table` and `td` elements

Next, I added a border to the `th` (heading) cells. I used a darker color for this border, because I also added a background color to these cells to highlight that they're headings rather than regular cells:

```
                                    chapter_05/spreadsheet.css (excerpt)

.datatable th {
  border: 1px solid #828282;
  background-color: #bcbcbc;
  font-weight: bold;
  text-align: left;
  padding: 0.2em;
}
```

To finish, I styled the caption to make it look visually part of the table, as shown in Figure 5.9.

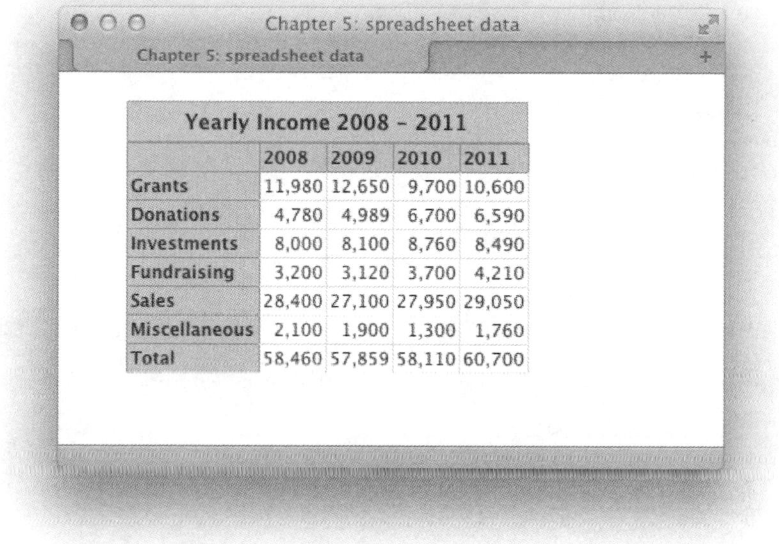

Yearly Income 2008 - 2011				
	2008	2009	2010	2011
Grants	11,980	12,650	9,700	10,600
Donations	4,780	4,989	6,700	6,590
Investments	8,000	8,100	8,760	8,490
Fundraising	3,200	3,120	3,700	4,210
Sales	28,400	27,100	27,950	29,050
Miscellaneous	2,100	1,900	1,300	1,760
Total	58,460	57,859	58,110	60,700

Figure 5.9. The finished table

How do I display table rows in alternating colors?

It can be difficult to stay on a particular row as your eyes work across a large table of data. Displaying table rows in alternating colors is a common way to help users stay focused on the row they're on.

Solution

Using the CSS3 `nth-child` selector, we can add a different style to every other row without needing to add anything to the markup.

Here's the table markup for our example:

chapter_05/alternate.html

```
<!DOCTYPE html>
<html>
<head>
  <meta charset="utf-8" />
```

```
  <title>Chapter 5: highlighting alternate rows</title>
  <link rel="stylesheet" href="alternate.css" />
</head>
<body>
  <div class="wrapper">
    <table class="datatable">
      <caption>Student List</caption>
      <tr>
        <th scope="col">Student Name</th>
        <th scope="col">Date of Birth</th>
        <th scope="col">Class</th>
        <th scope="col">ID</th>
      </tr>
      <tr>
        <td>Joe Bloggs</td>
        <td>27/08/1997</td>
        <td>Mrs Jones</td>
        <td>12009</td>
      </tr>
      <tr>
        <td>William Smith</td>
        <td>20/07/1997</td>
        <td>Mrs Jones</td>
        <td>12010</td>
      </tr>
      <tr>
        <td>Jane Toad</td>
        <td>21/07/1997</td>
        <td>Mrs Jones</td>
        <td>12030</td>
      </tr>
      <tr>
        <td>Amanda Williams</td>
        <td>19/03/1997</td>
        <td>Mrs Edwards</td>
        <td>12021</td>
      </tr>
      <tr>
        <td>Kylie Jameson</td>
        <td>18/05/1997</td>
        <td>Mrs Jones</td>
        <td>12022</td>
      </tr>
      <tr>
        <td>Louise Smith</td>
```

```
        <td>17/07/1997</td>
        <td>Mrs Edwards</td>
        <td>12019</td>
      </tr>
      <tr>
        <td>James Jones</td>
        <td>04/04/1997</td>
        <td>Mrs Edwards</td>
        <td>12007</td>
      </tr>
    </table>
  </div>
</body>
</html>
```

And here's the CSS to style it:

```css
body {
  background-color: #fff;
  color: #111;
  margin: 0;
  padding: 0;
  font: 0.75em/1.3 "Lucida Grande", "Lucida Sans Unicode",
    "Lucida Sans", Verdana, Tahoma, sans-serif;
}

.wrapper {
  width: 80%;
  margin: 20px auto 40px auto;
}

.datatable {
  width: 100%;
  border: 1px solid #d6dde6;
  border-collapse: collapse;
}

.datatable td {
  border: 1px solid #d6dde6;
  padding: 0.3em;
}

.datatable th {
```

```
    border: 1px solid #828282;
    background-color: #bcbcbc;
    font-weight: bold;
    text-align: left;
    padding-left: 0.3em;
}

.datatable caption {
    font: bold 110% Arial, Helvetica, sans-serif;
    color: #33517a;
    text-align: left;
    padding: 0.4em 0 0.8em 0;
}

.datatable tr:nth-child(odd) {
    background-color: #dfe7f2;
    color: #000000;
}
```

The result can be seen in Figure 5.10.

Student List

Student Name	Date of Birth	Class	ID
Joe Bloggs	27/08/1997	Mrs Jones	12009
William Smith	20/07/1997	Mrs Jones	12010
Jane Toad	21/07/1997	Mrs Jones	12030
Amanda Williams	19/03/1997	Mrs Edwards	12021
Kylie Jameson	18/05/1997	Mrs Jones	12022
Louise Smith	17/07/1997	Mrs Edwards	12019
James Jones	04/04/1997	Mrs Edwards	12007

Figure 5.10. Alternate table rows with `nth-child`

Discussion

The nth-child selector makes it very easy to target the odd and even rows in your table using the keywords odd and even:

chapter_05/alternate.css *(excerpt)*

```
.datatable tr:nth-child(odd) {
  background-color: #dfe7f2;
  color: #000;
}
```

Prior to widespread support for this selector, we'd have to add a class to every other row and then use the class to target the row:

```
.datatable tr.altrow {
  background-color: #dfe7f2;
  color: #000;
}
```

In Chapter 7, we will look at some other ways to deal with the lack of support for selectors such as nth-child in older browsers.

How do I change a row's background color when the mouse hovers over it?

One way to boost the readability of tabular data is to change the color of rows as users move the cursor over them to highlight the row they're reading. This can be seen in Figure 5.11.

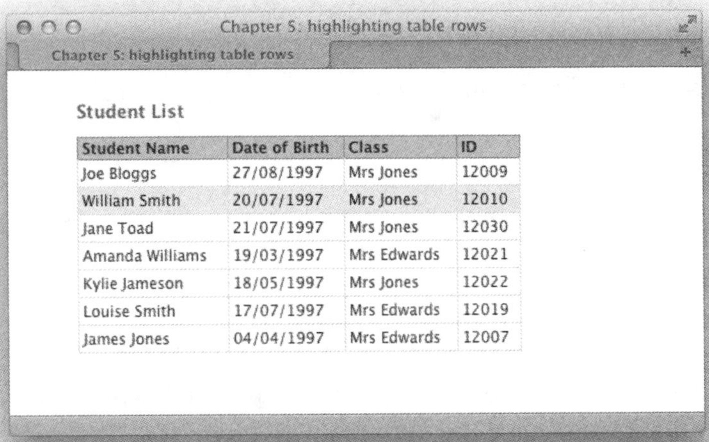

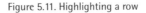

Figure 5.11. Highlighting a row

Solution

This can be a very simple solution; all you need to do is add the following rule to your CSS:

chapter_05/hiliterow.css *(excerpt)*

```
.datatable tr:hover {
  background-color: #DFE7F2;
  color: #000;
}
```

Job done!

Discussion

When we discussed `:hover` on links, I mentioned that you can also use `:hover` on other elements to create attractive effects; in addition, these serve to give the user feedback as to what they're interacting with.

This solution will work in all modern browsers including Internet Explorer 7—but not in Internet Explorer 6. But as long as your tables are clear, the highlight feature could be regarded as a "nice to have," rather than a necessary tool.

How do I display table columns in alternating colors?

While alternate row colors are a common feature of data tables, we see alternately colored columns less frequently. However, they can be a helpful way to show groupings of data.

Solution

If we use the `col` element to describe our table's columns, we can employ CSS to add a background to those columns. You can see the `col` elements I've added—one for each column—in the following table markup:

chapter_05/columns.html (excerpt)

```
<table class="datatable">
  <col />
  <col />
  <col />
  <col />
  <tr>
    <th>Pool A</th>
    <th>Pool B</th>
    <th>Pool C</th>
    <th>Pool D</th>
  </tr>
  <tr>
    <td>England</td>
    <td>Australia</td>
    <td>New Zealand</td>
    <td>France</td>
  </tr>
  <tr>
    <td>South Africa</td>
    <td>Wales</td>
    <td>Scotland</td>
    <td>Ireland</td>
  </tr>
  <tr>
    <td>Samoa</td>
    <td>Fiji</td>
    <td>Italy</td>
    <td>Argentina</td>
```

```
    </tr>
    <tr>
      <td>USA</td>
      <td>Canada</td>
      <td>Romania</td>
      <td>Europe 3</td>
    </tr>
    <tr>
      <td>Repechage 2</td>
      <td>Asia</td>
      <td>Repechage 1</td>
      <td>Namibia</td>
    </tr>
</table>
```

We can add style rules for our `col` elements using `nth-child` as shown here; the result is depicted in Figure 5.12:

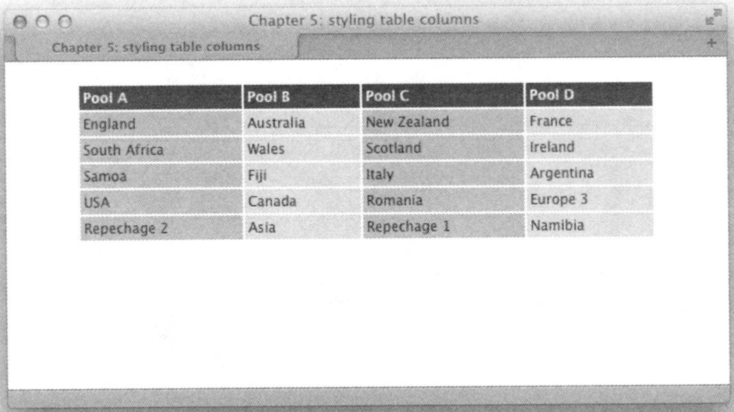

Figure 5.12. Using `nth-child` to target the `col` element

Discussion

The `col` element provides us with further flexibility for styling a table's columns, thus making our table attractive and easier to understand. It's also possible to nest `col` elements within a `colgroup` element, which allows us to change the column's appearance by applying style rules to the parent `colgroup` element.

Here's an example of nested col elements:

chapter_05/colgroups.html (excerpt)

```
<table class="datatable">
  <colgroup>
    <col />
    <col />
  </colgroup>
  <colgroup>
    <col />
    <col />
  </colgroup>
  <tr>
    <th>Pool A</th>
    <th>Pool B</th>
    <th>Pool C</th>
    <th>Pool D</th>
  </tr>
```

Here are the styles that are applied to the colgroup element rather than col:

chapter_05/colgroups.css (excerpt)

```
.datatable colgroup: nth-child(odd) {
  background-color: #80c9ff;
  color: #000;
}

.datatable colgroup: nth-child(even) {
  background-color: #bfe4ff;
  color: #000;
}
```

The result of this change is as shown in Figure 5.13.

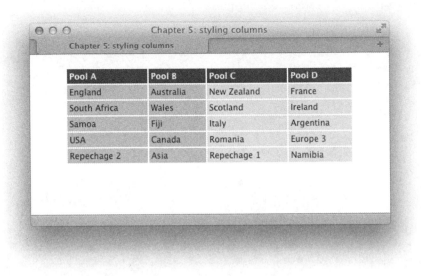

Figure 5.13. Styling columns using `colgroup`

How do I display a calendar using CSS?

Calendars, such as the example from a desktop application in Figure 5.14, also involve tabular data. The days of the week along the top of the calendar represent the headings of the columns. As such, a calendar's display constitutes the legitimate use of a table, but you can keep markup to a minimum by using CSS to control the look and feel.

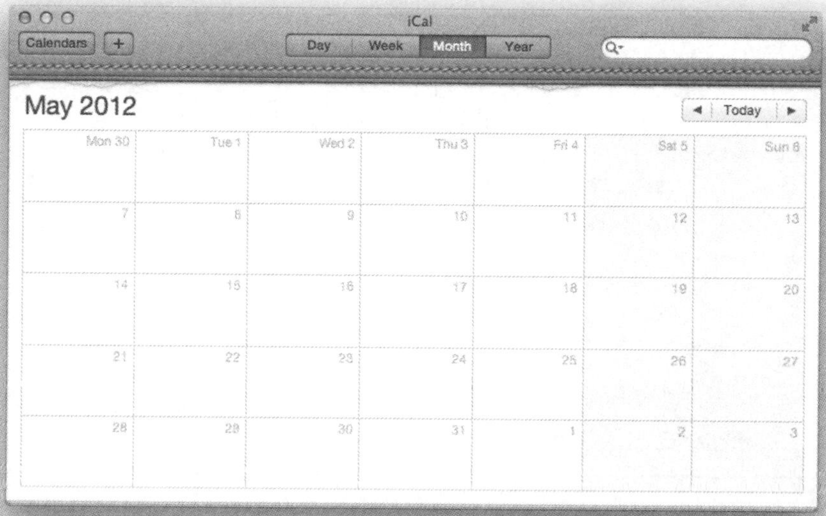

Figure 5.14. A desktop calendar

Solution

Our solution uses an accessible, simple table that leverages CSS styles to create the attractive calendar shown in Figure 5.15. Given its basic structure, it's ideal for use in a database-driven application in which the table is created via server-side code:

```
                                                    chapter_05/cal.html
<!DOCTYPE html>
<html>
<head>
  <meta charset="utf-8" />
  <title>Chapter 5: calendar</title>
  <link rel="stylesheet" href="cal.css" />
</head>
<body>
  <div class="wrapper">
    <table class="clmonth">
      <caption>November 2011</caption>
      <tr>
        <th scope="col">Monday</th>
        <th scope="col">Tuesday</th>
        <th scope="col">Wednesday</th>
```

```
      <th scope="col">Thursday</th>
      <th scope="col">Friday</th>
      <th scope="col">Saturday</th>
      <th scope="col">Sunday</th>
    </tr>
    <tr>
      <td class="previous">31</td>
      <td class="active">1
        <ul>
          <li>New pupils' open day</li>
          <li>Year 8 theater trip</li>
        </ul>
      </td>
      <td>2</td>
      <td>3</td>
      <td>4</td>
      <td>5</td>
      <td>6</td>
    </tr>
    <tr>
      <td class="active">7
        <ul>
          <li>Year 7 English exam</li>
        </ul>
      </td>
      <td>8</td>
      <td>9</td>
      <td>10</td>
      <td>11</td>
      <td>12</td>
      <td>13</td>
    </tr>
    <tr>
      <td>14</td>
      <td>15</td>
      <td>16</td>
      <td class="active">17
        <ul>
          <li>Sports Day</li>
        </ul>
      </td>
      <td class="active">18
        <ul>
          <li>Year 7 parents' evening</li>
          <li>Prizegiving</li>
```

```
        </ul>
      </td>
      <td>19</td>
      <td>20</td>
    </tr>
    <tr>
      <td>21</td>
      <td>22</td>
      <td>23</td>
      <td class="active">24
        <ul>
          <li>Year 8 parents' evening</li>
        </ul>
      </td>
      <td>25</td>
      <td>26</td>
      <td>27</td>
    </tr>
    <tr>
      <td>28</td>
      <td>29</td>
      <td class="active">30
        <ul>
          <li>First night of school play</li>
        </ul>
      </td>
      <td class="next">1</td>
      <td class="next">2</td>
      <td class="next">3</td>
      <td class="next">4</td>
    </tr>
    </table>
  </div>
</body>
</html>
```

```
body {
  background-color: #fff;
  color: #111;
  margin: 0;
  padding: 0;
  font: 0.75em/1.3 "Lucida Grande", "Lucida Sans Unicode",
    "Lucida Sans", Verdana, Tahoma, sans-serif;
```

```
}

.wrapper {
  width: 80%;
  margin: 20px auto 40px auto;
}

.clmonth {
  border-collapse: collapse;
  width: 100%;
}

.clmonth caption {
  text-align: left;
  font-weight: bold;
  font-size: 116.7%;
  padding-bottom: 0.4em;
}

.clmonth th {
  border: 1px solid #aaa;
  border-bottom: none;
  padding: 0.2em 0.6em 0.2em 0.6em;
  background-color: #ccc;
  color: #3f3f3f;
  min-width: 8em;
}

.clmonth td {
  border: 1px solid #eaeaea;
  padding: 0.2em 0.6em 0.2em 0.6em;
  vertical-align: top;
}

.clmonth td.previous, .clmonth td.next {
  background-color: #f6f6f6;
  color: #c6c6c6;
}

.clmonth td.active {
  background-color: #b1cbe1;
  color: #2b5070;
  border: 2px solid #4682b4;
}
```

```
.clmonth ul {
  list-style-type: none;
  margin: 0;
  padding-left: 1em;
  padding-right: 0.6em;
}

.clmonth li {
  margin-bottom: 1em;
}
```

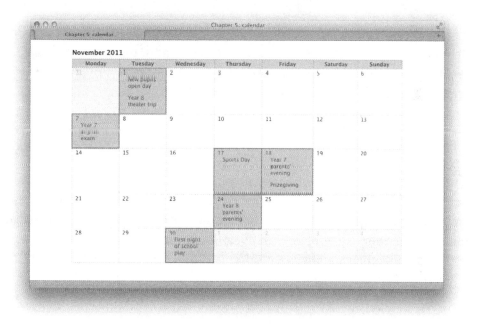

Figure 5.15. A calendar marked up as a table and styled with CSS

Discussion

This example starts out as a very simple table. It has a caption—the month we're working with—and I've marked up the days of the week as table headers using the th element:

```
<table class="clmonth">
  <caption>November 2011</caption>
  <tr>
    <th scope="col">Monday</th>
    <th scope="col">Tuesday</th>
    <th scope="col">Wednesday</th>
    <th scope="col">Thursday</th>
    <th scope="col">Friday</th>
    <th scope="col">Saturday</th>
    <th scope="col">Sunday</th>
  </tr>
```

The table has a `class` of `clmonth`. I've used a class rather than an ID because, in some situations, you might want to display more than one month on the page. If you then found that you needed to give the table an ID—perhaps to allow you to show and hide the table using JavaScript—you could add an ID as well as the class.

The days are held within individual table cells, and the events for each day are marked up as a list within the appropriate table cell.

In the following markup, you can see that I've added classes to two of the table cells. The class `previous` is applied to cells containing days that fall within the preceding month (we'll use `next` later for days in the following month), while the class `active` is applied to cells that contain event information, so that we may highlight them:

```
<tr>
  <td class="previous">31</td>
  <td class="active">1
    <ul>
      <li>New pupils' open day</li>
      <li>Year 8 theater trip</li>
    </ul>
  </td>
  <td>2</td>
  <td>3</td>
  <td>4</td>
  <td>5</td>
  <td>6</td>
</tr>
```

The table, without CSS, displays as shown in Figure 5.16.

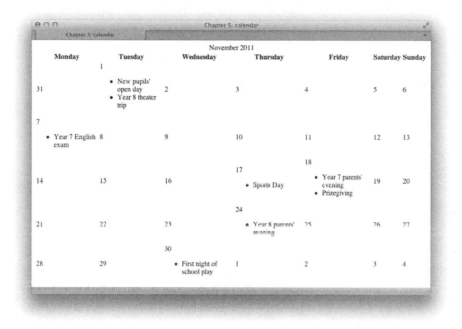

Figure 5.16. The table without CSS

Now that we have the structural markup in place, we can style the calendar. I set a standard style for the body, including a base font size. Then I set a style for the class `clmonth` for the borders to collapse, leaving no space between cells:

```
                                        chapter_05/cal.css (excerpt)
body {
  background-color: #fff;
  color: #111;
  margin: 0;
  padding: 0;
  font: 0.75em/1.3 "Lucida Grande", "Lucida Sans Unicode",
    "Lucida Sans", Verdana, Tahoma, sans-serif;
}

.wrapper {
  width: 80%;
  margin: 20px auto 40px auto;
}
```

```
.clmonth {
  border-collapse: collapse;
}
```

I styled the `caption` within the class `clmonth`, then created styles for the table headers (`th`) and table cells (`td`):

chapter_05/cal.css *(excerpt)*

```
.clmonth caption {
  text-align: left;
  font-weight: bold;
  font-size: 116.7%;
  padding-bottom: 0.4em;
}

.clmonth th {
  border: 1px solid #aaa;
  border-bottom: none;
  padding: 0.2em 0.6em 0.2em 0.6em;
  background-color: #ccc;
  color: #3f3f3f;
  min-width: 8em;
}

.clmonth td {
  border: 1px solid #eaeaea;
  padding: 0.2em 0.6em 0.2em 0.6em;
  vertical-align: top;
}
```

As you can see in Figure 5.17, our calendar is beginning to take shape.

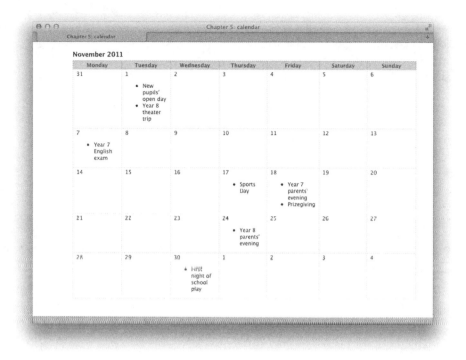

Figure 5.17. After styling the calendar cells, it's starting to look more like a desktop calendar

We can now style the list of events within each table cell, removing the bullet and adding space between list items:

chapter_05/cal.css *(excerpt)*

```
.clmonth ul {
  list-style-type: none;
  margin: 0;
  padding-left: 1em;
  padding-right: 0.6em;
}

.clmonth li {
  margin-bottom: 1em;
}
```

Finally, we add styles for the `previous` and `next` classes, giving the effect of graying out the days not part of the current month. We also style the `active` class, which highlights those days on which events take place:

```css
.clmonth td.previous, .clmonth td.next {
  background-color: #f6f6f6;
  color: #c6c6c6;
}

.clmonth td.active {
  background-color: #b1cbe1;
  color: #2b5070;
  border: 2px solid #4682b4;
}
```

This is just one of many ways to create a calendar. Online calendars are commonly used on blogs, where they have clickable days, and visitors can view entries made that month. By removing the events from our HTML markup, representing the day names with single letters—M for Monday, and so on—and making a few simple changes to our CSS, we can create a simple mini calendar that's suitable for this purpose, like the one shown in Figure 5.18.

Figure 5.18. Creating a mini calendar

Here's the HTML and CSS you'll need to create this version of the calendar:

```html
<!DOCTYPE html>
<html>
<head>
  <meta charset="utf-8" />
  <title>Chapter 5: mini calendar</title>
  <link rel="stylesheet" href="cal_mini.css" />
</head>
<body>
  <div class="wrapper">
    <table class="clmonth">
      <caption>November 2011</caption>
      <tr>
        <th scope="col">M</th>
        <th scope="col">T</th>
        <th scope="col">W</th>
        <th scope="col">T</th>
        <th scope="col">F</th>
        <th scope="col">S</th>
        <th scope="col">S</th>
      </tr>
      <tr>
        <td class="previous">31</td>
        <td class="active">1</td>
        <td>2</td>
        <td>3</td>
        <td>4</td>
        <td>5</td>
        <td>6</td>
      </tr>
      <tr>
        <td class="active">7</td>
        <td>8</td>
        <td>9</td>
        <td>10</td>
        <td>11</td>
        <td>12</td>
        <td>13</td>
      </tr>
      <tr>
        <td>14</td>
        <td>15</td>
        <td>16</td>
        <td class="active">17</td>
```

```
            <td class="active">18</td>
            <td>19</td>
            <td>20</td>
          </tr>
          <tr>
            <td>21</td>
            <td>22</td>
            <td>23</td>
            <td class="active">24</td>
            <td>25</td>
            <td>26</td>
            <td>27</td>
          </tr>
          <tr>
            <td>28</td>
            <td>29</td>
            <td class="active">30</td>
            <td class="next">1</td>
            <td class="next">2</td>
            <td class="next">3</td>
            <td class="next">4</td>
          </tr>
        </table>
      </div>
    </body>
</html>
```

chapter_05/cal_mini.css

```
body {
  background-color: #fff;
  color: #111;
  margin: 0;
  padding: 0;
  font: 0.75em/1.3 "Lucida Grande", "Lucida Sans Unicode",
    "Lucida Sans", Verdana, Tahoma, sans-serif;
}

.wrapper {
  width: 80%;
  margin: 20px auto 40px auto;
}

.clmonth {
  border-collapse: collapse;
```

```
}

.clmonth caption {
  text-align: left;
  font-weight: bold;
  font-size: 116.7%;
  padding-bottom: 0.4em;
}

.clmonth th {
  border: 1px solid #aaa;
  border-bottom: none;
  padding: 0.2em 0.4em 0.2em 0.4em;
  background-color: #ccc;
  color: #3f3f3f;
}

.clmonth td {
  border: 1px solid #eaeaea;
  padding: 0.2em 0.4em 0.2em 0.4em;
  vertical-align: top;
}

.clmonth td.previous, .clmonth td.next {
  background-color: #f6f6f6;
  color: #c6c6c6;
}

.clmonth td.active {
  background-color: #b1cbe1;
  color: #2b5070;
  border: 2px solid #4682b4;
}
```

How do I create a pricing table?

Pricing tables are a customary feature of websites offering a range of pricing plans. We can have a look at a common example—a pricing table for a web-hosting company—to see how we can combine some of tricks we've covered in this chapter to style a more complicated table.

Solution

The table in Figure 5.19 is created using the following markup and CSS:

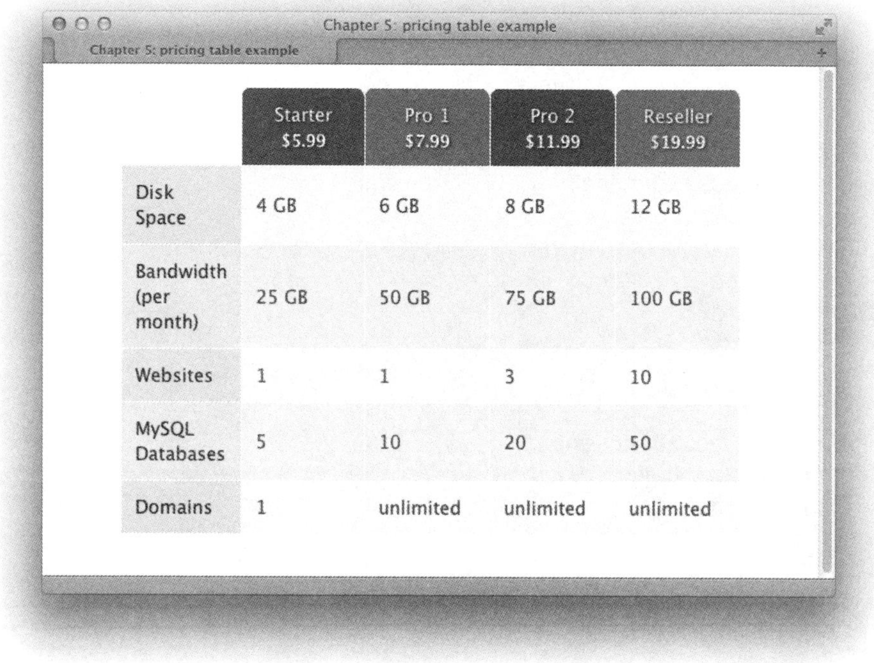

Figure 5.19. A pricing table

```
chapter_05/pricing.html

<!DOCTYPE html>
<html>
<head>
  <meta charset="utf-8" />
  <title>Chapter 5: pricing table example</title>
  <link rel="stylesheet" href="pricing.css" />
</head>
<body>
  <div class="wrapper">
    <table class="pricing">
      <col />
      <col />
      <col />
      <col />
```

```
<col />
<tr>
  <td></td>
  <th scope="col">Starter
  <span class="price">$5.99</span></th>
  <th scope="col">Pro 1
  <span class="price">$7.99</span></th>
  <th scope="col">Pro 2
  <span class="price">$11.99</span></th>
  <th scope="col">Reseller
  <span class="price">$19.99</span></th>
</tr>
<tr>
  <th scope="row">Disk Space</th>
  <td>4 GB</td>
  <td>6 GB</td>
  <td>8 GB</td>
  <td>12 GB</td>
</tr>
<tr>
  <th scope="row">Bandwidth (per month)</th>
  <td>25 GB</td>
  <td>50 GB</td>
  <td>75 GB</td>
  <td>100 GB</td>
</tr>
<tr>
  <th scope="row">Websites</th>
  <td>1</td>
  <td>1</td>
  <td>3</td>
  <td>10</td>
</tr>
<tr>
  <th scope="row">MySQL Databases</th>
  <td>5</td>
  <td>10</td>
  <td>20</td>
  <td>50</td>
</tr>
<tr>
  <th scope="row">Domains</th>
  <td>1</td>
  <td>unlimited</td>
  <td>unlimited</td>
```

```
        <td>unlimited</td>
      </tr>
    </table>
  </div>
</body>
</html>
```

```css
body {
  background-color: #fff;
  color: #111;
  margin: 0;
  padding: 0;
  font: 1em/1.4 "Lucida Grande", "Lucida Sans Unicode",
    "Lucida Sans", Verdana, Tahoma, sans-serif;
}

.wrapper {
  width: 80%;
  margin: 20px auto 40px auto;
}

.pricing {
  border-collapse: collapse;
}

.pricing col {
  width: 7em;
}

.pricing col:first-child {
  width: auto;
}

.pricing td {
  color: rgb(51,51,51);
  border: 1px solid rgb(255,255,255);
  padding: 0.75em;
}

.pricing tr:nth-child(odd) {
  background-color: rgb(246,246,246);
}
```

```
.pricing tr:nth-child(odd):hover td {
  background-color: rgba(59,87,98,.2);
}

.pricing tr:nth-child(even) {
  background-color: rgba(246,246,246,.5);
}

.pricing tr:nth-child(even):hover td {
  background-color: rgba(91,124,121,.2);
}

.pricing tr:first-child, .pricing tr:first-child:hover td {
  background-color: transparent;
}

.pricing th[scope="col"] {
  background-color: rgb(59,87,98);
  color: rgb(255,255,255);
  border: 1px solid rgb(255,255,255);
  font-weight: normal;
  padding: 0.75em;
  -moz-border-radius-topleft: 10px;
  -moz-border-radius-topright: 10px;
  -moz-border-radius-bottomright: 0px;
  -moz-border-radius-bottomleft: 0px;
  -webkit-border-radius: 10px 10px 0px 0px;
  border-radius: 10px 10px 0px 0px;
  text-shadow: 1px 1px 3px #111111;
}

.pricing th[scope="col"]:nth-child(odd) {
  background-color: rgb(91,124,121);
}

.pricing th span.price {
  display: block;
  padding: 0.2em 0 0 0;
  font-size: 87.5%;
  font-weight: bold;
}

.pricing th[scope="row"] {
  background-color: rgb(232,232,232);
  color: rgb(0,0,0);
```

```
    border: 1px solid rgb(255,255,255);
    padding: 0.75em;
    font-weight: normal;
    text-align: left;
}

.pricing tr:nth-child(odd) th[scope="row"] {
    background-color: rgba(232,232,232,.5);
}
```

Discussion

This solution really pulls together much of what we've covered in this chapter. I start out with my pricing information marked up as a table. The table has headers (th elements) across the top and down the left-hand side; I've used the scope attribute to explain which fields the headers are for, and this attribute becomes useful once we start to add CSS.

In my CSS, the first task is set border-collapse to collapse, and then use the col element to give my columns a width. After setting all the columns to 7em, I then use first-child to target the very first column and set the width back to auto, allowing the longer headers to take up more space:

chapter_05/pricing.css *(excerpt)*

```
.pricing {
    border-collapse: collapse;
}

.pricing col {
    width: 7em;
}

.pricing col:first-child {
    width: auto;
}
```

I next look at the td elements within my table—adding a color, border, and padding:

chapter_05/pricing.css *(excerpt)*

```
.pricing td {
  color: rgb(51,51,51);
  border: 1px solid rgb(255,255,255);
  padding: 0.75em;
}
```

I've yet to give my `td` elements a background color as I'm going to set this on the rows using `nth-child` to create a striped table effect:

chapter_05/pricing.css *(excerpt)*

```
.pricing tr:nth-child(odd) {
  background-color: rgb(246,246,246);
}

.pricing tr:nth-child(even) {
  background-color: rgba(246,246,246,.5);
}
```

If we take a look at the table now, we can see this effect:

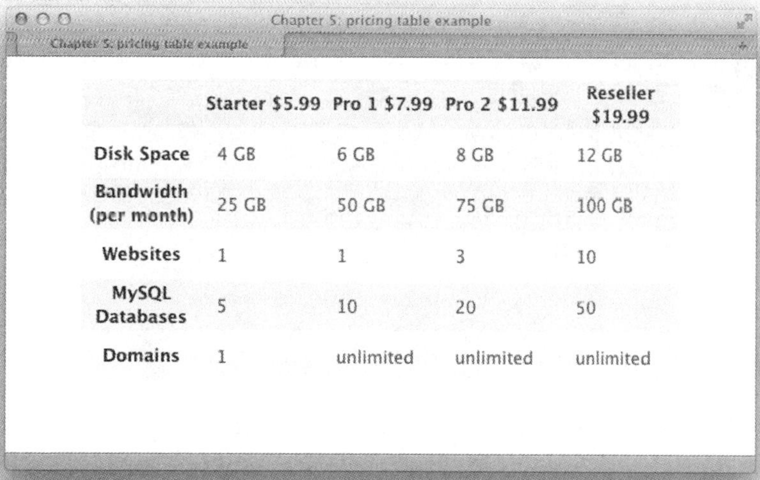
Chapter 5: pricing table example
Chapter 5: pricing table example
Starter $5.99
Pro 1 $7.99
Pro 2 $11.99
Reseller $19.99
Disk Space 4 GB 6 GB 8 GB 12 GB
Bandwidth (per month) 25 GB 50 GB 75 GB 100 GB
Websites 1 1 3 10
MySQL Databases 5 10 20 50
Domains 1 unlimited unlimited unlimited

Figure 5.20. After styling columns, cells, and rows

I am now going to look at the headings for the columns. These can be targeted separately from the th elements down the left-hand side by using an attribute selector and looking for scope="col". I'm styling my headings to look a bit like tabs by using border-radius to round the top corners, and adding a text shadow to the text. Then I use nth-child to select every other heading for a different background-color. Finally, I style the span element within each heading that contains the pricing information:

chapter_05/pricing.css *(excerpt)*

```
.pricing th[scope="col"] {
  background-color: rgb(59,87,98);
  color: rgb(255,255,255);
  border: 1px solid rgb(255,255,255);
  font-weight: normal;
  padding: 0.75em;
  -moz-border-radius-topleft: 10px;
  -moz-border-radius-topright: 10px;
  -moz-border-radius-bottomright: 0px;
  -moz-border-radius-bottomleft: 0px;
  -webkit-border-radius: 10px 10px 0px 0px;
  border-radius: 10px 10px 0px 0px;
  text-shadow: 1px 1px 3px #111111;
}

.pricing th[scope="col"]:nth-child(odd) {
  background-color: rgb(91,124,121);
}

.pricing th span.price {
  display: block;
  padding: 0.2em 0 0 0;
  font-size: 87.5%;
  font-weight: bold;
}
```

I can now take a look at the headings down the left, selecting these with an attribute selector and adding some style information. Again, I'm using nth-child to stripe these heading rows:

chapter_05/pricing.css (excerpt)

```css
.pricing th[scope="row"] {
  background-color: rgb(232,232,232);
  color: rgb(0,0,0);
  border: 1px solid rgb(255,255,255);
  padding: 0.75em;
  font-weight: normal;
  text-align: left;
}

.pricing tr:nth-child(odd) th[scope="row"] {
  background-color: rgba(232,232,232,.5);
}
```

Now for some final touches. On :hover of a table row, I change the rgba alpha value of the td to give a visual indication of the rollover:

chapter_05/pricing.css (excerpt)

```css
.pricing tr:nth-child(odd):hover td {
  background-color: rgba(59,87,98,.2);
}

.pricing tr:nth-child(even):hover td {
  background-color: rgba(91,124,121,.2);
}
```

A final rule removes the background color from the heading row, both on the tr and on the td when hovered, so that no background color displays behind the tabs:

chapter_05/pricing.css (excerpt)

```css
.pricing tr:first-child, .pricing tr:first-child:hover td {
  background-color: transparent;
}
```

The nice aspect about this solution is that I've had no need to add very much in the way of classes or additional markup to be able to style it. I've used the correct markup for a table, and then used that markup as a way to attach CSS to the table to make it look appealing.

Tables Topped

In this chapter, we've discovered that tables are alive and well—when used for their original purpose of displaying tabular data, that is! CSS gives you the ability to turn data tables into really attractive interface items, without negatively impacting their accessibility. So, please, embrace tables and use them to display tabular data—that's their job!

Chapter

Forms and User Interfaces

Forms are an inescapable part of web design and development. We use them to capture information from our users, to post information to message boards, to add items to shopping carts, and to update our blogs—to name but a few.

CSS gives us plenty of options with which to style our forms; however, forms are unlike the other HTML elements that we've encountered so far. Form elements—for example, fields, buttons, and any other input element—are included as a "replaced element" in the spec. Replaced elements are those whose appearance is defined by an external source. In the case of form elements, this is the browser or operating system UI. Due to this, user agents can provide interface controls that best suit the environment they're running in; for example, a browser on a phone may deal with a select list in a different way from a desktop browser. This is helpful in terms of usability, in that a user grows used to the control offered by the device they're using; however, it can be frustrating to web designers who feel they should have more control over these interface elements.

Since this book's last edition, new form elements and attributes that are part of HTML5 have become included in browsers, offering their own styling opportunities and challenges. In this chapter, we'll explore some of the ways we can create attractive forms without compromising their usability across different devices.

How do I lay out a form with CSS?

While you may still sometimes see a form laid out using a table, it's straightforward to lay out your forms using CSS, as the following example shows.

Solution

The form layout in Figure 6.1 is created using the following markup and CSS:

chapter_06/form.html

```html
<!DOCTYPE html>
<html>
<head>
  <meta charset="utf-8" />
  <title>Chapter 6: Styling a form</title>
  <link rel="stylesheet" href="form.css" />
</head>
<body>
  <div class="wrapper">
    <form method="post" action="/contact" id="contact-form">
      <div>
        <label for="fName">Name</label>
        <input type="text" name="fName" id="fName" required=
          "required" />
      </div>
      <div>
        <label for="fEmail">Email address</label>
        <input type="text" name="fEmail" id="fEmail" />
      </div>
      <div>
        <label for="fQuestion">Question / Comments</label>
        <textarea name="fQuestion" id="fQuestion" rows="10"
          cols="30"></textarea>
      </div>
      <div class="submit">
        <input type="submit" name="contact-submit"
          id="contact-submit" value="Submit" />
      </div>
    </form>
```

```
    </div>
  </body>
</html>
```

```css
body {
  background-color: #fff;
  color: #111;
  margin: 0;
  padding: 0;
  font: 0.75em/1.3 "Lucida Grande", "Lucida Sans Unicode",
    "Lucida Sans", Verdana, Tahoma, sans-serif;
}

.wrapper {
  width: 80%;
  margin: 20px auto 40px auto;
}

form {
  width: 400px;
}

form div {
  float: left;
  width: 400px;
  padding: 0 0 0.75em 0;
}

form label {
  float: left;
  width: 120px;
}

form textarea, form input {
  float: right;
  width: 260px;
}

form input[type="submit"] {
  float: none;
  width: auto;
}
```

```
form div.submit {
  text-align: right;
}
```

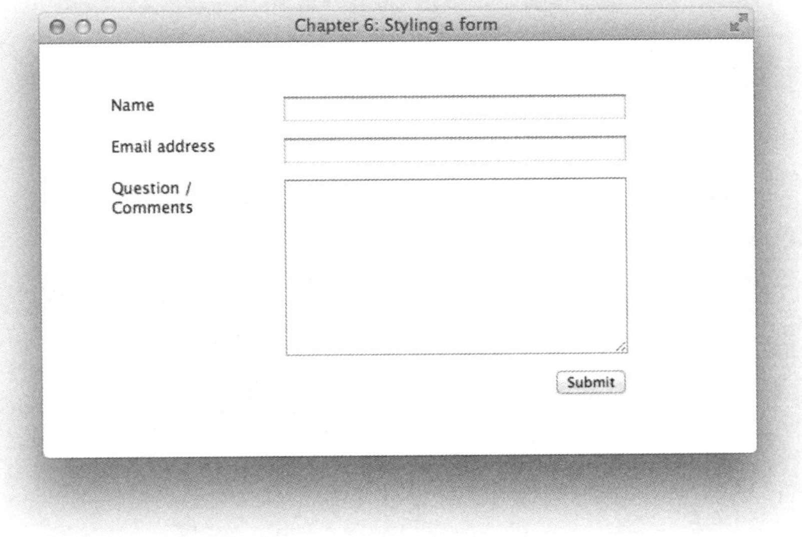

Figure 6.1. A simple form laid out using CSS

Discussion

Our form consists of `div` elements containing a label and field pair. The label is linked to the form field using the ID of the field:

chapter_06/form.html *(excerpt)*

```
<div>
  <label for="fName">Name</label>
  <input type="text" name="fName" id="fName" required="required" />
</div>
```

Without any CSS applied, the form will look as in Figure 6.2.

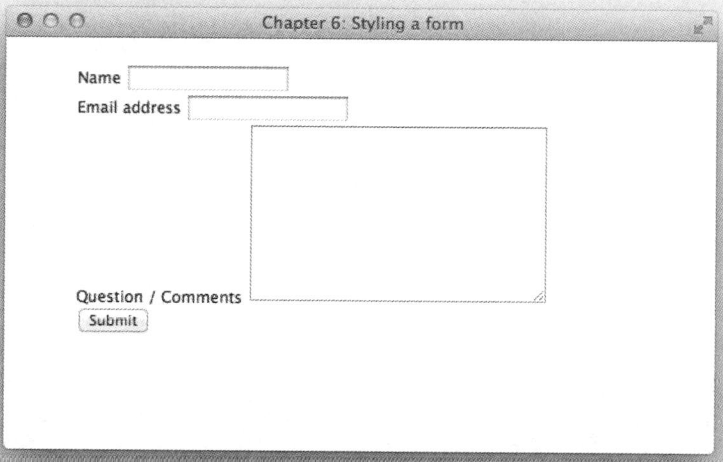

Figure 6.2. The unstyled form

First, I give the form a width and then float the label element left:

```
                                              chapter_06/form.css (excerpt)

form {
  width: 400px;
}

form div {
  float: left;
  width: 400px;
  padding: 0 0 0.75em 0;
}

form label {
  float: left;
  width: 120px;
}
```

Immediately the form starts to look better, as you can see in Figure 6.3.

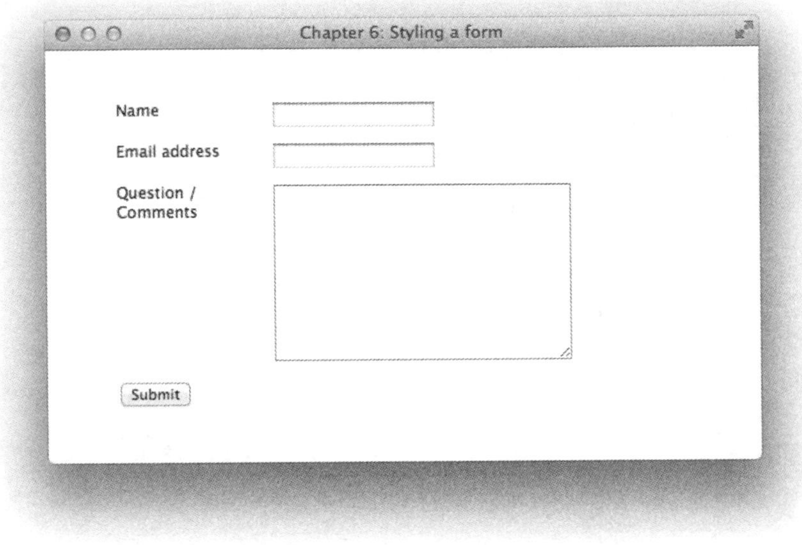

Figure 6.3. After styling the div and label elements

I now want to give my text input elements and textarea a width, which I can do with the following rule:

```
form textarea, form input {
  float: right;
  width: 260px;
}
```

Unfortunately, this has an unwanted effect, as you can see in Figure 6.4.

The CSS changes the **Submit** button, because we're targeting the input element and the **Submit** button is also an input element with a type of submit.

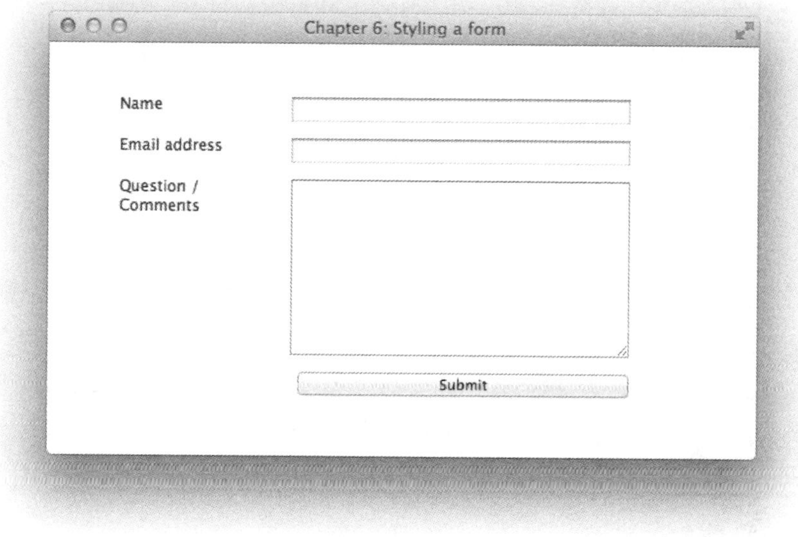

Figure 6.4. The CSS affects the **Submit** button in addition to the text input element

To sort this out, we can use an attribute selector to address the **Submit** button and overwrite the CSS used for input. I have also used the class applied to the div surrounding the **Submit** button to right-align the button. This gives us our completed form:

chapter_06/form.css *(excerpt)*

```
form input[type="submit"] {
  float: none;
  width: auto;
}

form div.submit {
  text-align: right;
}
```

Using the :not pseudo-class

Rather than overwriting the CSS using an attribute selector, we could also choose to use the :not pseudo-class. The following code would target input elements as long as they weren't a type of submit:

```
form textarea, form input:not([type="submit"]) {
  float: right;
  width: 260px;
}
```

I chose to use the attribute selector method due to there being better browser support.

Can I change the look and feel of form elements with CSS?

In the previous example, we set widths on the form elements, but it's possible to style them in other ways, too.

Solution

Using the same markup as before, I've added some additional styling to my form elements:

chapter_06/form2.css *(excerpt)*

```
form {
  width: 400px;
}

form div {
  float: left;
  width: 400px;
  padding: 0 0 0.75em 0;
}

form label {
  float: left;
  width: 120px;
}

form textarea, form input {
  float: right;
  width: 250px;
  border-top: 1px solid #999;
  border-right: 1px solid #ccc;
  border-bottom: 1px solid #cfcfcf;
```

```
  border-left: 1px solid #cfcfcf;
  -webkit-box-shadow: inset -2px 1px 2px 2px rgba(0, 0, 0, 0.1);
  -moz-box-shadow: inset -2px 1px 2px 2px rgba(0, 0, 0, 0.1);
  box-shadow: inset -2px 1px 2px 2px rgba(0, 0, 0, 0.1);
  padding: 4px;
}

form input[type="submit"] {
  float: none;
  width: auto;
  padding: 0.25em;
  -webkit-box-shadow: -2px 1px 2px 2px rgba(0, 0, 0, 0.1);
  -moz-box-shadow: -2px 1px 2px 2px rgba(0, 0, 0, 0.1);
  box-shadow: -2px 1px 2px 2px rgba(0, 0, 0, 0.1);
  font-size: 125%;
  -webkit-border-radius: 3px;
  -moz-border-radius: 3px;
  border-radius: 3px;
}

form div.submit {
  text-align: right;
}
```

The new styles can be seen in Figure 6.5.

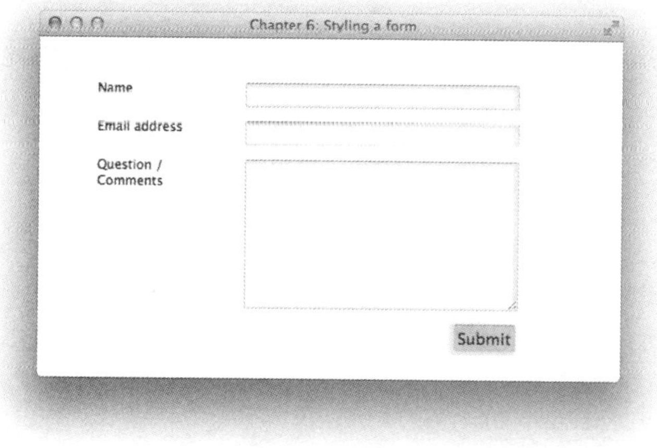

Figure 6.5. The form, now with added style

Discussion

I've used CSS to add a border to the input elements in my form. By using different shades for the borders, I can create a beveled effect. I've added to this effect by using box-shadow as an inset shadow; this creates the shadow inside the element rather than outside:

chapter_06/form2.css (excerpt)

```
form textarea, form input {
  float: right;
  width: 250px;
  border-top: 1px solid #999;
  border-right: 1px solid #ccc;
  border-bottom: 1px solid #cfcfcf;
  border-left: 1px solid #cfcfcf;
  -webkit-box-shadow: inset -2px 1px 2px 2px rgba(0, 0, 0, 0.1);
  -moz-box-shadow: inset -2px 1px 2px 2px rgba(0, 0, 0, 0.1);
  box-shadow: inset -2px 1px 2px 2px rgba(0, 0, 0, 0.1);
  padding: 4px;
}
```

For the submit button, I've used border-radius to round the corners, and added a box-shadow, this time to fall outside the element.

The font size of the text inside this button has also been increased:

chapter_06/form2.css (excerpt)

```
form input[type="submit"] {
  float: none;
  width: auto;
  padding: 0.25em;
  -webkit-box-shadow: -2px 1px 2px 2px rgba(0, 0, 0, 0.1);
  -moz-box-shadow: -2px 1px 2px 2px rgba(0, 0, 0, 0.1);
  box-shadow: -2px 1px 2px 2px rgba(0, 0, 0, 0.1);
  font-size: 125%;
  -webkit-border-radius: 3px;
  -moz-border-radius: 3px;
  border-radius: 3px;
}
```

You can set many properties that affect the look and feel of form fields, but it will depend on the browser and operating system as to what can actually be applied. As replaced elements, form fields don't have to take on the CSS provided by the author. This means that you do need to test form elements very carefully across browsers and devices. Personally, I feel that less is more when it comes to styling forms, so I tend to leave the elements alone as much as I can. Instead, I concentrate on providing good help text and error messaging to make the forms as usable as possible.

How do I highlight a field when the user tabs into or clicks on it?

It's a nifty effect to highlight a field when it has focus and is ready to be typed in.

Solution

The effect we can see in Figure 6.6 is created by adding rules for the :focus dynamic pseudo-class to our stylesheet. I'm using the same markup as used in the previous example:

```
                                          chapter_06/form-highlight.css (excerpt)
form {
  width: 400px;
}

form div {
  float: left;
  width: 400px;
  padding: 0 0 0.75em 0;
}

form label {
  float: left;
  width: 120px;
}

form textarea, form input {
  float: right;
  width: 250px;
  border-top: 1px solid #999;
```

```
    border-right: 1px solid #ccc;
    border-bottom: 1px solid #cfcfcf;
    border-left: 1px solid #cfcfcf;
    -webkit-box-shadow: inset -2px 1px 2px 2px rgba(0, 0, 0, 0.1);
    -moz-box-shadow: inset -2px 1px 2px 2px rgba(0, 0, 0, 0.1);
    box-shadow: inset -2px 1px 2px 2px rgba(0, 0, 0, 0.1);
    padding: 4px;
}

form textarea:focus, form input:focus {
    background-color: #adb3c5;
}

form input[type="submit"] {
    float: none;
    width: auto;
    padding: 0.25em;
    -webkit-box-shadow: -2px 1px 2px 2px rgba(0, 0, 0, 0.1);
    -moz-box-shadow: -2px 1px 2px 2px rgba(0, 0, 0, 0.1);
    box-shadow: -2px 1px 2px 2px rgba(0, 0, 0, 0.1);
    font-size: 125%;
    -webkit-border-radius: 3px;
    -moz-border-radius: 3px;
    border-radius: 3px;
}

form input[type="submit"]:focus {
    background-color: #fbef8e;
}

form div.submit {
    text-align: right;
}
```

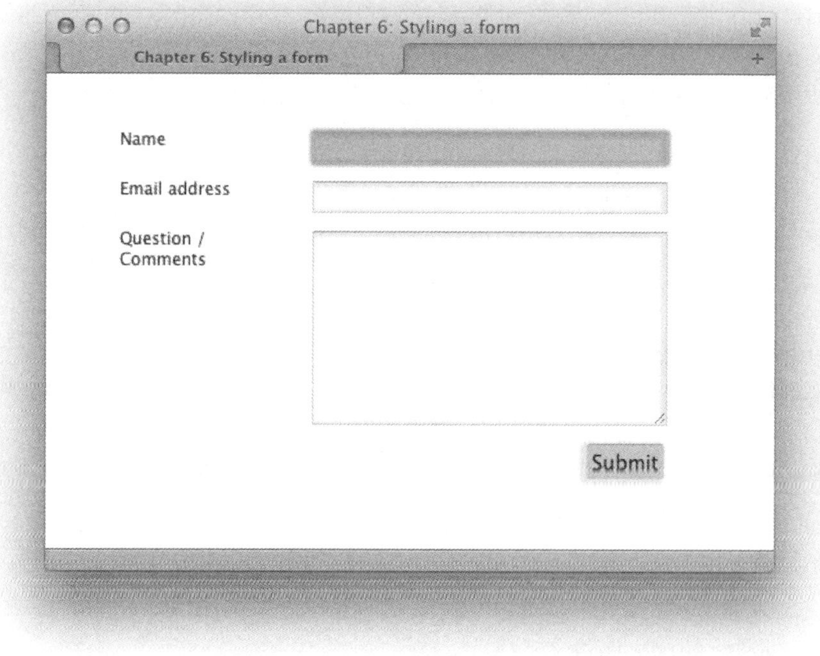

Figure 6.6. Highlighting a form field on focus

Discussion

We can simply use the :focus pseudo-class to target the field when it has focus, meaning it is ready to be used; for example, entering text into a text field, making a selection using a select box, or clicking a button. Some browsers may implement something like this effect natively.

This gives the user a nice way to see where they are in the form. Such feedback may be helpful when they're working with a very long or complex form.

What additional elements and attributes are part of the HTML5 forms spec?

We've so far looked at some fairly basic form elements. These elements have been in the HTML specification for a long time without much changing about them. HTML5 has brought with it some new form elements and attributes, and consequently a much richer interface to form-based web applications.

Many of the new elements react poorly to attempts at styling them with CSS; they rely heavily on the UI provided by the operating system or browser. The new attributes are interesting, though, for the front-end developer or designer as they offer some additional aspects we can target using CSS.

Solution

A practical example of HTML5 in forms can be seen by making a small change to our existing contact form markup: changing the email field from `type="text"` to the HTML5 type—`type="email"`, adding a `placeholder` attribute with some placeholder text, and setting a `required` flag, indicating that the field is a required field:

chapter_06/form-html5.html (excerpt)

```
<form method="post" action="/contact" id="contact-form">
  <div>
    <label for="fName">Name</label>
    <input type="text" name="fName" id="fName"
      required="required" />
  </div>

  <div>
    <label for="fEmail">Email address</label>
    <input type="email" name="fEmail" id="fEmail"
      required="required"
      placeholder="name@example.com" />
  </div>

  <div>
    <label for="fQuestion">Question / Comments</label>
    <textarea name="fQuestion" id="fQuestion" rows="10" cols="30">
      </textarea>
  </div>

  <div class="submit">
    <input type="submit" name="contact-submit" id="contact-submit"
      value="Submit" />
  </div>
</form>
```

You can see that the value of the `placeholder` attribute—**name@example.com**, an example of a valid email address in Figure 6.7—is inside the form field on load of the form. Otherwise, the form looks much the same.

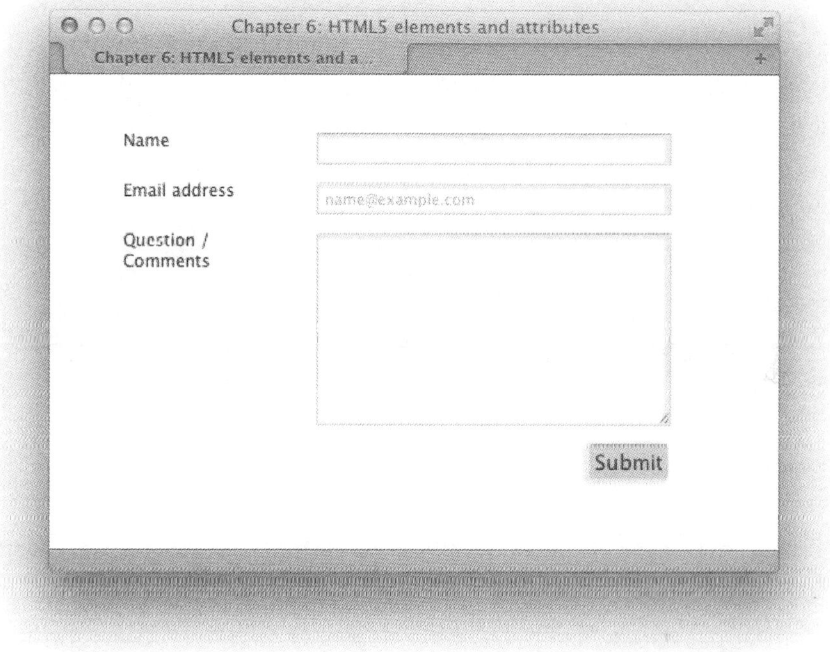

Figure 6.7. The form after adding an input field with a `type` of `email`

In a supporting browser, however, if you try and submit the form without completing the fields, or if you enter something other than an email address in the email field, you'll receive a validation error message, as shown in Figure 6.8 below. This all happens through the browser with no JavaScript required.

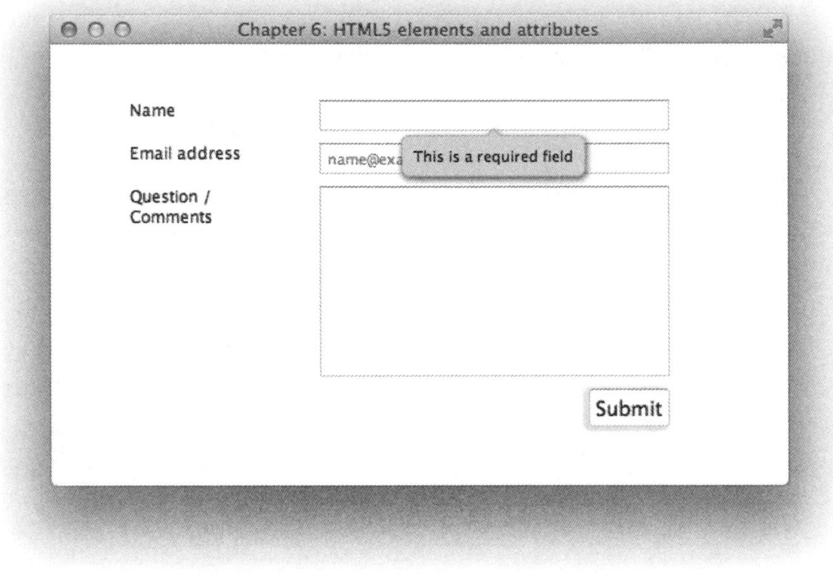

Figure 6.8. Opera shows the validation messages when the form is submitted without completing it correctly

At the time of writing, Safari and IE9 does not support `required`, while Opera, Chrome, and Firefox do. This situation is likely to change fairly quickly, though, so you may find by the time you read this that all the mainstream browsers support this feature.

Discussion

The new HTML5 elements and attributes offer a lot of potential to those of us who develop web applications and need to use forms frequently. The prospect of being able to do client-side validation simply by adding the relevant HTML element is very appealing, and by using built-in browser handling for this validation, we use a feature that users will be accustomed to—once there's good browser support.

In our solution, we looked at the use of the `required` attribute to perform client-side validation; however, these new built-in browser validation techniques should never suffice alone for testing user input. It's still essential you validate any input from your form with server-side code, just as you would when using JavaScript validation functions. Currently, bypassing the HTML5 `required` field just needs the user to be using Internet Explorer 9, because it doesn't support `required` and so allows the user to submit the form.

The `required` attribute is ignored by browsers without support for it, so there's no harm in using it. You could even inspect the `input` field using JavaScript to see if it's `required` and, for browsers without support for HTML5 form validation, create your own JavaScript validation.

Can we style the validation messages using CSS?

The question that may now be in your mind is whether we can style the messages that appear, and the answer is: not in any standard way, although browser vendors themselves may have their own pseudo-classes that you can apply CSS to. These messages are generated by the operating system and browser, so they take on a default style. This is good in some ways, as it enables people to become used to these messages and how they look and act; however, it may be frustrating to designers who find the alerts ugly—there's certainly a difference between browsers. Figure 6.9 reveals the same form, this time in Firefox on OS X.

Figure 6.9. The form alerts in Firefox

Form Input Types

The `type="email"` used for the email field is one of the new values for the `type` attribute brought to us by HTML5 forms. What's good about these new input types is that where browsers fail to recognize one, they just display a regular text input. In the case of our email field, a browser without support for `type="email"` simply treats this as `type="text"`. While there's no additional format validation, the data is collected as normal and any error is caught by your server-side validation routine.

The `email` input type is quite well supported, however. The full list of input types can be seen in Table 6.1.

Table 6.1. HTML5 form input type values

type=""	Input device / validation
search	takes on the look and feel of an operating system search element
tel	is a text field input for telephone numbers (no syntax is enforced and telephone numbers vary worldwide)
url	is a text field input validating that the format is a URL
email	is a text field input validating that the format is an email address
datetime	displays a date and time picker
date	displays a date picker
month	displays a date picker that allows selection of a month only
week	displays a date picker that allows selection of a week only
time	displays a time picker
datetime-local	displays a date and time picker
number	displays a widget that allows you to increment a number
range	displays a range slider selector
color	presents a color-picker widget

Support for these types is fairly patchy. Opera typically has the most advanced support. Figure 6.10 and Figure 6.11 show Opera with the `number`, `date`, and `color` values.

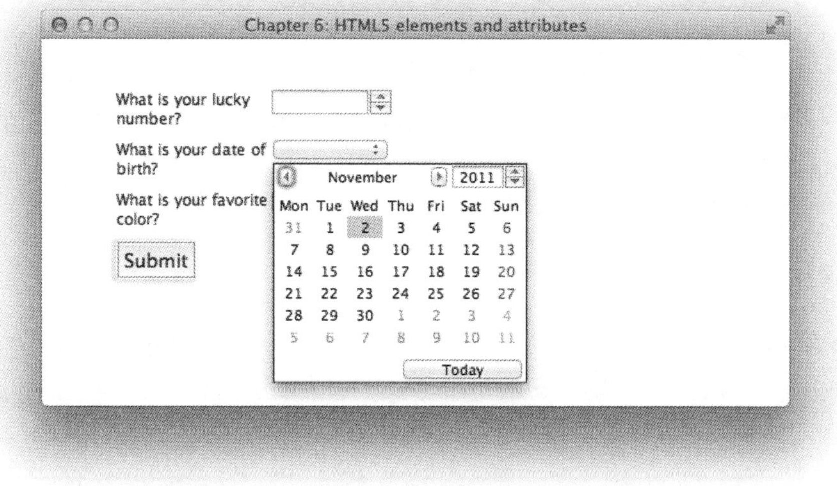

Figure 6.10. The date picker active

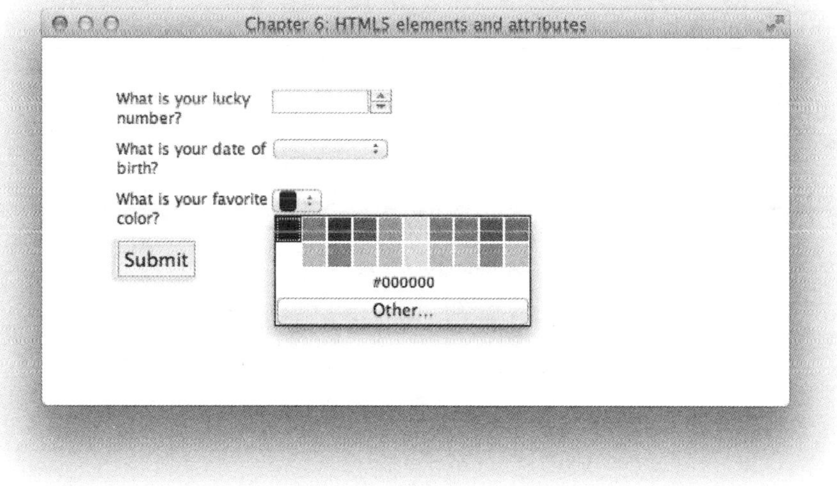

Figure 6.11. The color picker active

Can I style `input` elements based on their validity?

Knowing that an element is required can obviously be useful, as we saw in the previous solution, let alone knowing whether the element has an error or is valid. Can we access these states using CSS?

Solution

The CSS3 Basic User Interface Module outlines several dynamic pseudo-classes that we can use to detect the various states of a field as it's interacted with by the user:

chapter_06/form-validation.html *(excerpt)*

```html
<!DOCTYPE html>
<html>
<head>
  <meta charset="utf-8" />
  <title>Chapter 6: Form validation</title>
  <link rel="stylesheet" href="form-validation.css" />
</head>
<body>
  <div class="wrapper">
    <form method="post" action="/contact" id="contact-form">
      <div>
        <label for="fName">Name</label>
        <input type="text" name="fName" id="fName"
          required="required" />
      </div>
      <div>
        <label for="fEmail">Email address</label>
        <input type="email" name="fEmail" id="fEmail"
          required="required" placeholder="name@example.com" />
      </div>
      <div>
        <label for="fQuestion">Question / Comments</label>
        <textarea name="fQuestion" id="fQuestion" rows="10"
          cols="30"></textarea>
      </div>
      <div class="submit">
        <input type="submit" name="contact-submit"
          id="contact-submit" value="Submit" />
```

```
      </div>
    </form>
  </div>
</body>
</html>
```

chapter_06/form-validation.css *(excerpt)*

```css
form {
  width: 400px;
}

form div {
  float: left;
  width: 400px;
  padding: 0 0 0.75em 0;
}

form label {
  float: left;
  width: 120px;
}

form textarea, form input {
  float: right;
  width: 250px;
  border-top: 1px solid #999;
  border-right: 1px solid #ccc;
  border-bottom: 1px solid #cfcfcf;
  border-left: 1px solid #cfcfcf;
  -webkit-box-shadow: inset -2px 1px 2px 2px rgba(0, 0, 0, 0.1);
  -moz-box-shadow: inset -2px 1px 2px 2px rgba(0, 0, 0, 0.1);
  box-shadow: inset -2px 1px 2px 2px rgba(0, 0, 0, 0.1);
  padding: 4px;
}

input:focus:required:invalid {
  background-image: url(error.png);
  background-position: 98% center;
  background-repeat: no-repeat;
}

input:required:valid {
  background-image: url(accept.png);
  background-position: 98% center;
```

```
    background-repeat: no-repeat;
}

input[type="email"]:focus:required:invalid {
    background-image: url(email_error.png);
}

form input[type="submit"] {
    float: none;
    width: auto;
    padding: 0.25em;
    -webkit-box-shadow: -2px 1px 2px 2px rgba(0, 0, 0, 0.1);
    -moz-box-shadow: -2px 1px 2px 2px rgba(0, 0, 0, 0.1);
    box-shadow: -2px 1px 2px 2px rgba(0, 0, 0, 0.1);
    font-size: 125%;
    -webkit-border-radius: 3px;
    -moz-border-radius: 3px;
    border-radius: 3px;
}

form div.submit {
    text-align: right;
}
```

You can see the text input field containing invalid input styled in Figure 6.12, and valid input styled in Figure 6.13.

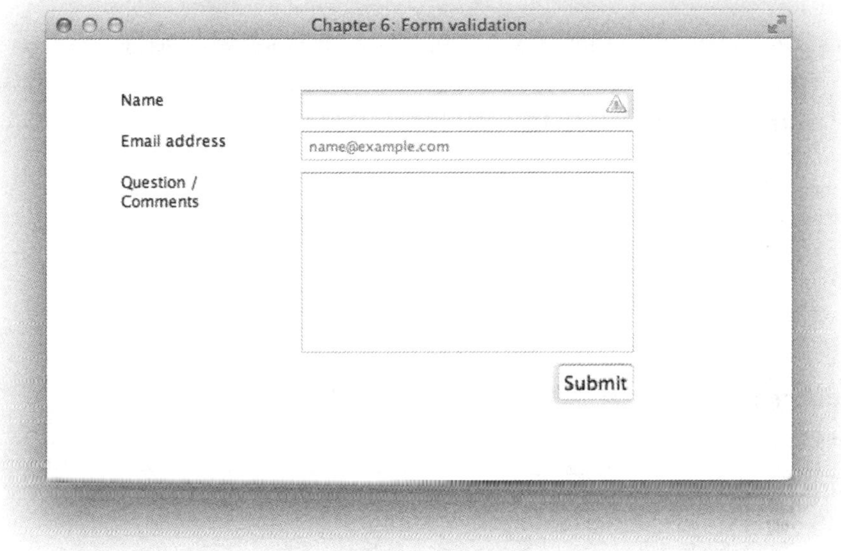

Figure 6.12. The field is invalid or incomplete

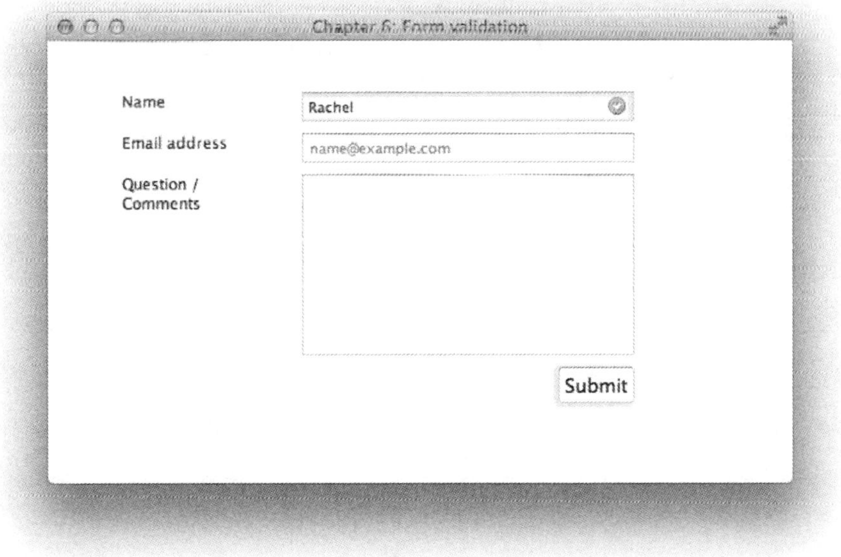

Figure 6.13. The field is valid

Discussion

We can style our fields using UI pseudo-classes in exactly the same way we use the dynamic pseudo-class :hover to target the hover state of a link. The pseudo-classes defined in the Basic User Interface Module are:

- :default
- :valid
- :invalid
- :in-range
- :out-of-range
- :required
- :optional
- :read-only
- :read-write

In this solution, we're looking at the valid and invalid pseudo-classes as they apply to our form fields. The first field—fName—is valid if any text is entered in the field:

chapter_06/form-validation.html *(excerpt)*

```
<div>
  <label for="fName">Name</label>
  <input type="text" name="fName" id="fName" required="required" />
</div>
```

The second field is only valid if a correctly formatted email address is entered into the field:

```
<div>
  <label for="fEmail">Email address</label>
  <input type="email" name="fEmail" id="fEmail" required=
    "required" placeholder="name@example.com" /></div>
```

In the CSS, I start by creating rules for text fields that are set to required:

```css
input:focus:required:invalid {
  background-image: url(error.png);
  background-position: 98% center;
  background-repeat: no-repeat;
}

input:required:valid {
  background-image: url(accept.png);
  background-position: 98% center;
  background-repeat: no-repeat;
}
```

The first slightly long-winded selector selects `input` elements that are focused (the user has tabbed or clicked into them), set to `required`, and invalid. This means that the invalid icon won't show when the user first arrives at the form—only once they start completing an input.

The second targets any `input` element that's required and valid. I've chosen not to set these to only show on focus. This is because it's comforting to see the confirmation that your input is correct, so they'll stay after the user clicks out of the field once it's completed it correctly. Next, I'm going to update the code to react differently when a field has a `type` of `email`. I'll use an attribute selector to target this field and use a different icon:

```css
input[type="email"]:focus:required:invalid {
  background-image: url(email_error.png);
}
```

So an invalid email field shows a little envelope with an error icon. Here you can see how simple it is to stack up your selectors so that they target elements precisely.

Required Information

This nifty technique will enhance your forms for the users who can see the icons; however, you should never rely on this or any other purely visual method to inform users that a field is required. A user who relies on a screen reader will be unaware that the icon is changing.

In time, I hope that screen readers will support the HTML5 `required` attribute and relay that information to the user, but until they do we need to provide this information ourselves. See the solution at the end of this chapter for details of how we can make our forms accessible while also making them attractive.

How do I group related fields?

We can group form fields logically using a `fieldset`, and then style the `fieldset` element to make the end result more attractive.

Solution

The form in Figure 6.14 comprises two `fieldsets`:

chapter_06/fieldsets.html

```
<!DOCTYPE html>
<html>
<head>
  <meta charset="utf-8" />
  <title>Chapter 6: grouping data with fieldsets</title>
  <link rel="stylesheet" href="fieldsets.css" />
</head>
<body>
  <div class="wrapper">
    <form method="post" action="/contact" id="contact-form">
      <p class="help">Please complete the form to register.
        Required fields are indicated by a <em>*</em>.</p>
      <fieldset>
        <legend>Create an account</legend>
        <div>
          <label for="fName">Name <em>*</em></label>
          <input type="text" name="fName" id="fName"
            required="required" />
        </div>
        <div>
          <label for="fEmail">Email address <em>*</em></label>
          <input type="email" name="fEmail" id="fEmail"
            required="required" placeholder="name@example.com" />
        </div>
        <div>
          <label for="fPassword">Password <em>*</em></label>
          <input type="text" name="fPassword" id="fPassword"
            required="required" />
```

```
          </div>
          <div>
            <label for="fPassword2">Confirm password <em>*</em>
              </label>
            <input type="text" name="fPassword2" id="fPassword2"
              required="required" />
          </div>
        </fieldset>
        <fieldset>
          <legend>Your address</legend>
          <div>
            <label for="fAddress1">Address Line 1 <em>*</em>
              </label>
            <input type="text" name="fAddress1" id="fAddress1"
              required="required" />
          </div>
          <div>
            <label for="fAddress2">Address Line 2</label>
            <input type="text" name="fAddress2" id="fAddress2" />
          </div>
          <div>
            <label for="fCity">Town / City <em>*</em></label>
            <input type="text" name="fCity" id="fCity"
              required="required" />
          </div>
          <div>
            <label for="fPostalCode">Zip / Post Code <em>*</em>
              </label>
            <input type="text" name="fPostalCode" id="fPostalCode"
              required="required" />
          </div>
        </fieldset>
        <div class="submit">
          <input type="submit" name="contact-submit"
            id="contact-submit" value="Submit" />
        </div>
      </form>
    </div>
  </body>
</html>
```

```css
form {
  background-color: rgb(244,252,232);
  width: 500px;
  padding: 1em;
  -webkit-border-radius: 10px;
  -moz-border-radius: 10px;
  border-radius: 10px;
}

fieldset {
  background-color: rgba(126,208,214,0.3);
  border: 3px solid rgb(255,255,255);
  -webkit-border-radius: 10px;
  -moz-border-radius: 10px;
  border-radius: 10px;
  margin: 0 0 1em 0;
}

fieldset:hover {
  background-color: rgba(126,208,214,0.5);
}

legend {
  font-size: 133%;
}

form div {
  float: left;
  width: 100%;
  padding: 0 0 0.75em 0;
  position: relative;
}

form p.help {
  font-style: italic;
  padding: 0 1em 1em 1em;
}

form p.help em {
  color: red;
}

form fieldset div:first-of-type {
```

```
    padding-top: 1em;
}

form label {
  float: left;
  width: 30%;
  font-size: 116.7%;
}

form div label em {
  position: absolute;
  color: red;
  right: 0;
}

form input {
  width: 65%;
  font-size: 133%;
  border: 0;
  -webkit-border-radius: 10px;
  -moz-border-radius: 10px;
  border-radius: 10px;
  padding: 0.25em;
}

div.submit {
  float: none;
  background-color: rgba(126,208,214,0.3);
  border: 3px solid rgb(255,255,255);
  -webkit-border-radius: 10px;
  -moz-border-radius: 10px;
  border-radius: 10px;
  margin: 0 0 1em 0;
  padding: 0.5em 0 0.5em 0;
  text-align: center;
}

form input[type="submit"] {
  width: auto;
  border: 3px solid rgb(126,208,214);
  background-color: rgba(78,150,137,0.5);
  color: rgb(255,255,255);
}
```

```
form input[type="submit"]:hover {
  background-color: rgb(78,150,137);
}
```

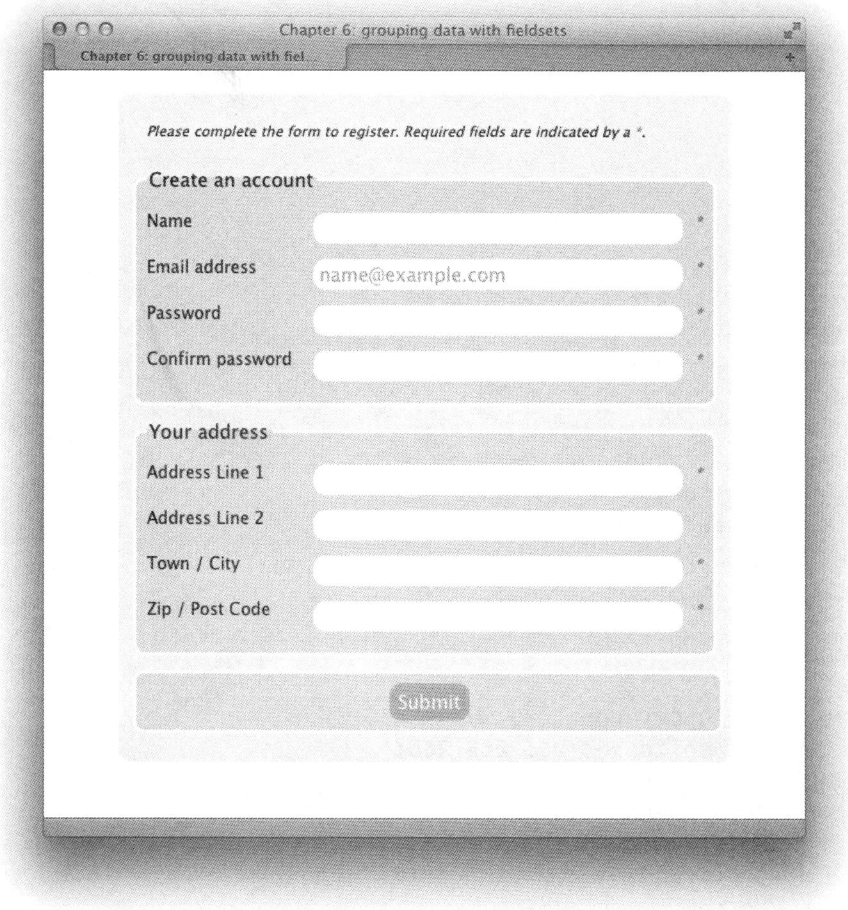

Figure 6.14. A finished form

Discussion

We start out with a marked-up form comprising two sections of information: basic account information and address details. In Figure 6.15, you can see the form without any CSS applied, and the two fieldsets clear—if a bit ugly—with a gray border.

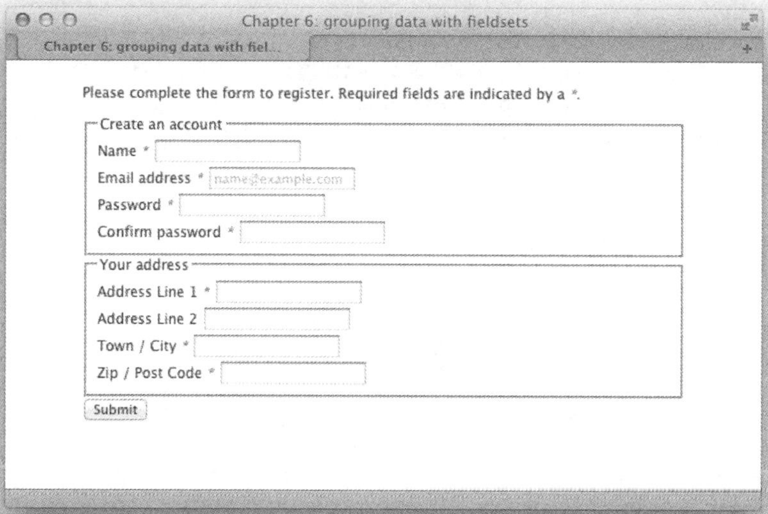

Figure 6.15. The form without any CSS

I start by styling the form, giving it a background color and some rounded corners. I'm also using padding to provide a bit of space between the edge of the form and the `fieldsets` within it:

chapter_06/fieldsets.css *(excerpt)*

```
form {
  background-color: rgb(244,252,232);
  width: 500px;
  padding: 1em;
  -webkit-border-radius: 10px;
  -moz-border-radius: 10px;
  border-radius: 10px;
}
```

Then I style the `fieldsets` by giving them a chunky rounded border. You can remove the borders altogether, but I want to maintain the visual distinction between the sections in my form. As an extra touch, I'm using `:hover` on the `fieldset` element to change the alpha value of my RGBA color when the user moves their pointer to that `fieldset`. After making these changes, my form now displays as in Figure 6.16:

chapter_06/fieldsets.css *(excerpt)*

```
fieldset {
  background-color: rgba(126,208,214,0.3);
  border: 3px solid rgb(255,255,255);
  -webkit-border-radius: 10px;
  -moz-border-radius: 10px;
  border-radius: 10px;
  margin: 0 0 1em 0;
}

fieldset:hover {
  background-color: rgba(126,208,214,0.5);
}
```

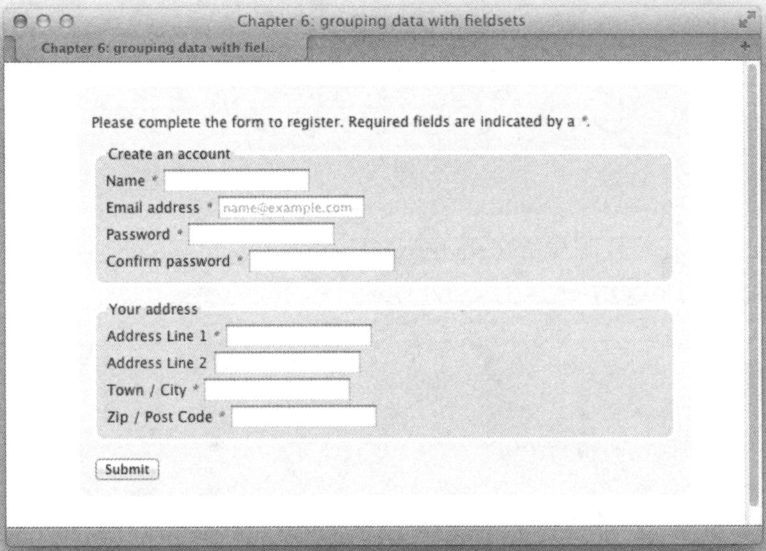

Figure 6.16. After styling the `form` and `fieldset`

The `legend` element is a label for the `fieldset`. I'm increasing the size of this to make it more of a heading:

chapter_06/fieldsets.css *(excerpt)*

```css
legend {
  font-size: 133%;
}
```

I can then style the `div` elements within the `fieldsets`—just as we have for the other solutions in this chapter. The CSS3 selector `first-of-type` is being used to add some extra padding to the top of the first `div` element:

chapter_06/fieldsets.css *(excerpt)*

```css
form div {
  float: left;
  width: 100%;
  padding: 0 0 0.75em 0;
}

form fieldset div:first-of-type {
  padding-top: 1em;
}
```

Then I float my labels left and style the `input` elements:

chapter_06/fieldsets.css *(excerpt)*

```css
form label {
  float: left;
  width: 30%;
  font-size: 116.7%;
}

form input {
  width: 65%;
  font-size: 133%;
  border: 0;
  -webkit-border-radius: 10px;
  -moz-border-radius: 10px;
  border-radius: 10px;
  padding: 0.25em;
}
```

Finally, I style the `div` wrapping the **Submit** button in a similar way to the `fieldset` elements. I also align the contents of the `div` center so that the **Submit** button now displays centrally.

As with the forms earlier in this chapter, I'm using an attribute selector to target the **Submit** button and give it appropriate styles:

chapter_06/fieldsets.css (excerpt)

```
div.submit {
  float: none;
  background-color: rgba(126,208,214,0.3);
  border: 3px solid rgb(255,255,255);
  -webkit-border-radius: 10px;
  -moz-border-radius: 10px;
  border-radius: 10px;
  margin: 0 0 1em 0;
  padding: 0.5em 0 0.5em 0;
  text-align: center;
}

form input[type="submit"] {
  width: auto;
  border: 3px solid rgb(126,208,214);
  background-color: rgba(78,150,137,0.5);
  color: rgb(255,255,255);
}

form input[type="submit"]:hover {
  background-color: rgb(78,150,137);
}
```

In Figure 6.17, you can see that an asterisk is used to indicate required fields in the form. This appears as part of the `label` element so that—in the case of a user using a screen reader—the required status of the field will be read out, along with the label for the field.

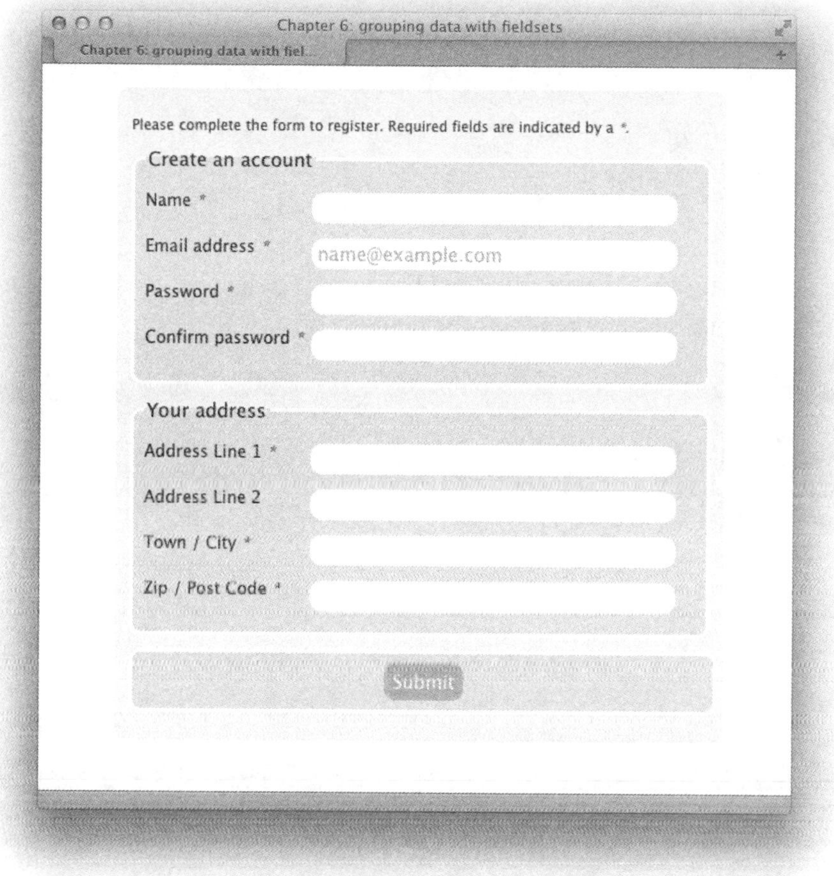

Figure 6.17. Our form is almost complete

For users with a regular web browser, however, I think the asterisk is better when placed visually after the form field, so that they all line up. I can use a technique described on Simply Accessible to achieve this.[1]

First, I need to add `position: relative` to the containing `div` (we will discuss `relative` and `absolute` positioning fully in Chapter 8). This simply means that we can now position content inside this `div` relative to it as a container:

---

[1] http://simplyaccessible.com/article/required-form-fields/

chapter_06/fieldsets.css *(excerpt)*

```
form div {
  float: left;
  width: 100%;
  padding: 0 0 0.75em 0;
  position: relative;
}
```

The asterisk is wrapped in an em element (for emphasis). I can use this and position it absolute to the right-hand side of the containing div element:

chapter_06/fieldsets.css *(excerpt)*

```
form div label em {
  position: absolute;
  color: red;
  right: 0;
}
```

I then style the help text at the top of the form so that the asterisk character looks the same there:

chapter_06/fieldsets.css *(excerpt)*

```
form p.help {
  font-style: italic;
  padding: 0 1em 1em 1em;
}

form p.help em {
  color: red;
}
```

This is a slightly more complex form, but it shows how we can use the semantic form elements to create appealing designs using CSS.

How do I create a form that reads like a sentence with inline fields?

Sometimes a short form can be displayed as if the user is filling in the words of a sentence. You can currently see this effect on the UK BUPA website,[2] where users are asked to complete a few details in order to obtain a quote.

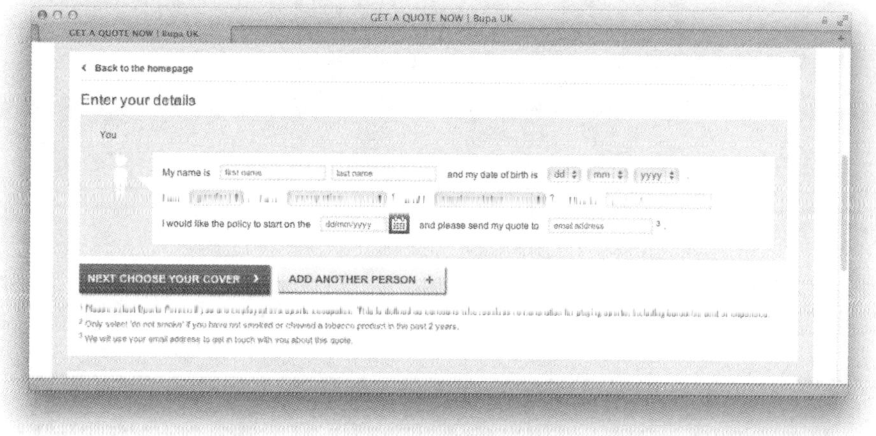

Figure 6.18. The form to add details for a BUPA quote

How can we create this style of form using CSS?

Solution

The below HTML and CSS creates the form seen in Figure 6.19:

chapter_06/form-inline.html

```
<!DOCTYPE html>
<html>
<head>
  <meta charset="utf-8" />
  <title>Chapter 6: Styling a form</title>
  <link rel="stylesheet" href="form-inline.css" />
</head>
<body>
```

---

[2] https://www.bupa.co.uk/individuals/health-insurance/quote/quote-process

```
<div class="wrapper">
  <h2>Subscribe</h2>
  <form method="post" action="/contact" id="contact-form">
    <p class="helptext">Hello! We need to take a few details to be
      able to process your subscription. Please fill in the form
      below - <strong>all fields are required</strong>.</p>
    <p>
      <label for="fName">My name is </label>
      <input type="text" name="fName" id="fName"
        required="required" />
      and
      <label for="fEmail">my email address is</label>
      <input type="email" name="fEmail" id="fEmail"
        required="required" placeholder="name@example.com" />
      <label for="fPaymentType">I would like to pay for my
        subscription using</label>
      <select name="fPaymentType" id="fPaymentType"
        required="required">
        <option value="">Please select</option>
        <option value="paypal">PayPal</option>
        <option value="creditcard">Credit Card</option>
      </select>.
    </p>
    <div class="submit"><input type="submit" name="contact-submit"
      id="contact-submit" value="Submit" />
    </div>
  </form>
</div>
</body>
</html>
```

chapter_06/form-inline.css *(excerpt)*

```
form {
  border: 3px solid #ccc;
  background-color: #fcfcfc;
  padding: 1em;
  -webkit-border-radius: 10px;
  -moz-border-radius: 10px;
  border-radius: 10px;
}

form p {
  line-height: 2.5;
}
```

```css
form p.helptext {
  line-height: 1.4;
  font-style: italic;
}

form input {
  border-top: 1px solid #999;
  border-right: 1px solid #ccc;
  border-bottom: 1px solid #cfcfcf;
  border-left: 1px solid #cfcfcf;
  -webkit-box-shadow: inset -2px 1px 2px 2px rgba(0, 0, 0, 0.1);
  -moz-box-shadow: inset -2px 1px 2px 2px rgba(0, 0, 0, 0.1);
  box-shadow: inset -2px 1px 2px 2px rgba(0, 0, 0, 0.1);
  padding: 4px;
}

input:focus:required:invalid {
  background-image: url(error.png);
  background-position: 98% center;
  background-repeat: no-repeat;
}

input:required:valid {
  background-image: url(accept.png);
  background-position: 98% center;
  background-repeat: no-repeat;
}

input[type="email"]:focus:required:invalid {
  background-image: url(email_error.png);
}

form input[type="submit"] {
  width: auto;
  border: 3px solid #ccc;
  background-color: #fff;
  color: #333;
  -webkit-border-radius: 5px;
  -moz-border-radius: 5px;
  border-radius: 5px;
  font-weight: bold;
}
```

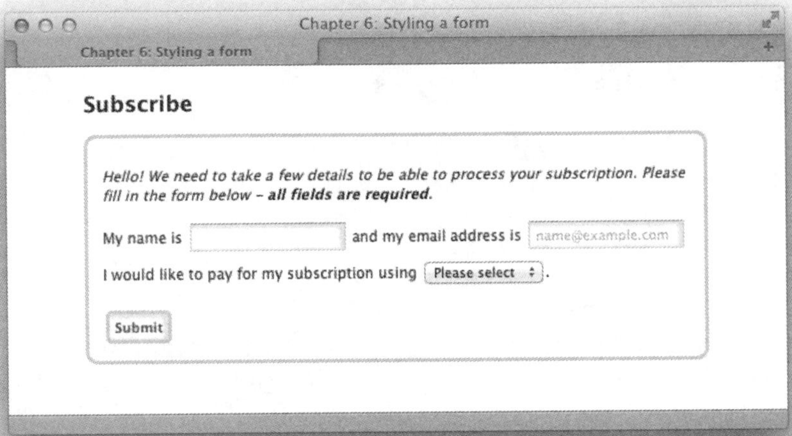

Figure 6.19. A form displayed as a paragraph with "fill in the blanks" fields

Discussion

Forms displayed in this way can seem more friendly than the alternative. In the case of the health insurance company example, it does seem less imposing answering a few questions asked as a sentence instead of a more formal-looking application.

In the form markup I've ensured that the `label` element is wrapped around text that explains what's required to complete the field. Therefore, each field has an associated label:

chapter_06/form-inline.html *(excerpt)*

```
<label for="fName">My name is </label>
<input type="text" name="fName" id="fName" required="required" />
```

Without any CSS applied, our form displays as in Figure 6.20. As you can see, we're quite close to the end result; our CSS should simply make this form a little easier to use and more attractive.

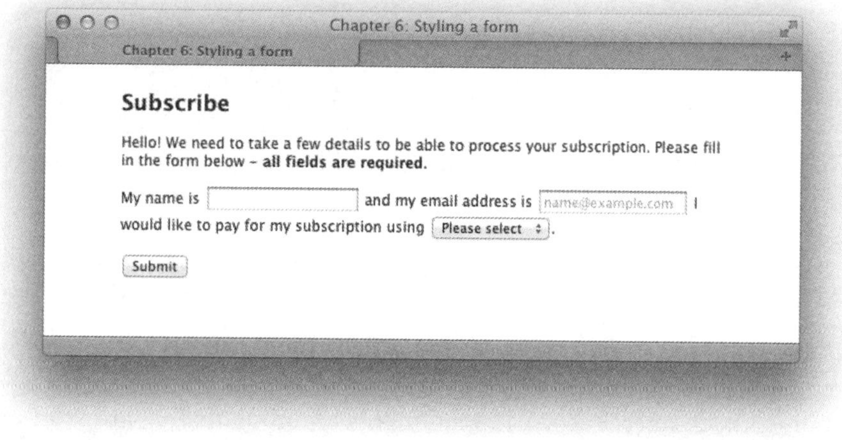

Figure 6.20. The form prior to adding CSS

I have then added some rules to the form itself—a border, background color, and padding:

chapter_06/form-inline.css *(excerpt)*

```css
form {
  border: 3px solid #ccc;
  background-color: #fcfcfc;
  padding: 1em;
  -webkit-border-radius: 10px;
  -moz-border-radius: 10px;
  border-radius: 10px;
}
```

Then I adjust the line-height on the form paragraphs to space the lines out, making more room for the fields.

I'd prefer the help text to be more compact, so I adjust that while also setting it to italic:

chapter_06/form-inline.css *(excerpt)*

```css
form p {
  line-height: 2.5;
}
```

```
form p.helptext {
  line-height: 1.4;
  font-style: italic;
}
```

The remaining CSS is simply to style the look of the form fields themselves, and it's similar to what was used earlier in the chapter.

What should I be aware of in terms of accessibility when creating forms?

Throughout this chapter, I've mentioned many components that are vital when creating accessible forms, because we do need to take special care to ensure our user interfaces are accessible to all our users. In this solution, I want to highlight the most important factors to consider, and I encourage you to keep these in mind when creating your own form designs.

Solution

The first thing we can do to ensure our forms are accessible is to use the correct markup. This helps those using screen-reading software make sense of our forms.

The `label` element, used in all our examples, links the text telling us what goes into a field with the field itself. This is vital for the screen reader user, who'd otherwise have no idea what should be put in any given field.

Labels are also helpful for users with a regular browser, as clicking the label will focus the form field (or make a selection in the case of a checkbox or radio button). This can make the experience of using a form less fiddly for a user who has trouble clicking accurately, or for one using an inaccurate touch interface.

In longer forms, grouping related fields using a `fieldset` with an appropriate `legend` element helps to ensure what needs to be inputted in this part of the form. The visual grouping that can be achieved with CSS may also assist in breaking up the form so that it's easier to understand.

Required fields

We discussed required fields earlier in this chapter where we discovered that HTML5 offers a way to flag a field as being `required`. Ultimately, screen readers may well catch up with this, and start to announce the `required` or `optional` status of a field. But until we know that browser support is across the board for these attributes, we need to add to our markup to ensure users know the field is required.

Using CSS alone to indicate that a field is required is insufficient, as screen reader users aren't supported. You should also avoid using color as the only way to indicate a field element is required, as it can be problematic due to the incidence of color-blindness among users.

In the solution in the section called "How do I group related fields?", I opted to use an asterisk to indicate that a field is required. I put this in the `label` element as, knowing that the label will be read out as an instruction, this would most likely ensure the required nature was indicated to a screen reader user. Then in the solution in the section called "How do I create a form that reads like a sentence with inline fields?", I simply stated that all fields were required when introducing the form; this is an option for short forms where all fields must be completed to submit the form.

You could also consider adding the ARIA-required flag[3] to the element as some screen readers understand it:

```
<label for="fName">My name is </label> <input type="text"
  name="fName" id="fName" required="required"
  aria-required="true" />
```

WAI-ARIA (Web Accessibility Initiative—Accessible Rich Internet Applications)

ARIA is a specification developed by the W3C.[4] It provides a method for User Interface widgets in a web application to describe what they are, so that they're usable for assistive technology users. ARIA also deals with the issue of updating

---

[3] http://www.alistapart.com/articles/aria-and-progressive-enhancement/
[4] http://www.w3.org/TR/wai-aria/

content using AJAX, as this can be particularly problematic to users of assistive technology. You can read a good Introduction to WAI-ARIA on Dev.Opera.[5]

In addition to ensuring that screen-reader users understand our forms, we should also test forms carefully in a range of desktop and mobile browsers, especially where we've added a lot of CSS. As mentioned at the start of the chapter, form elements' status as replaced content means that they may not take on all of your CSS—and you can easily end up with very different effects across browsers. Often the most robust action to take is concentrate on the elements around the fields, rather than go crazy with the fields themselves.

If you design in Photoshop or similar, you may find that dropping in standard UI form elements when creating your designs helps you to remember that sometimes these elements are outside your control, and see them as part of the design. A good set of these elements can be found at Designers Toolbox.[6]

You've Got Form

In this chapter, we've looked at a variety of ways to style forms using CSS, from simply changing the look of form elements to using CSS to lay forms out. We've seen how CSS can greatly enhance the appearance and usability of forms. We have also touched on the accessibility of forms for users of alternative devices, and we've seen how, by being careful when marking forms up, you can make it easier for all visitors to use your site or web application.

[5] http://dev.opera.com/articles/view/introduction-to-wai-aria/
[6] http://designerstoolbox.com/designresources/elements/

Chapter

7

Cross-browser Techniques

At the time of writing this current edition of *The CSS Anthology*, we're in an exciting period of web design and development. The latest versions of browsers have great support for CSS, including much of CSS3. The majority of techniques shown so far in this book will work in the most current versions of desktop browsers and most mobile browsers. Browser manufacturers are working to faster release schedules and implementing new parts of CSS3 far more swiftly than a few years ago, which means that we can start experimenting with new features quicker.

With modern browsers, we're dealing less frequently with browser bugs than we were in the past. Our issues now tend to center on whether or not a browser supports a certain feature. However, in the real world there are clients using older browsers containing significant bugs, as well as a complete lack of support for CSS3. A question we all need to ask is: how should we balance using CSS3 to create modern web designs with supporting these older browsers?

This chapter outlines how to create a browser support policy for each site that you work on, and demonstrates how to provide good experiences for users of older browsers. We'll also cover some testing tips, as well as details of some of the main bugs that come with very old versions of Internet Explorer, so that if you come across them, you're able to fix them quickly.

In which browsers should I test my sites?

When I started working in web development, we talked about testing in "both browsers"—that was Internet Explorer and Netscape. Today, we're faced with a large number of browsers and rendering engines.

Solution

The answer is to test your sites in as many browsers as you can. The types of browsers that you're able to install will depend on the operating systems to which you have access. At the very least, you should test in Internet Explorer 6, 7, 8, and 9, as well as the latest versions of Firefox, Opera, Safari, and Chrome. Additionally, even if you're not providing a different experience for mobile users, it's worth checking how the site behaves on the iPhone, iPad, and other mobile devices, making sure that everything is usable via a touch interface.

That's not to say that the site should look identical in all of these browsers. The experience for an IE6 user could be very different from an IE9 user—but you should aim to have the content accessible and the site usable.

In the Engine Room

You may have come across the term **browser rendering engine**. If we conceive of the browser as the complete software package, including the application interface and features, the browser rendering engine is the part that interprets the HTML and CSS, rendering the web pages for you to view and interact with. Some engines are separate software products that are used by more than one browser. For example, the Gecko engine developed by the Mozilla Foundation is used by Firefox, as well as Camino and the last versions of Netscape Navigator, among others. The WebKit engine powers Safari and Chrome, and was originally derived from the KHTML engine that powers the Konqueror web browser on Linux. WebKit is also particularly interesting as it is the rendering engine behind mobile Safari (used on iPhones and iPads) and also browsers for Android and modern Blackberry devices.

You may be thinking that if two browsers use the same rendering engine, you only need to test in one. While true to a certain extent, there can still be differences, especially across versions and operating systems. Some browsers, like Internet Explorer and Opera, use their own internal engines.

Can I just ignore older browsers?

With the latest versions of browsers having good support for many of the interesting CSS3 properties, and far fewer browser bugs than we have seen in the past, it is tempting to consider dropping support completely for old versions of Internet Explorer. How do we decide which browsers to support, and what level of support to provide them?

Solution

When starting work on a new site, you should first consider the kind of person who will be using the site, as well as the likely browsers and devices that they'll be using. If you are redesigning a website, you're in luck! There should be some existing information in the web statistics as to which browsers are being used.

Even if it is a brand new site, you should be able to draw some conclusions based on the audience. For example, many really old Internet Explorer browsers (IE6 and 7) can be found in large companies in the UK who require it for legacy internal products. If your site is aimed at these users, you may find that you need to provide more support for these old browsers. If your site is aimed at young people, or is particularly useful to people on the go, you might have more mobile devices than average browsing the site.

You might also have other sites, for which you have access to statistics, that serve a similar audience. There are also a number of sites that publish statistics, such as StatCounter.[1] It offers an analytics service, collating the data from all the sites that run its service to provide some idea of browser and version trends.

By looking at the browsers and devices that your users most frequently employ, you can put together a browser support policy for your site. This can outline the browsers that you test in, and the level of support you offer in terms of the design.

---

[1] http://gs.statcounter.com

Support Doesn't Mean "Looks the Same"

When discussing the support of older browsers, it doesn't mean we need to make the design look or function in an identical way in all those browsers. If your site happens to have a large number of people using old versions of Internet Explorer, you may find that there's pressure from your boss or client to try and make the design consistent across the browsers; this generally translates to you needing to simplify your design and avoid using newer techniques. However, for most sites it's appropriate to serve a simpler design to these older browsers. What's important is that the content is still accessible in a usable manner.

We can take as an example a layout created in Chapter 3. In Figure 7.1, we can see it displayed in Safari on OS X.

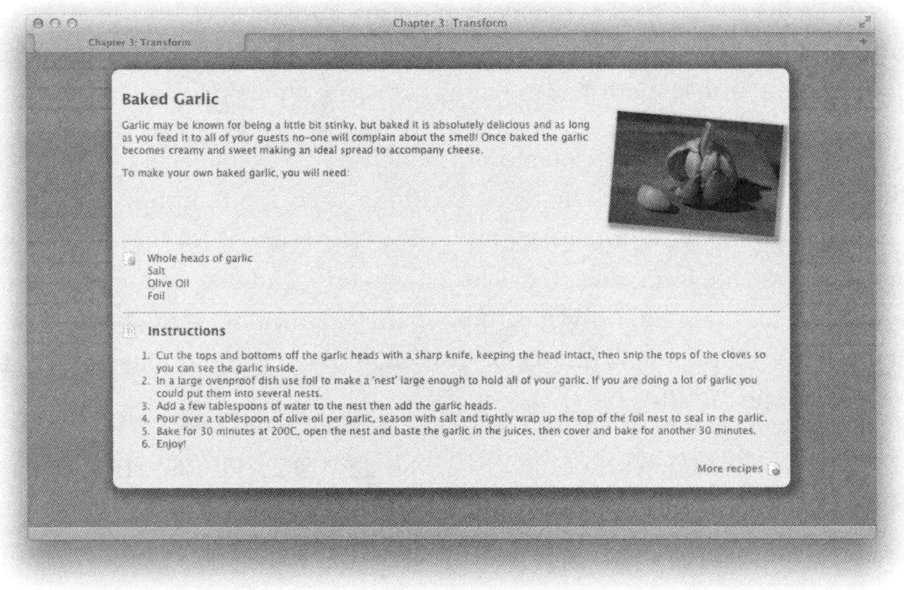

Figure 7.1. The layout in Safari

It uses a number of CSS3 properties, highlighted in the CSS here:

```
                                                       chapter_07/example1.css
body {
  background-color: #333;
  background-image: url(brushed_alu_dark.png);
```

```css
  color: #fff;
  margin: 0;
  padding: 0;
  font: 0.75em/1.3 "Lucida Grande", "Lucida Sans Unicode",
    "Lucida Sans", Verdana, Tahoma, sans-serif;
}

.wrapper {
  width: 80%;
  margin: 20px auto 40px auto;
  background-color: #fff;
  color: #333;
  background-image: url(brushed_alu.png);
  -webkit-box-shadow: 3px 3px 10px 8px rgba(0, 0, 0, 0.4);
  -moz-box-shadow: 3px 3px 10px 8px rgba(0, 0, 0, 0.4);
  box-shadow: 3px 3px 10px 8px rgba(0, 0, 0, 0.4);
  -webkit-border-radius: 10px;
  -moz-border-radius: 10px;
  border-radius: 10px;
}

.recipe {
  padding: 1em;
}

.recipe img {
  float:right;
  width: 200px;
  margin: 0 0 1em 1em;
  -webkit-box-shadow: 3px 3px 5px 3px rgba(0, 0, 0, 0.4);
  -moz-box-shadow: 3px 3px 5px 3px rgba(0, 0, 0, 0.4);
  box-shadow: 3px 3px 5px 3px rgba(0, 0, 0, 0.4);
  -webkit-transform: rotate(5deg);
  -moz-transform: rotate(5deg);
  -o-transform: rotate(5deg);
  -ms-transform: rotate(5deg);
  transform: rotate(5deg);
}

h1 {
  font-size: 150%;
}

h2 {
  font-size: 125%;
```

```
}

h2.instructions {
  background-image: url(instructions.png);
  background-repeat: no-repeat;
  background-position: left center;
  padding-left: 30px;
}

ul.ingredients {
  clear:both;
  border-top: 1px solid #999;
  border-bottom: 1px solid #999;
  list-style: none;
  margin: 1em 0 1em 0;
  padding: 1em 0 1em 30px;
  background-image: url(ingredients.png);
  background-repeat: no-repeat;
  background-position: 0 1em;
}

a.more:link, a.more:visited {
  display: block;
  padding: 0.3em 20px 0.3em 0;
  text-align: right;
  color: #666;
  font-weight: bold;
  background-image: url(arrow.png);
  background-position: right center;
  background-repeat: no-repeat;
  text-decoration: none;
}
```

Internet Explorer 9 also supports the CSS properties that we've used. We can see that the design in Internet Explorer 9, shown in Figure 7.2, looks as it does in Safari.

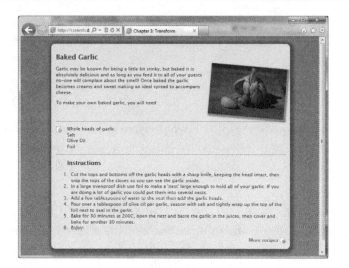

Figure 7.2. The same layout in Internet Explorer 9

Figure 7.3 shows the same layout in Internet Explorer 6.

Figure 7.3. The layout in Internet Explorer 6

Here we can see a few issues:

- The rounded corners on the main content area are missing.
- The shadow on the main content area is missing.
- The shadow on the feature image is missing.
- The `transform` does not rotate the main image.

Overall, the page content is perfectly accessible and looks good in all the browsers; however, where the very old browsers are concerned, we do lose some of the finer detail.

Discussion

This approach is a simple example of **progressive enhancement**. Essentially our IE6 layout has all the basics in place. By using CSS, we've added detail that's unsupported in the older browsers, though those browsers still display a basic, readable experience. This concept of progressive enhancement is crucial to robust front-end development. You start simple for the browsers that have little support, and layer in CSS properties, JavaScript, and other enhancements for the most capable browsers. Everyone then has a decent experience, and those with newer, more capable devices gain all the additional finesse of a modern user interface.

For very complex layouts that rely heavily on new CSS features and have very little traffic from browsers such as IE6, you may wish to take this approach a step further and serve a very simple stylesheet to IE6. Andy Clarke has popularized this approach,[2] and his Universal IE6 Stylesheet is available on Google Code.[3]

My advice is not to ignore older browsers while we still see some traffic from them; however, it's appropriate with these problematic browsers to serve something different. Keep your content accessible, but there's no need to try to replicate the modern web experience for ten-year-old browsers.

How can I add support for CSS3 selectors in older browsers?

CSS3 selectors are incredibly useful, as we've already seen in earlier chapters of this book. If you're relying on them in your design, though, it could look a little strange in older browsers lacking support.

Solution

CSS3 selectors are one of the simplest aspects of CSS3 to create support for using JavaScript. You can do so by writing JavaScript yourself, or by writing functions to

---

[2] http://www.stuffandnonsense.co.uk/blog/about/universal_internet_explorer_6_css/
[3] http://code.google.com/p/universal-ie6-css/

use with another library such as jQuery, or by including a JavaScript plugin that automatically adds support for selectors.

We'll take a look at an example from an earlier chapter where we learned how to stripe alternate table rows using `nth-child`, as seen in Figure 7.4.

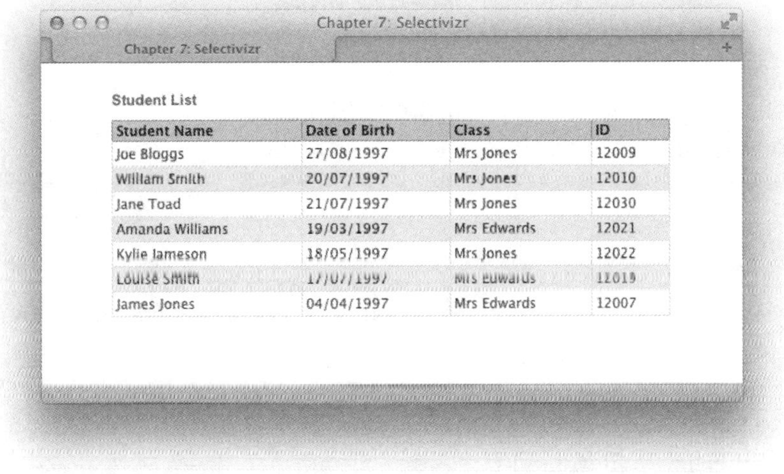

Figure 7.4. Striped table rows in Safari using nth-child

The CSS3 `nth-child` selector is used as follows:

```css
.datatable tr:nth-child(odd) {
  background-color: #dfe7f2;
  color: #000000;
}
```

Internet Explorer 8 has no support for `nth-child`, so there are no striped rows, as you can see in Figure 7.5.

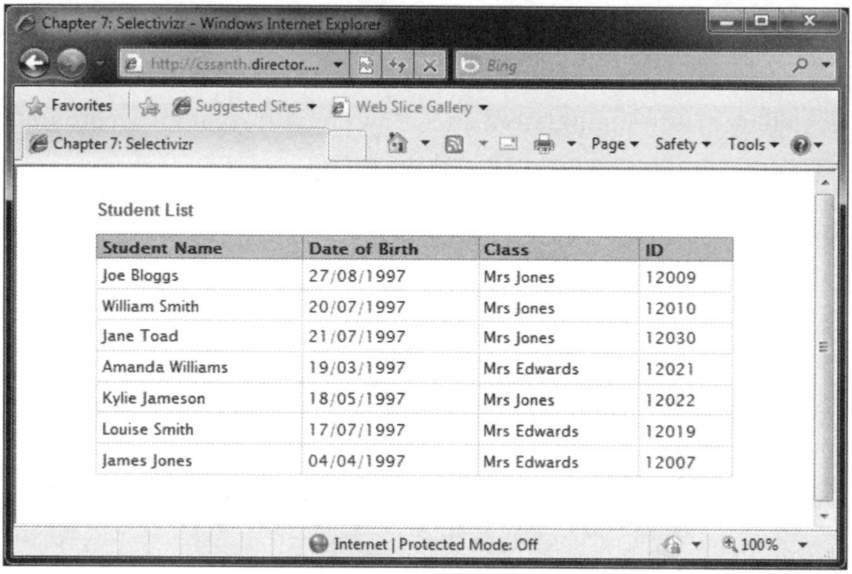

Figure 7.5. Internet Explorer 8 sans the striped rows

One way to patch this is by using Selectivizr.[4] This script provides CSS3 selector support to Internet Explorer, and does so without you needing to make any other changes to your CSS. A script that adds in support like this is sometimes referred to as a **polyfill**.

What is a polyfill?

A polyfill, sometimes referred to as a shim, is a piece of code that provides support for technology that you would expect the browser to provide itself.[5] Here we're looking at CSS3 polyfills, though the same approach is also used to provide support for HTML5 features.[6]

Selectivizr requires another JavaScript library to work. You can see on the website which libraries it works with, but if you're already using a library, it's quite likely to be included. As my page doesn't already use a library, I've chosen to include jQuery.

I add the jQuery include, and then download and link in Selectivizr:

---

[4] http://selectivizr.com/

[5] http://remysharp.com/2010/10/08/what-is-a-polyfill/

[6] https://github.com/Modernizr/Modernizr/wiki/HTML5-Cross-browser-Polyfills

chapter_07/selectors.html *(excerpt)*

```
<head>
  <meta charset="utf-8" />
  <title>Chapter 7: Selectivizr</title>
  <link rel="stylesheet" href="selectors.css" />
  <script src="//ajax.googleapis.com/ajax/libs/jquery/1.7.1/
➥jquery.min.js"></script>
  <script type="text/javascript" src="selectivizr-min.js"></script>
</head>
```

If I reload my page in Internet Explorer, I can see the striped table rows as evident in Figure 7.6.

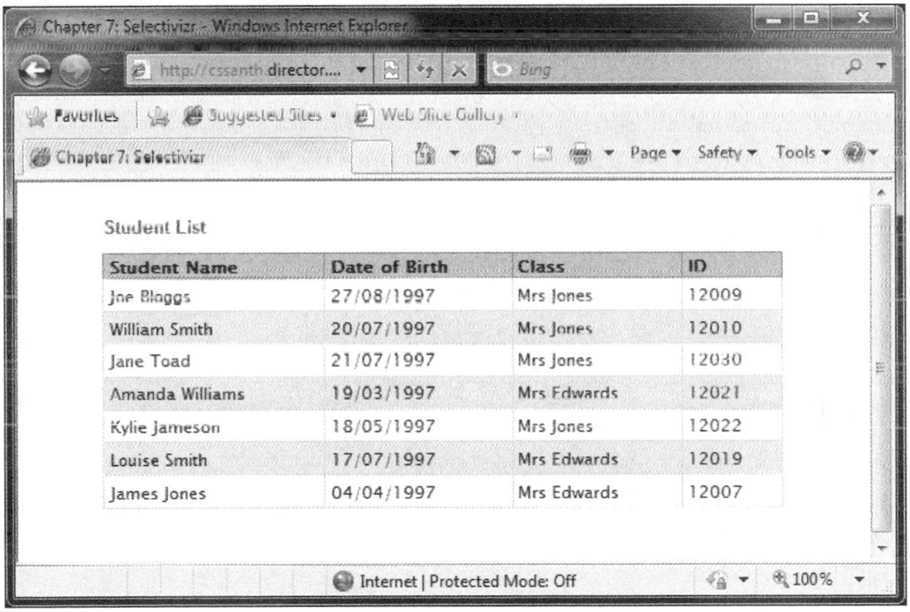

Figure 7.6. The striped table rows in Internet Explorer 8 using Selectivizr

Discussion

Using Selectivizr is a great solution if you have a lot of CSS3 selectors in use; however, you should take care that your pages are still comprehensible without it being included just in case a user has an old version of IE and JavaScript disabled, blocked, or failing to load for some reason.

If you only have one or two CSS3 selectors to patch, and would rather skip the inclusion of Selectivizr or its ilk, you could write your own JavaScript to plug this particular hole. Again, I'm using jQuery as the library. One very nice benefit of jQuery is that it uses CSS selectors to target elements. So if you know how to access an element using CSS, you should find jQuery quite straightforward to use for these patches.

I include jQuery, then write a simple little function that adds a class of odd to every other table row. In reality, you'd probably include a JavaScript file here with a number of functions in it:

chapter_07/selectors-jquery.html *(excerpt)*

```
<script src="//ajax.googleapis.com/ajax/libs/jquery/1.7.1/
➥jquery.min.js"></script>
<script>
  $(document).ready(function(){
    $("tr:nth-child(odd)").addClass("odd");
  });
</script>
```

We now need to make a small change to our CSS: adding a selector that looks for a class of odd alongside our nth-child selector:

chapter_07/selectors-jquery.css *(excerpt)*

```
.datatable tr:nth-child(odd), .datatable tr.odd {
  background-color: #dfe7f2;
  color: #000000;
}
```

This will cause the rows to be striped in older browsers as long as they support JavaScript.

Whether you use Selectivizr or decide to write your own JavaScript is up to you. As most of our projects use jQuery anyway, and we tend to have a JavaScript file that deals with any UI requirements, I often create a fixSelectors function that goes through and adds classes to enable support for CSS3 selectors. This does involve a little more work than just including Selectivizr; however, it does mean that I'm always aware of what the JavaScript is doing. For very rapid development, or when you are prototyping layouts, scripts such as Selectivizr are very useful. Browsers lacking support for these selectors are going to become far less commonly used, making the employment of Selectivizr more compelling as there's no need for additional CSS selectors. If the browsers eventually stop registering in the stats on your site, you can simply remove the JavaScript include.

Can I add CSS or JavaScript and have it served only to older versions of IE?

The previous solution used a script that polyfills support for older versions of Internet Explorer. Is it possible to only serve this script to those browsers?

Solution

The Selectivizr polyfill is designed to provide CSS3 selector support in Internet Explorer 6, 7, and 8, so there's no reason to have WebKit or Gecko browsers downloading it. We can use conditional comments to serve this script to only certain versions of IE:

chapter_07/selectors-conditional.html *(excerpt)*

```html
<head>
  <meta charset="utf-8" />
  <title>Chapter 7: Selectivizr</title>
  <link rel="stylesheet" href="selectors.css" />
  <script src="//ajax.googleapis.com/ajax/libs/jquery/1.7.1/
➥jquery.min.js"></script>

  <!--[if (gte IE 6)&(lte IE 8)]>
  <script type="text/javascript" src="selectivizr-min.js"></script>
  <![endif]-->
</head>
```

Discussion

Conditional comments were introduced by Internet Explorer as a proprietary method of serving content to specific versions of Internet Explorer. They can be used to include an additional stylesheet to fix problems in certain versions of IE, or, as we're doing in this example, to include polyfills that only target certain versions of IE.

In our example, we're stating that if the browser is greater than or equal to IE6 AND less than or equal to IE8, it should load the JavaScript. Non-IE browsers and Internet Explorer 9 and above will ignore it.

Here are some further examples of useful conditional comments. This would include **ie6fixes.css** if the browser is IE6:

```
<!--[if IE 6]>
<link rel="stylesheet" type="text/css" href="ie6fixes.css" />
<![endif]-->
```

This includes **ie7fixes.css** if the browser is equal to IE7:

```
<!--[if IE 7]>
<link rel="stylesheet" type="text/css" href="ie7fixes.css" />
<![endif]-->
```

This code will reveal a stylesheet to all versions of Internet Explorer less than or equal to version 7. It's useful if you have some layout fixes for both these old browsers:

```
<!--[if lte IE 7]>
<link rel="stylesheet" type="text/css" href="iefixes.css" />
<![endif]-->
```

For further examples of conditional comments and a full guide to their use, see the SitePoint CSS Reference page.[7]

How do I achieve rounded corners in browsers without support for `border-radius`?

As we saw in Figure 7.3, it's often perfectly acceptable not to try to support CSS3 features in old browsers. Making your design fall back to square corners where `border-radius` is unsupported can be a reasonable solution. But what if your client or boss is insistent that the rounded corners work in older browsers?

---

[7] http://reference.sitepoint.com/css/conditionalcomments

Solution

One solution is to use a polyfill script that adds support for border-radius along with other CSS3 properties. CSS3 PIE (Progressive Internet Explorer) is one such script. We can take a look at how this works using our example page. In Internet Explorer 8, our layout displays very much as it does in earlier versions of Internet Explorer, with no rounded corners or drop shadows as in Figure 7.7.

Figure 7.7. Our page in Internet Explorer 8

Download CSS PIE and unzip the files. The file **PIE.htc** needs to be placed into your site.

In any rule set that contains rounded corners or drop shadows, add the behavior as shown in our code. The path to **PIE.htc** needs to be relative to the page rather than the CSS file, so I would suggest that in a live site you make it a path from root; for example, behavior: url(/path/to/PIE.htc);:

```
.wrapper {
  width: 80%;
  margin: 20px auto 40px auto;
  background-color: #fff;
  color: #333;
  background-image: url(brushed_alu.png);
  -webkit-box-shadow: 3px 3px 10px 8px rgba(0, 0, 0, 0.4);
  -moz-box-shadow: 3px 3px 10px 8px rgba(0, 0, 0, 0.4);
  box-shadow: 3px 3px 10px 8px rgba(0, 0, 0, 0.4);
  -webkit-border-radius: 10px;
  -moz-border-radius: 10px;
  border-radius: 10px;
  behavior: url(PIE.htc);
}

.recipe img {
  float:right;
  width: 200px;
  margin: 0 0 1em 1em;
  -webkit-box-shadow: 3px 3px 5px 3px rgba(0, 0, 0, 0.4);
  -moz-box-shadow: 3px 3px 5px 3px rgba(0, 0, 0, 0.4);
  box-shadow: 3px 3px 5px 3px rgba(0, 0, 0, 0.4);
  -webkit-transform: rotate(5deg);
  -moz-transform: rotate(5deg);
  -o-transform: rotate(5deg);
  -ms-transform: rotate(5deg);
  transform: rotate(5deg);
  behavior: url(PIE.htc);
}
```

If you now view your page in Internet Explorer 6, 7, or 8, you should find that rounded corners and drop shadows are working. Although not quite as slick as the pure CSS implementation, it does work, as you can see in Figure 7.8.

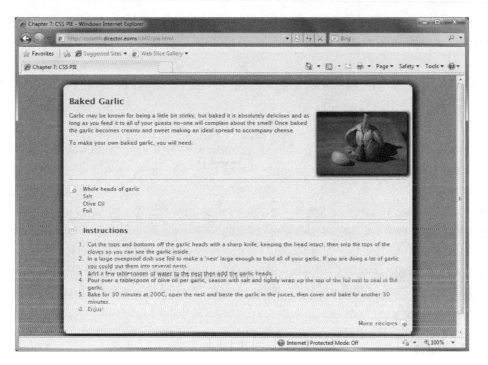

Figure 7.8. Internet Explorer 8 after adding PIE

Discussion

PIE is added to your site using a proprietary Internet Explorer property: the behavior property. This property enables you to attach a script to your CSS. The script is in a **.htc** file (HTML component). Other browsers will ignore this property, and only Internet Explorer will attempt to run your **.htc** files.

Similar scripts are available that attempt to support other unsupported features such as CSS3 transforms. It's worth mentioning that whenever you use one of these scripts, you should carefully test all the target browsers, as it's possible that problems will be introduced by their inclusion.

An alternative solution would be to avoid using CSS3 at all and return to older methods of using images to achieve this effect. Depending on the number of older browser users and the particular effect you require, this may sometimes be necessary. What's great about using a polyfill like PIE is that at the point in time when these older browser users cease to visit your site, you can simply remove the behavior. Otherwise, if you add extra markup and images to create the layout without using

CSS3, this weight is then downloaded by all users, and you'd need to rebuild the site in the future to take advantage of CSS3.

How do I deal with the most common issues in IE6 and IE7?

The most troublesome browsers that you're likely to come across today are Internet Explorer 6 and 7. They're particularly troublesome because they have significant rendering bugs. Other older browsers that you might come across, including Internet Explorer 8, tend to have issues that stem from a lack of support for some CSS. As we've seen, a lack of support is often a manageable problem, as you can decide whether to allow that browser to show a simpler rendering of the site, or attempt to use polyfills to patch in support. Browser bugs, however, can cause perfectly valid markup and CSS to display in very strange ways, and even supporting IE6 and 7 at a basic level could cause you to run into some of these.

Solution

I'd advise you to avoid worrying too much about these old browsers while developing your site unless you're in the unfortunate position of having a large number of users on such browsers (a situation that is becoming less common each month). Develop in an up-to-date browser, validate your markup and CSS, and get everything working as you want it for modern browsers first. I believe strongly that you should refrain from cluttering your markup with fixes for very old browsers, and continually checking and trying to fix issues as you go tends to lead to that temptation.

There will probably be some problems in IE6 when you first look at your layout. These might be small predicaments such as incorrect padding between page elements, or larger issues such as huge sections of your page disappearing or displaying in an odd place. There's no need to panic! Most IE6 issues can be easily resolved by specifying some different style rules for this particular browser.

The same goes for IE7, although I find there are fewer layout problems to fix in this browser.

Adding Browser-specific Stylesheets Using Conditional Comments

At this point, I'd suggest that you place an additional stylesheet—as described in the previous section—using conditional comments to target IE6, 7, or both. You add this stylesheet to your document head (after the existing stylesheets in your HTML) so that any rules you place in your IE6- and IE7-specific stylesheet will overwrite the same rules in the main stylesheet.

Fixing Internet Explorer Problems

You can now work through any problems that you can see in IE6 and 7 in a methodical way, applying fixes in your alternate stylesheet, safe in the knowledge they'll only ever be applied by the browsers that need them. The following tips solve most of the issues that we see in IE6. For IE7, I usually find that there's no need for all the rules used for IE6, but some are still required. It's rare that I find a brand new issue in IE7 that I've yet to see in IE6, and the fixes are generally the same.

Checking Your `doctype`

Make sure that you're using a correct `doctype` as the first line in your markup; for most new sites, this will be the HTML5 `doctype` as used in all the examples in this book. If you need to use HTML4 or XHTML, make sure you use a full Strict or Transitional `doctype`, including the URI. Omitting a `doctype` or using an incorrect `doctype` may cause your layout to display in quirks mode in some browsers.[8] This implements an old, incorrect box model used in very early browsers—best avoided in modern sites. If you want to know more about this, see the article at Activating Browser Modes with Doctype.[9]

Fixing the Lack of `min-height` Support in IE6

Internet Explorer 6 has no support for `min-height` (the minimum height an element should take), but it incorrectly interprets `height` as `min-height`. So, even though `height` is used to specify a fixed height in other browsers, Internet Explorer 6 takes it to mean the minimum height; therefore a block element will expand taller than its specified height if need be.

---

[8] Many modern browsers have two rendering modes. Quirks mode renders documents according to the buggy implementations of older browsers such as Internet Explorer 6. Standards or compliance mode renders documents as per the W3C specifications, or as close to them as they can.

[9] http://hsivonen.iki.fi/doctype/

To work around this issue, we simply use the `height` property in our IE6-specific stylesheet wherever we've used `min-height` in our main stylesheet.

Triggering the `hasLayout` Property

IE6 and 7 have a mysterious scripting property called `hasLayout` that's an internal component of the rendering engine, and the source of many seemingly bizarre rendering bugs. When an element is responsible for sizing and arranging its contents, it's said to have a layout. If an element is without a layout, it relies on its parent or an ancestor element to take care of its size and position. When an element has no layout, there's the potential for weird stuff to happen—like content disappearing and the layout behaving erratically. Some elements, like table cells, automatically have a layout; however, `div` elements do not. Specifying some CSS properties, such as setting `float` to `left` or `right`, also cause an element to gain a layout. In making an element gain a layout, most of these problems disappear. The trick is to find a CSS property that gives an element a layout without having a detrimental effect on your overall design.

In IE6, I find the simplest way to trigger a layout on an element is to give it a height value of 1%. As I just mentioned, IE6 treats height as `min-height`, so a height of 1% actually renders as a minimum height of 1%—so this is perfectly safe to apply and the box will still be sized to suit its contents. Obviously you need to do this in your IE6-specific stylesheet that's included with conditional comments.

IE7, by contrast, supports the `height` property correctly, so we're unable to use it as we might with IE6. However, setting the `min-height` property to any value—even to 0—in IE7 causes the element to gain a layout. This is a safe approach because the default value for `min-height` is 0 anyway.

It isn't always apparent which element is going to need the layout trigger applied, but if you work methodically, you may well find the one that causes everything to jump into shape. I usually work from the innermost container out, so if I have a `div` nested inside two more `div`s, I add the `height` to the inner `div` and refresh to see if it made a difference. Otherwise, I remove it and try the next `div`, and so on.

Adding `Position: Relative` to Elements

If gaining a layout fails to work, setting `position` to `relative` on an element will sometimes fix a problem. Keep in mind that setting `position` to `relative` on an element will mean all its child elements will now use that element for a positioning context. Otherwise this should be safe to do.

And If All Else Fails

The above tips should fix the worst problems, but you may still be left with slight alignment, margin, or padding issues. At this point remind yourself that what you're dealing with are old, buggy browsers, so you should feel quite at liberty in your IE6- and IE7-specific stylesheets to manipulate elements by adjusting the margin, padding, or positioning until it does work. This will have no effect on any other browser if you've used conditional comments, so no harm is done. It's to be hoped there's little to do, because it will need to be redone if the layout ever changes. Sometimes, with a very complex layout, you do need to just hammer bits into place!

How do I style HTML5 semantic elements that are unsupported in older browsers?

HTML5 brings us new elements for marking up sections of our pages; however, these cause problems in older browsers that prohibit CSS from being applied to them.

Solution

Internet Explorer below version 9 won't recognize the new HTML5 elements, and will not apply CSS to elements that it fails to recognize. If you want to use these elements, you can add the HTML5 shiv[10] to your document as demonstrated in this boilerplate document from HTML5 Doctor:[11]

```
<!DOCTYPE html>
<html>
<head>
  <meta charset="utf-8" />
  <title>HTML 5 complete</title>
  <!--[ lte IE 8]>
  <script src="http://html5shiv.googlecode.com/svn/trunk/html5.js">
    </script>
  <![endif]-->
```

[10] See http://ejohn.org/blog/html5-shiv/ for an explanation of this tool.
[11] http://html5doctor.com/html-5-boilerplates/

```
<style>
  article, aside, details, figcaption, figure, footer, header,
  hgroup, menu, nav, section { display: block; }
</style>
</head>
<body>
  <p>Hello World</p>
</body>
</html>
```

In this document, you can also see that the HTML5 structural elements have been set to `display: block`. This would normally happen inside your stylesheet for the page. We'll be covering the `display` property in Chapter 9 more thoroughly; but by setting these elements to `display: block`, we're able to apply CSS to them much as we would a `div` element on our page.

Discussion

The new HTML5 semantic elements offer far better ways of marking up sections of your pages than simply using a `div` element. If navigation is marked up using the `nav` element, a device could indicate to the user where the navigation was on the page; knowing where the header and footer of a document is offers potential in terms of being able to parse and extract content for reuse.

If you decide to take advantage of these elements, you need to be aware that any CSS used to style them won't be applied by Internet Explorer 8 and below. The HTML5 shiv JavaScript will enable these elements to be styled; however, you are then building in a reliance on JavaScript for users of those browsers.

Depending on the traffic to your site, you can decide whether using these semantic elements and thus requiring JavaScript is acceptable. The alternative is to continue using the `div` element to mark up areas on your page (perhaps adding a class or ID using the HTML5 semantic element name) until such time as the nonsupporting browsers are enough of an acceptable minority for you to feel happy about switching. The decisions you make are likely to be different for each site depending on the site and audience.

How can I test in many browsers when I only have access to one operating system?

If you are a Windows, Mac, or Linux user with access to only one operating system, testing across all the browsers can be a bit of a struggle. How does the web developer without access to a full test suite deal with cross-browser testing?

Solution

There are now far fewer serious browser bugs in commonly used CSS, but new issues mean that we can't afford to test in just one modern browser before launching a site. We need to check that our content is readable in older browsers when using CSS3, and we're likely to find that fonts (especially custom fonts imported using @font face) render differently across operating systems.

Some browsers are available across all operating systems; Firefox, Chrome, and Opera, for example, can be installed on Windows, OS X, and Linux. There is a version of Safari, the default browser on OS X, for Windows. As Chrome is based on WebKit—the same rendering engine as Safari—there are many similarities across these two browsers; however, it's unwise to assume that if it works in one it will work in the other (such as the support of CSS3, for example). They are, after all, on different release cycles.

Virtual Machines on OS X

If you use a Mac running OS X, you're probably in the most fortunate position. You can natively test any Mac-specific browsers, and by installing virtualization software such as VMware Fusion,[12] Parallels,[13] or the free VirtualBox,[14] you can install Windows and Linux operating systems in a virtual machine and then install whichever browsers you like; you can even have multiple virtual machines with different versions of browsers and operating systems installed. Windows and Linux users can install virtual machines to test browsers for Windows and Linux. There are attempts to get OS X working either in a virtual machine or on non-Apple

---

[12] http://www.vmware.com/products/fusion/overview.html
[13] http://www.parallels.com/au/products/desktop/
[14] https://www.virtualbox.org/

hardware, creating a "Hackintosh";[15] however, this is unsupported by Apple and less than straightforward to set up.

Browser "Snapshot" Tools

If you simply want to check a layout, there are a number of sites that offer you the ability to take a screen capture of your site across multiple browsers. Examples of these are Adobe BrowserLab and Browsershots, the latter of which can be seen in Figure 7.9. These can be useful for a quick overview of how your site renders. They're particularly handy if you're checking what a certain font looks like across different operating systems and browsers; however, their limitation is that you just get a picture of your site. You're unable to test whether any JavaScript is working properly, or whether a bug in some browser has made your form fields impossible to focus.

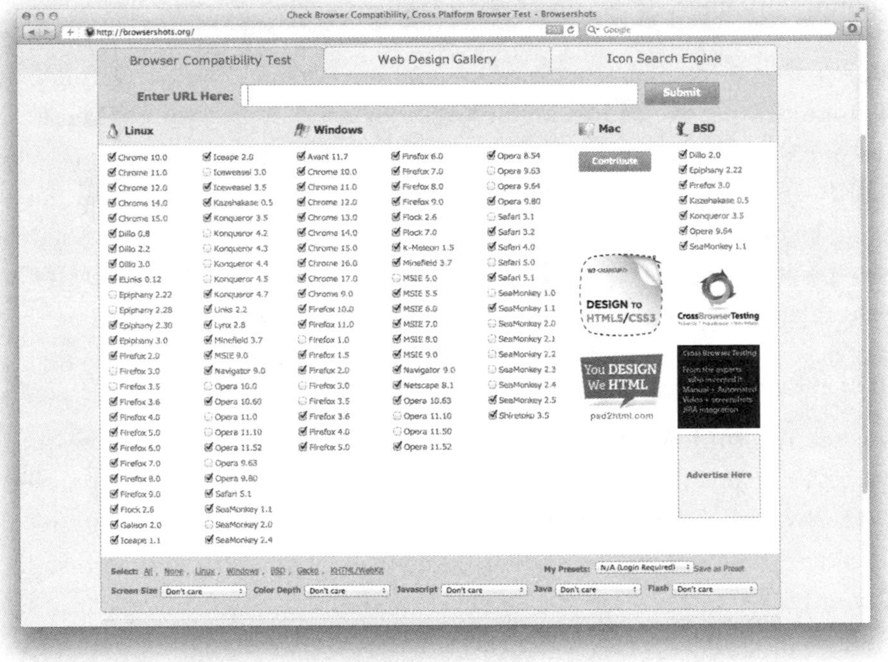

Figure 7.9. Browsershots enables us to view a screenshot of our site in a wide range of browsers

A better option than third-party browser-screen-capture tools, although one that's likely to cost some money, is third-party-hosted browser-testing services such as

---

[15] http://www.windows7hacker.com/index.php/2011/09/how-to-install-fully-functional-mac-os-x-lion-virtual-machine-inside-windows-7/

BrowserStack, seen in Figure 7.10. BrowserStack allows you to test your sites on a range of browsers and operating systems via the Web. You can load up your site in your browser of choice, and even set up a tunnel (accessing your local files on BrowserStack's remote browser) in order to view files that are on your computer (rather than needing to set up a live development site).

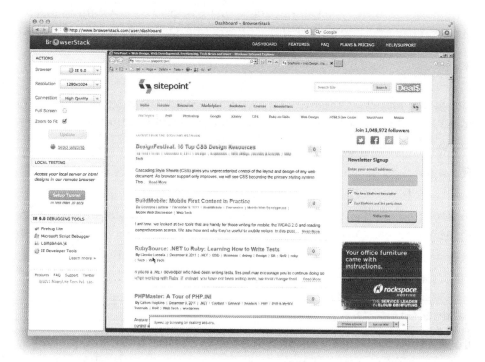

Figure 7.10. Viewing the SitePoint website in Internet Explorer 9 via BrowserStack

It Stacks Up

Remote testing tools such as BrowserStack are very useful, even if you have a decent test suite. If a site user is experiencing a problem in a particular browser that you don't have installed—such as an older version of Firefox—you can quickly go to BrowserStack and load up your site in the exact browser, rather than having to work out how to access an old version of a browser you already run.

Can I install multiple versions of Internet Explorer on Windows?

As already discussed in this chapter, older versions are very different from the most recent version of Internet Explorer, and they're particularly problematic; however, it's only possible to run one version of Internet Explorer on a Windows machine at a time. So what's the best way to test multiple Internet Explorer browser versions?

Solution

In my experience, the best way to test Internet Explorer is to use a proper version of Internet Explorer in a virtual machine. The free virtualization software, Virtual-Box,[16] is very capable when used for this purpose.

You do need a reasonable amount of disk space and memory to run virtual machines—especially if you have several open at once. If this is a problem for you, Utilu IE Collection[17] may be helpful; it installs a collection of standalone versions of Internet Explorer. I would suggest doing this inside a virtual machine even if you are a Windows user, to avoid creating any issues with your primary Internet Explorer browser.

Discussion

There are simpler solutions for Internet Explorer testing. Internet Explorer itself, in recent versions, has a method for rendering pages as if it's an earlier version. In Internet Explorer 9 Developer Tools, you can switch browser mode and view a page as if using the earlier browser. While this works reasonably well, in some cases what you see in browser mode through IE9 is different to the real browser, and browser mode itself may well have its own quirks not present in the original browser. So it might be good for a quick look during development, but I'd always suggest doing proper testing in the real browser.

There are also multiple IE testing tools such as IETester;[18] however, in my experience these are unreliable. In particular, conditional comments are often ignored (so a stylesheet or script file targeted solely at this browser may be bypassed). I've spent

---

[16] https://www.virtualbox.org/
[17] http://utilu.com/IECollection/
[18] http://www.my-debugbar.com/wiki/IETester/HomePage

many a frustrating hour trying to work out why a client was seeing something different to us in IE6, only to discover they were running IETester to test the site and not a real IE6 browser! Therefore, I cannot advise using these tools. For an excellent write-up of Internet Explorer testing, including many of the tools I've mentioned in this section and much more, read "Reliable Cross-browser Testing" on *Smashing Magazine*.[19]

How should I go about testing on mobile browsers?

All smartphones have capable browsers, and are increasingly used for viewing websites. In addition, we're seeing a rise in the number of tablets, such as the iPad, in use. So considering that most of us tend to own just the one phone, how can we test across devices?

Solution

There are two issues when it comes to testing on mobile devices. One is that they have smaller screen sizes than their desktop counterparts; the second is that the experience of using a mobile touchscreen device is different from using a desktop computer with a keyboard and mouse. So your testing needs to cover "does it look okay?" and "is it usable?"

The browsers used by mobile devices tend to be fairly up to date. The iPhone and iPad use mobile Safari, which uses Webkit as its rendering engine—the same engine behind the default Android browser, and the browser used in newer Blackberry devices. In addition, there are mobile versions of Opera and Firefox. Windows phone uses a mobile browser based on the rendering engine in Internet Explorer 9. Due to these up-to-date browsers, you can often be more confident using CSS3 for phones than on the desktop. The rendering is generally the same as desktop versions of these rendering engines—albeit at a small screen size, and in Chapter 9 we'll be discussing how you might support those smaller screens in particular. For current information on mobile browsers and devices, I'd suggest visiting the mobile section of QuirksMode.org[20] run by Peter-Paul Koch and Mobile HTML5[21] by Maximiliano

---

[19] http://smashingmagazine.com/2011/09/02/reliable-cross-browser-testing

[20] http://www.quirksmode.org/mobile/

[21] http://mobilehtml5.org/

Firtman, where a large amount of information on mobile devices and browsers is being collated.

There are services that let you view how the site might display on a small device; for example, Screenfly.[22] There are also options for taking a screen capture on mobile devices—just as with the desktop services I described earlier in the chapter. BrowserCam[23] is one such service that covers desktop and mobile, and gives access to a wide range of different devices. Then there are some services that give remote access to a variety of devices—for example, Perfecto Mobile[24]—although these are quite expensive.

Given that the rendering engines of mobile browsers are similar to desktop rendering engines, and that the browsers tend to be up to date, you generally won't hit too many problems in terms of layout for modern mobile phones. Where you do need to test more thoroughly is in terms of the actual experience of using your site with a touchscreen device, especially if you are using drop-down menus or any other interactions that might become fiddly on a touchscreen.

If possible, I'd recommend that you have access to a couple of devices: a higher-end device such as an iPhone or Android phone with a larger screen and reasonable specs, and a cheaper device. I have a tiny Android phone that I use for this purpose; it's the kind of phone that, in the UK, you get free on inexpensive phone plans, so it's the sort of device that many people might be using. You can then test the experience for users of high-end phones and lower spec phones, making sure that everything is usable. At the very least, you should be checking your site on one-touch devices at this point in time.

What do I do if I hit a CSS issue I'm unable to fix?

We all find ourselves in situations where our CSS will just *not* work. Though you've tried every solution you can think of, the margins on an element continue to be twice the size you expect, or content is pushing a page wide. Before the bug drives you mad, take a deep breath and relax. There is a solution!

---

[22] http://quirktools.com/screenfly/
[23] http://www.browsercam.com/
[24] http://www.perfectomobile.com/

Solution

This is a solution that helps you find the solution.

Take a Break

Once we're frustrated with battling a problem, applying any kind of rational process for finding a solution is difficult at best. So take a break. Go for a walk, tidy your desk, or do some housework. If you're at work with your boss looking over your shoulder (and so unable to make it to the coffee machine in peace), work on another task: answer some mail or tidy up some content. Do anything to take your mind off the problem for a while.

Validate Your Stylesheet and Document

If you've yet to do so, your next step should be to validate the CSS and the markup (although you may come across some validation problems regarding CSS3; see the section called "The validator complains about my vendor-specific extensions, so how do I validate CSS3?" for details). Errors in your CSS or markup may well cause problems and, even if your problem is actually caused by another issue, they often make it more difficult to find a solution.

Double-check that the Properties You're Using Are Supported in the Browser You're Testing

It's very easy to forget at which point a CSS3 property made it into a particular browser. If, for example, you're using `first-child` to remove a margin on the first element, this will fail to work in Internet Explorer 6, and you'll need to patch this with a JavaScript polyfill, use some alternate CSS, or live with the difference in spacing. The website When can I use ...[25] is an excellent resource for checking which browsers support which properties.

Isolate the Problem

Can you make your issue occur in isolation from the rest of your document? CSS problems often display only when a certain group of conditions is met, so finding out exactly where the problem occurs may help you work out how it can be fixed. Try to reproduce the problem in a document separate from the rest of your layout.

---

[25] caniuse.com

If you are using JavaScript polyfills, does the issue go away if you remove the JavaScript? You may have encountered a bug in a third-party polyfill script, in which case the script's support would be the best place to start asking questions.

Search the Web

If your issue is with a very old browser, in particular Internet Explorer 6 and 7, it's highly likely to be a problem that's been previously experienced. Bugs with the IE6 and 7 rendering engine are very well documented. Searching the Web should turn up plenty of sites with details of these issues; and don't worry if the websites look out of date—the browsers are too!

There are far fewer actual CSS rendering bugs with the newer browsers; the most likely issues for those will be in the lack of support for properties you're using. Google can also help you find answers to problems, as it's fairly rare to come up against completely new issues.

Ask for Help

If you're yet to find a solution as you've moved through the aforementioned steps, ask for help. Even the most experienced developers hit problems that they're unable to see past. Sometimes, just talking through the issue with a bunch of people with fresh eyes can help you resolve the problem, or come up with new ideas to test—even if no one has an immediate solution.

If you have a reasonable number of front-end developer followers on Twitter, simply posting an example of the issue may well prompt a user familiar with the issue to come to your aid. There are also various forums and lists where help can be found, such as the SitePoint forums[26] or Stack Overflow.[27]

When you post to a website, forum, or mailing list, remember these rules of thumb:

■ Search the site or list archives, just in case your question is common enough to be asked at least once a day.

■ Make sure that your CSS and HTML validates; otherwise, the answer you'll receive is most likely to be "Go and validate your document and see if that helps."

---

[26] http://www.sitepoint.com/forums/forum.php
[27] http://stackoverflow.com/

- Upload an example to a location to which you can link from your forum post. If you manage to reproduce the problem outside a complex layout,[28] so much the better—this will make it easier for others to work out what's going on. If you can recreate your problem in a tool like jsFiddle,[29] better still. This will allow other people to play around with the issue and see if they can solve it for you.

- Explain the solutions you've tried so far. This saves the recipients of your message from pursuing those same dead-ends, and shows that you've attempted to fix the problem yourself before asking for help.

- Give your message a descriptive subject line. People are more likely to read a post entitled "Double height margin in Internet Explorer 8" than one that screams, "HELP!" Descriptive titles also make the list archives more useful, as people can see at a glance the post topics in a thread.

- Be polite and to the point.

- Be patient while you wait for answers. If you fail to receive a reply after a day or so and it's a busy list, it's usually acceptable to post again with the word "REPOST" in the subject line. Posts can be overlooked in particularly large boards, and this is a polite way to remind users that you've yet to receive any assistance with your problem.

- When you receive answers, try implementing the poster's suggestions. Avoid becoming upset or angry if the recommendations fail to work, or you feel that the poster is asking you to try very basic measures. I've seen threads go on for many posts as different posters weigh in to help a user solve a problem, continuing the discussion until a solution is found. Give people a chance to help!

- If you find a solution, or you have no success and decide instead to change your design to avoid the problem, post to the thread to explain what worked and what failed. This shows good manners towards those who helped you, and will also aid anyone who searches the archive for information on the same problem. It's very frustrating to search an archive and find several possible solutions to a problem, but be unsure which (if any) were successful!

---

[28] http://css-tricks.com/reduced-test-cases/

[29] http://jsfiddle.net/

The validator complains about my vendor-specific extensions, so how do I validate CSS3?

When trying out the examples in this book, or using the techniques in your own work, you may find that the validator displays warnings due to proprietary extensions used in your CSS.

Solution

Vendor-specific extensions, starting with `-moz`, `-webkit`, and so on, are not part of the CSS3 specification, so they'll be unrecognized by the validator and throw a warning or error. The syntax of beginning an extension to CSS with a "`-`" is correct, however, so the validator does understand about the existence of these extensions. Therefore, you can use the additional options fields at the W3C Markup Validator to hide these messages.

At the CSS Validator,[30] seen in Figure 7.11, open the **More Options** area and make sure that under **Profile** you have selected **CSS level 3**. You can then select **No warnings** and set the **Vendor Extensions** notification to show up as **Warnings**. This will allow you to validate your CSS for the important errors. I'd advise you to also check the warnings as well, but it can be hard to start looking for problems if you're swamped with hundreds of messages about the legitimate use of prefixed properties.

---

[30] http://jigsaw.w3.org/css-validator/

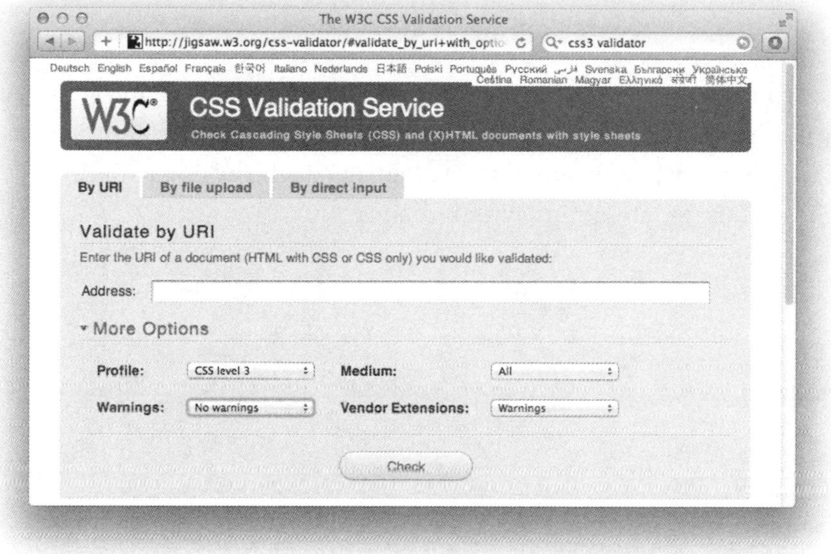

Figure 7.11. Setting options on the CSS Validator

Discussion

Another point to note with regards to the Validator is that when you first validate your page, don't panic if you see lots and lots of error messages. Deal with the first one, then validate again. Often the messages cascade from that one problem, so fixing it will also "fix" further errors. Fix each issue, then validate, and see what you're left with.

All Users Catered For

This chapter has aimed to shed some light on the thorny subject of browser testing. It can't be a complete guide—and the browsers and devices that we deal with are changing on a very regular basis. My best advice is to test often, in as many browsers and devices as you can get your hands on.

In the last few years we've seen browsers move to a more consistent rendering of CSS 2.1, and other than dealing with old browsers, the modern web developer has far fewer browser bugs to fight with. Nowadays, we need to keep up with which browsers support which parts of CSS3 and HTML5, and there are also the issues of designing sites that work for touch interfaces! That said, we are now in a far better situation with our browsers than we've ever been.

With regard to mobile browsers and touch interfaces, there's a lot of information already on the Web about how best to design for smartphones and tablets. It's an area in which many people are working to make the browsing experience better for designers and users interacting with our sites.

CSS Positioning Basics

In this chapter, we will look in further depth at some of the vital concepts when positioning page elements using CSS. If you're reading this book chapter by chapter, you'll already have come across some of these concepts used in the examples. Here we'll take a proper look at them, and see how they can be used in combination to layout our pages and components.

How do I decide when to use a class and when to use an ID?

At first glance, classes and IDs seem to be used in much the same way: you can assign CSS properties to both classes and IDs, and apply them to change the way HTML elements look. But in which circumstances are classes and IDs best applied?

Solution

The most important rule where classes and IDs are concerned is that an ID must be only used once in a document, as it uniquely identifies the element to which it's applied. Once you've assigned an ID to an element, you cannot use that ID again within that document.

Classes, on the other hand, may be used as many times as you like within the same document. If there's a feature on a page that you wish to repeat, a class is the ideal choice. Even if you don't wish to repeat the element on the page, if there's a chance you might use it again in the future, use a class.

You can apply both a class and an ID to any given element. For example, you might be required to add an ID to an unordered list, so that some JavaScript you're using can target it. If you were to create CSS for the ID, you would only be able to use that once within the page. However, you could instead add a class to the element as well as the ID and write CSS for the class selector, making it possible to reuse the CSS multiple times in the page.

What are block-level and inline elements in CSS, and can I change how these display?

In CSS, most elements are categorized as block or inline, and this affects the default way they behave in browsers. This default display method can be changed using the `display` property.

Solution

In Figure 8.1, we can see some HTML elements, each describing their default display (block or inline) with an example of what happens if we change the `display` property on that element.

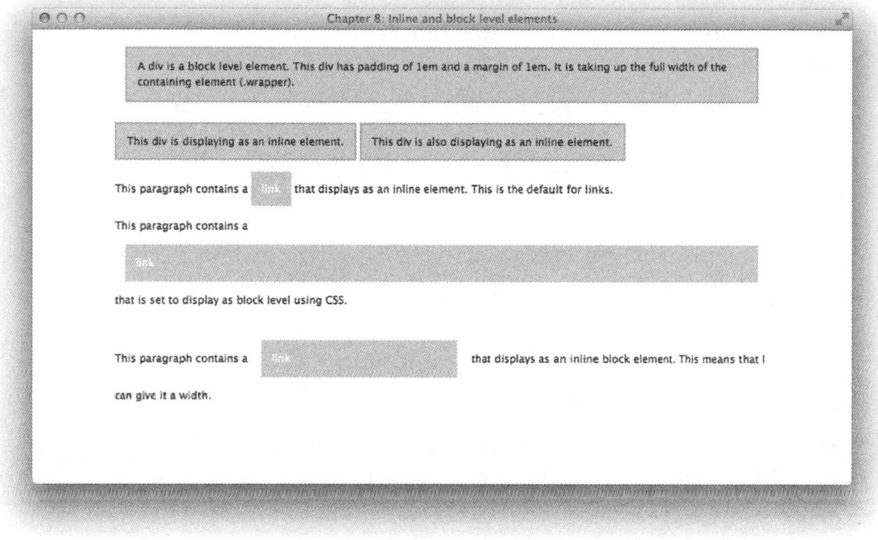

Figure 8.1. Changing the default display property of elements

In this example, six elements are used to demonstrate display properties. The first div is block by default, with the second and third divs specifically set to inline. The fourth element is a p containing a link which is inline by default, and the fifth element is a p containing a link set to block. The final element is a p containing a link set to inline-block:

```
                                              chapter_08/inline-block.html
<!DOCTYPE html>
<html>
<head>
  <meta charset="utf-8" />
  <title>Chapter 8: Inline and block-level elements</title>
  <link rel="stylesheet" href="inline-block.css" />
</head>
<body>
  <div class="wrapper">
    <div class="one">A div is a block-level element. This div has
      padding of 1em and a margin of 1em. It is taking up the full
      width of the containing element (.wrapper).</div>
    <br /><br />
    <div class="two">This div is displaying as an inline element.
      </div>
    <div class="two">This div is also displaying as an inline
```

```
      element.</div>
    <br /><br />
    <p>This paragraph contains a <a href=
➥"http://www.sitepoint.com/">link</a> that displays as an inline
      element. This is the default for links.</p>
    <p>This paragraph contains a <a class="block" href=
➥"http://www.sitepoint.com/">link</a> that is set to display as
      block-level using CSS.</p>
    <p>This paragraph contains a <a class="inline-block" href=
➥"http://www.sitepoint.com/">link</a> that displays as an inline
      block element. This means that I can give it a width.</p>
  </div>
</body>
</html>
```

chapter_08/inline-block.css

```
body {
  background-color: #fff;
  color: #000;
  margin: 0;
  padding: 0;
  font: 0.75em/1.5 "Lucida Grande", "Lucida Sans Unicode",
    "Lucida Sans", Verdana, Tahoma, sans-serif;
}

p {
  margin: 0;
  padding: 1em 0 1em 0;
}

.wrapper {
  width: 80%;
  margin: 20px auto 40px auto;
}

.one {
  background-color: #ccc;
  color: #000;
  border: 2px solid #aaa;
  padding: 1em;
  margin: 1em;
}

.two {
```

```
  background-color: #ccc;
  color: #000;
  border: 2px solid #aaa;
  padding: 1em;
  display: inline;
}

a {
  background-color: #ccc;
  color: #fff;
  text-decoration: none;
  padding: 1em;
}

a.block {
  display: block;
  margin: 1em;
  padding: 1em;
}

a.inline-block {
  display: inline-block;
  margin: 1em;
  padding: 1em;
  width: 200px;
}
```

Discussion

Understanding the `display` property is important because it explains why certain CSS rules will appear to work on one element and not on another. Knowing whether an item is set to `inline` or `block` (and that you can change this) also means that you're aware of when it's necessary to set widths or other properties on an element, and when you can simply let it take up the room it requires.

Inline Elements

An element set to display inline will only take up the space it needs. In our previous example, the default display of the a element is to remain inline with the text. It won't force a line break and the background color is simply behind the element itself—it does not extend out further than this. In addition, inline elements:

■ ignore top and bottom margins if applied

- disregard `height` and `width` properties
- can be affected by the `vertical-align` property

An inline element will become block-level if you set the `display` property to `block`, or if you float the element. Floated elements automatically become block-level and so height, width, and all margins will start to take effect.

Block-level Elements

Block-level elements will force a line break and drop to the next line in your document (unless a float is in effect above the element—see the section called "How do I stop the next item floating up once I've floated an element?" on `float` and `clear` for more information). They expand to fill the parent element unless a width has been given to them. In addition, block-level elements:

- respect all `margin` and `padding` properties
- expand in height to fit everything they contain; therefore, a `div` will expand to contain any amount of text and images as long as the text and images are not positioned or floated, as we'll see later in this chapter
- are not affected by `vertical-align`

Inline-block Elements

While discussing block and inline elements, it's worth noting another value for the `display` property: `inline-block`. If you set an element to `display: inline-block`, it will behave like a block-level element in terms of respecting all margins, padding, height, and width; however, it will not force a line break. Note that `inline-block` has no support in Internet Explorer 6 and 7.

How do margins and padding work in CSS?

What's the difference between the `margin` and `padding` properties, and how do they affect elements?

Solution

The `margin` properties add space to the outside of an element. You can set margins individually:

```
margin-top: 1em;
margin-right: 2em;
margin-bottom: 0.5em;
margin-left: 3em;
```

You can also set margins using a shorthand property:

```
margin: 1em 2em 0.5em 3em;
```

If all the margins are to be equal, simply use a rule like this:

```
margin: 1em;
```

This rule applies a 1em margin to all sides of the element.

Figure 8.2 shows what a block-level element—a paragraph—looks like when we add margins to it.

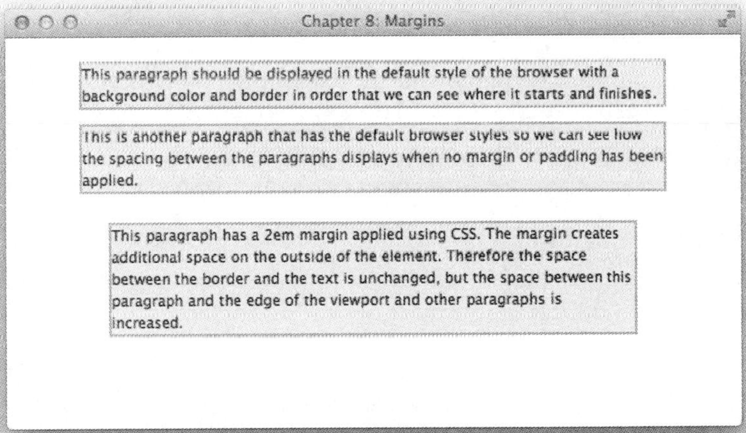

Figure 8.2. What happens when we add a margin to a paragraph element

The code for this page is as follows:

chapter_08/margin.html

```html
<!DOCTYPE html>
<html>
<head>
  <meta charset="utf-8" />
  <title>Chapter 8: Inline and block-level elements</title>
  <link rel="stylesheet" href="inline-block.css" />
</head>
<body>
  <div class="wrapper">
    <div class="one">A div is a block-level element. This div has
      padding of 1em and a margin of 1em. It is taking up the full
      width of the containing element (.wrapper).</div>
    <div class="two">This div is displaying as an inline element.
      </div>
    <div class="two">This div is also displaying as an inline
      element.</div>
    <p>This paragraph contains a <a href=
➥"http://www.sitepoint.com/"> link</a> that displays as an inline
      element. This is the default for links.</p>
    <p>This paragraph contains a <a class="block" href=
➥"http://www.sitepoint.com/">link</a> that is set to display as
      block-level using CSS.</p>
    <p>This paragraph contains a <a class="inline-block" href=
➥"http://www.sitepoint.com/">link</a> that displays as an
      inline-block element. This means that I can give it a width.
      </p>
  </div>
</body>
</html>
```

chapter_08/margin.css

```css
body {
  background-color: #fff;
  color: #000;
  margin: 0;
  padding: 0;
  font: 0.75em/1.5 "Lucida Grande", "Lucida Sans Unicode",
    "Lucida Sans", Verdana, Tahoma, sans-serif;
}

.wrapper {
  width: 80%;
```

```
    margin: 20px auto 40px auto;
}

p {
  border: 2px solid #aaa;
  background-color: #eee;
}

p.margintest {
  margin: 2em;
}
```

The padding properties add space inside the element, between its borders and its content. You can set padding individually for the top, right, bottom, and left sides of an element:

```
padding-top: 1em;
padding-right: 1.5em;
padding-bottom: 0.5em;
padding-left: 2em;
```

You can also apply padding using this shorthand property:

```
padding: 1em 1.5em 0.5em 2em;
```

As with margins, if the padding is to be equal all the way around an element, you can simply use a rule like this:

```
padding: 1em;
```

Figure 8.3, which results from the following code, shows what a block looks like with padding applied. Compare it to Figure 8.2 to see the differences between margins and padding.

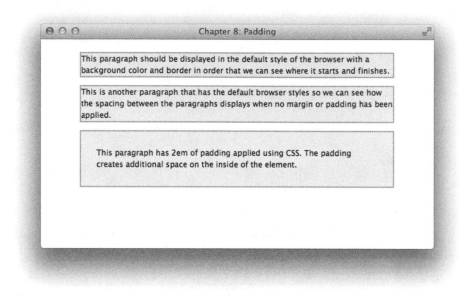

Figure 8.3. Applying padding using CSS

To see the same page use padding instead of margin, try this:

```
chapter_08/padding.html
<!DOCTYPE html>
<html>
<head>
  <meta charset="utf-8" />
  <title>Chapter 8: Padding</title>
  <link rel="stylesheet" href="padding.css" />
</head>
<body>
  <div class="wrapper">
    <p>This paragraph should be displayed in the default style of
      the browser with a background color and border in order that
      we can see where it starts and finishes.</p>
    <p>This is another paragraph that has the default browser
      styles so we can see how the spacing between the paragraphs
      displays when no margin or padding has been applied.</p>
    <p class="paddingtest">This paragraph has 2em of padding applied
      using CSS. The padding creates additional space on the inside
      of the element.</p>
```

```
    </div>
  </body>
</html>
```

```css
body {
  background-color: #fff;
  color: #000;
  margin: 0;
  padding: 0;
  font: 0.75em/1.5 "Lucida Grande", "Lucida Sans Unicode",
    "Lucida Sans", Verdana, Tahoma, sans-serif;
}

.wrapper {
  width: 80%;
  margin: 20px auto 40px auto;
}

p {
  border: 2px solid #aaa;
  background-color: #eee;
}

p.paddingtest {
  padding: 2em;
}
```

Discussion

The above solution demonstrates the basics of margins and padding. As we've seen, the margin properties create space between the element to which they're applied and the surrounding elements, while padding creates space inside the element to which it's applied. This is part of the CSS **box model** and is illustrated in Figure 8.4. (The markup for this box model is in the code archive as **boxmodel.html** and **boxmodel.css**.)

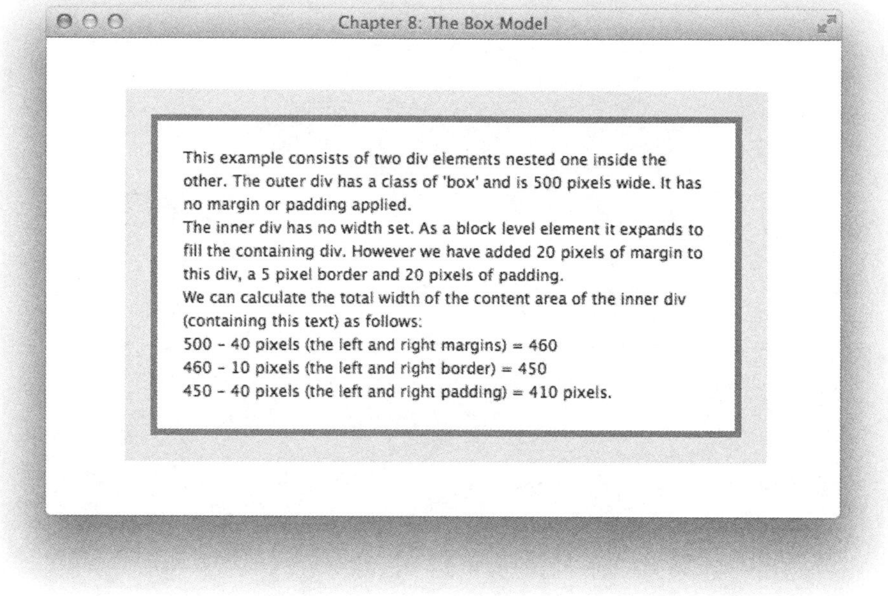

Figure 8.4. Reducing the width of an inner element's area

In our example, the containing element has a width set to 500 pixels. The inner `div` has no width set, and as we learned in the previous section, block-level elements expand in width to fill their container. The padding and margins set on the inner element pushes the content in, while the outer element remains a fixed size.

Contrast this with a similar example in Figure 8.5 with no inner element. (The markup for this box model has been included in the code archive as **boxmodel2.html** and **boxmodel2.css**.)

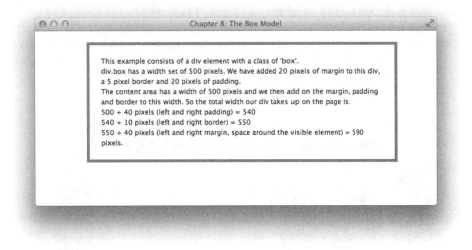

Figure 8.5. A single div with margins and padding applied

If you're applying margins and padding to a fixed-width element, they'll be added to the specified width to produce the total width for that element. So, if your element has a width of 500 pixels, and you add 20 pixels' worth of padding on all sides, you'll make the element take up 540 pixels of total width (500 pixels wide plus 20 pixels on each side). Add 20 pixels of margin to that, and the element will occupy a width of 580 pixels (a visible width of 540 pixels with 20 pixels of spacing on either side). If you have a very precise layout, remember to calculate your element sizes carefully, including any added margins and padding.

It's All Collapsing!

You may notice strange behavior where two elements have margins and you would expect both margins to take effect, but you seem to end up with only one margin. As margins are essentially invisible, this can be really confusing! The culprit is **margin collapsing**, and this is part of the CSS specification.

Essentially, if you have two margins adjacent to each other, or "touching" due to there being a parent-child relationship between the elements, they'll collapse, with only the largest margin honored. You can read an in-depth discussion of margin collapsing, complete with examples, in the SitePoint CSS Reference.[1]

---

[1] http://reference.sitepoint.com/css/collapsingmargins

How do I wrap text around an image?

If you add an image and then a paragraph of text to a page, the text will display after the image, as seen in Figure 8.6. How do we use CSS to wrap the image with the text?

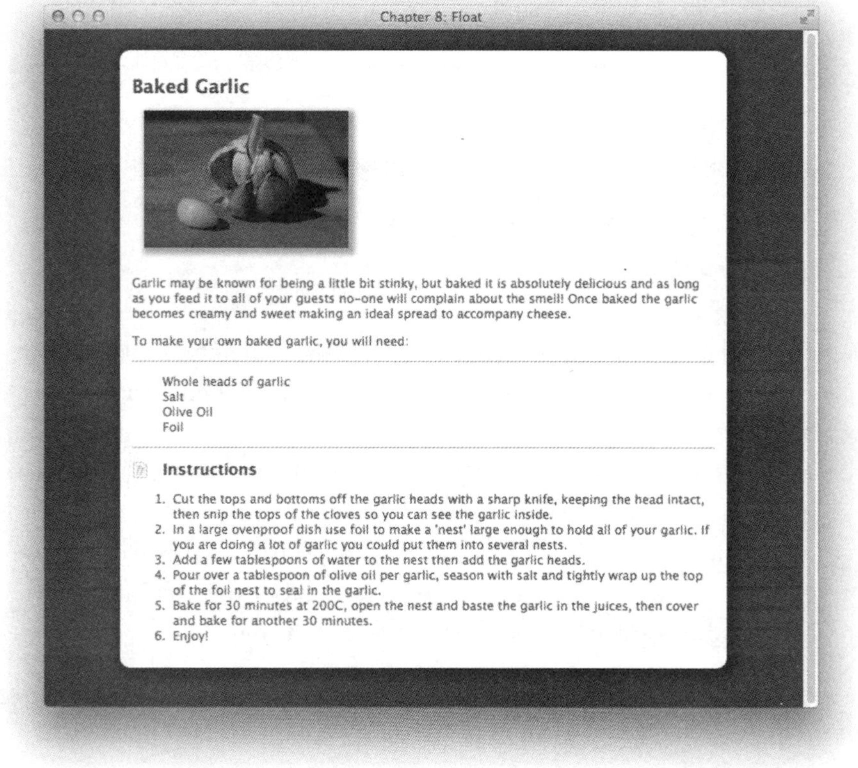

Figure 8.6. Text wrapping is the best solution when there's too much whitespace

Solution

We use the CSS `float` property to float an image left or right. This enables the text to flow around it, as you can see in Figure 8.7.

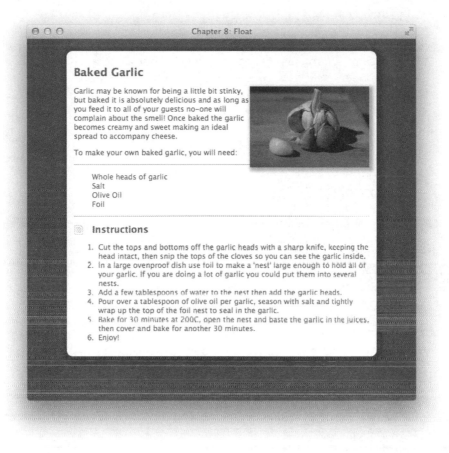

Figure 8.7. The page after text has been flowed around the image

The code to float the garlic image right is as follows:

<div class="code-heading">chapter_08/float.html</div>

```
<!DOCTYPE html>
<html>
<head>
  <meta charset="utf-8" />
  <title>Chapter 8: Float</title>
  <link rel="stylesheet" href="float.css" />
</head>
<body>
  <div class="wrapper">
    <div class="recipe">
      <h1>Baked Garlic</h1>
```

```
          <img src="garlic.jpg" alt="Garlic" height="134" width="200" />
          <p>Garlic may be known for being a little bit stinky, but
            baked it is absolutely delicious and as long as you feed it
            to all of your guests no-one will complain about the smell!
            Once baked the garlic becomes creamy and sweet making an
            ideal spread to accompany cheese.</p>
          <p>To make your own baked garlic, you will need:</p>
          <ul class="ingredients">
            <li>Whole heads of garlic</li>
            <li>Salt</li>
            <li>Olive Oil</li>
            <li>Foil</li>
          </ul>

          <h2 class="instructions">Instructions</h2>
          <ol>
            <li>Cut the tops and bottoms off the garlic heads with a
              sharp knife, keeping the head intact, then snip the tops
              of the cloves so you can see the garlic inside.</li>
            <li>In a large ovenproof dish use foil to make a 'nest'
              large enough to hold all of your garlic. If you are doing
              a lot of garlic you could put them into several nests.
              </li>
            <li>Add a few tablespoons of water to the nest then add the
              garlic heads.</li>
            <li>Pour over a tablespoon of olive oil per garlic, season
              with salt and tightly wrap up the top of the foil nest to
              seal in the garlic.</li>
            <li>Bake for 30 minutes at 200C, open the nest and baste the
              garlic in the juices, then cover and bake for another
              30 minutes.</li>
            <li>Enjoy!</li>
          </ol>
        </div>
      </div>
    </body>
  </html>
```

chapter_08/float.css *(excerpt)*

```css
.recipe img {
  float: right;
  width: 200px;
  …
  -webkit-box-shadow: 3px 3px 5px 3px rgba(0, 0, 0, 0.4);
```

```
    -moz-box-shadow: 3px 3px 5px 3px rgba(0, 0, 0, 0.4);
    box-shadow: 3px 3px 5px 3px rgba(0, 0, 0, 0.4);
}
```

Discussion

The `float` property *floats* the image against the edge of the block-level element that contains it. Other block-level elements will ignore the floated element and render as if it's absent. Inline elements such as content, however, will make space for the floated element, which is why we can use float to wrap our text around an image.

As we can clearly see in Figure 8.7, the text collides against the side of the image. If we add a border to that image, the text will bump against the side of the border.

To create space between our image and the text, we need to add a margin to the image. Since the image is aligned against the left-hand margin, we only need to add right and bottom margins to move the text slightly away from the image:

chapter_08/float.css *(excerpt)*

```
.recipe img {
    float: right;
    width: 200px;
    margin: 0 0 1em 1em;
    -webkit-box-shadow: 3px 3px 5px 3px rgba(0, 0, 0, 0.4);
    -moz-box-shadow: 3px 3px 5px 3px rgba(0, 0, 0, 0.4);
    box-shadow: 3px 3px 5px 3px rgba(0, 0, 0, 0.4);
}
```

Figure 8.8 shows the resulting display, with the extra space around the floated image.

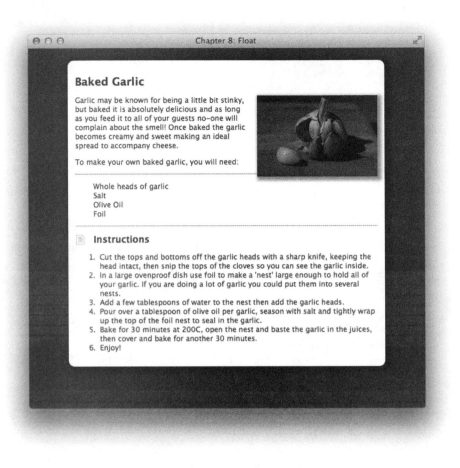

Figure 8.8. Adding a margin to the floated image

You can float elements right or left, and `float` is currently one of the main building blocks of CSS layout, so we'll be working with it a lot in Chapter 9.

How do I stop the next item floating up once I've floated an element?

You may have spotted in the previous float examples that the border on the ingredients section runs underneath the floated image. How can we make this element begin *after* the floated image has finished?

Solution

We can use the `clear` property to clear block-level elements so that they only render once the floated element is complete. Take a look at Figure 8.9.

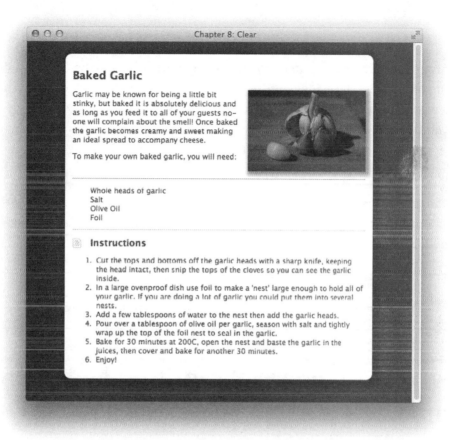

Figure 8.9. Our page is much neater after clearing the ingredients list

We can make room for the ingredients list by using these styles:

```
chapter_08/float-clear.css (excerpt)

ul.ingredients {
  clear: both;
  border-top: 1px solid #999;
  border-bottom: 1px solid #999;
  list-style: none;
  margin: 1em 0 1em 0;
```

```
    padding: 1em 0 1em 30px;
    background-image: url(ingredients.png);
    background-repeat: no-repeat;
    background-position: 0 1em;
}
```

Discussion

The float property changes the way other elements respond to the floated element, causing other block-level elements to ignore it altogether. So the border on the top of the ingredients list was correctly taking the full width of the container, as if there were no floated image. The floated image essentially sits on top of any block-level elements, whereas space is made for it by inline elements. We'll see a lot more of this behavior in the next chapter.

The clear property tells the block-level elements below any floated images that they should clear those floated elements; that is, only start once the floats have finished. The clear property can take the following values:

- left: clear only items floated left
- right: clear only items floated right
- none: clear nothing
- both: clear items floated left and right

How do I set an item's position on the page using CSS?

We can use CSS to position elements using absolute positioning.

Solution

If you set the value of the position property to absolute, you can position your element top, left, bottom, and right. This positioning will happen in relation to the viewport unless you've given absolute or relative positioning to a parent element of the element that you're trying to position. This is easier to understand with a series of examples.

The image shown in Figure 8.10 has two boxes that are positioned using absolute positioning, from the top-left and bottom-right of the viewport.

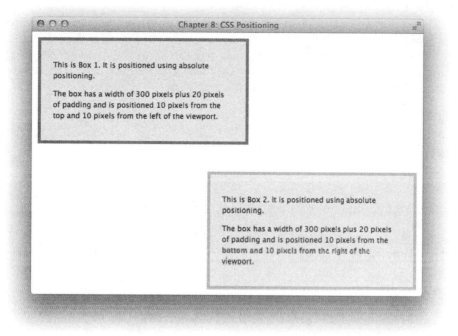

Figure 8.10. An example of absolute positioning

The code and CSS for this document is as follows:

```
                                    chapter_08/position.html (excerpt)
<!DOCTYPE html>
<html>
<head>
  <meta charset="utf-8" />
  <title>Chapter 8: CSS Positioning</title>
  <link rel="stylesheet" href="position.css" />
</head>
<body>
  <div class="wrapper">
    …
    <div class="box1">
      <p>This is Box 1. It is positioned using absolute positioning.
        </p>
      <p>The box has a width of 300 pixels plus 20 pixels of padding
        and is positioned 10 pixels from the top and 10 pixels from
        the left of the viewport.</p>
    </div>
```

```
    <div class="box2">
      <p>This is Box 2. It is positioned using absolute positioning.
        </p>
      <p>The box has a width of 300 pixels plus 20 pixels of padding
        and is positioned 10 pixels from the bottom and 10 pixels
        from the right of the viewport.</p>
    </div>
  </div>
</body>
</html>
```

chapter_08/position.css

```
body {
  background-color: #fff;
  color: #000;
  margin: 0;
  padding: 0;
  font: 0.75em/1.5 "Lucida Grande", "Lucida Sans Unicode",
    "Lucida Sans", Verdana, Tahoma, sans-serif;
}

.wrapper {
  width: 80%;
  margin: 20px auto 40px auto;
  position: relative;
}

.box1 {
  width: 300px;
  padding: 20px;
  border: 5px solid rgb(130,108,84);
  background-color: rgb(244,234,199);
  position: absolute;
  top: 10px;
  left: 10px;
}

.box2 {
  width: 300px;
  padding: 20px;
  border: 5px solid rgb(216,174,158);
  background-color: rgb(250,230,232);
  position: absolute;
```

```
    bottom: 10px;
    right: 10px;
}
```

Note that if we resize to make the window smaller, the second box will overlap the first as in Figure 8.11. The boxes are completely independent of each other and everything else on the page.

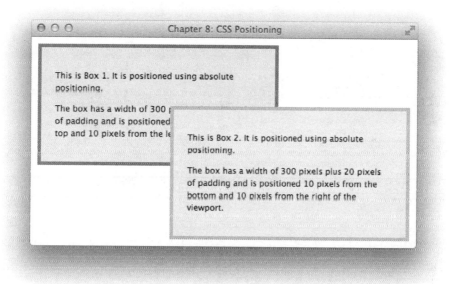

Figure 8.11. When the browser is resized, the boxes overlap

The markup for the boxes is inside another div with a class of wrapper. If we add some text inside this wrapper, we can see that the boxes completely ignore the new content and sit on top of it.

You can also see in Figure 8.12 that the boxes overlap the edges of wrapper; they're positioning themselves from the edge of the viewport, and not respecting their containing element anymore. Here we can say that absolutely positioned elements are "removed from the document flow."

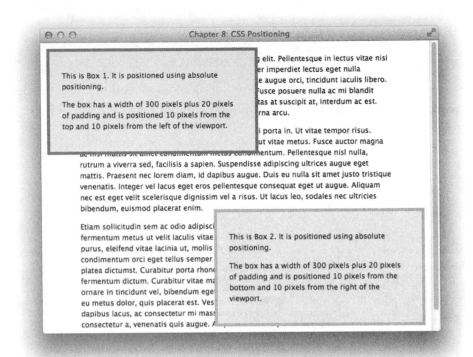

This is Box 1. It is positioned using absolute positioning.

The box has a width of 300 pixels plus 20 pixels of padding and is positioned 10 pixels from the top and 10 pixels from the left of the viewport.

This is Box 2. It is positioned using absolute positioning.

The box has a width of 300 pixels plus 20 pixels of padding and is positioned 10 pixels from the bottom and 10 pixels from the right of the viewport.

Figure 8.12. The boxes sit on top of any other content

A common rookie error of those who are just beginning to use CSS is to think that they can simply position everything on the page using `position absolute`. This might work in their own browsers, but in another browser with a larger default text-size set, or if more content is added, everything starts to overlap!

Discussion

We've seen how it's possible to position items from the edge of the viewport, but this is unlikely to be very useful. What can be useful (when done carefully) is the ability to position items within a container.

If, in our previous example, we wanted our positioned elements to respect the parent wrapper `div`, we could do so by setting `.wrapper` to `position: relative` as follows:

```
.wrapper {
  width: 80%;
  margin: 20px auto 40px auto;
  position: relative;
}
```

In Figure 8.13, you can see what happens. The boxes now take their position from the height and width of the wrapper and position themselves 10 pixels from the top-left and bottom-right of the wrapper. So box2 is now below the bottom of the viewport with our browser window at this size, rather than sticking to the viewport as it did before.

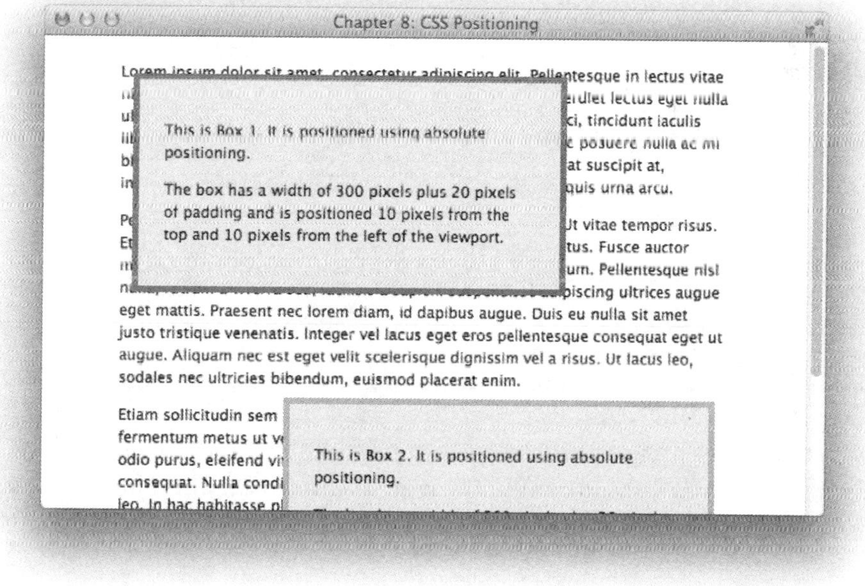

Figure 8.13. The boxes are now positioned inside the .wrapper div

The wrapper becomes the new "positioning context" for the absolutely positioned elements and this behavior is important to remember. If you position anything absolutely, it will take its position from the next parent element that has position: relative or position: absolute set. If it does not find anything, it will take its position from the viewport.

Relative Positioning

Setting position: relative as in our example will have no effect on the wrapper other than to cause it to become a positioning context for the items inside it. If you set top, left, bottom, or right values on an element that is set to position: relative, the item will shift from its original position by those pixels. This can be useful to shift an item a small distance from the position it ends up in by way of the document flow, but it can cause elements to overlap.

How do I center a layout on the page?

A common page layout has the main content area of the page as a fixed or flexible width box centered in the browser window. How do we achieve this centering?

Solution

Figure 8.14 shows a centered box. It's done by setting the left and right margins on the div with a class of wrapper to a value of auto.

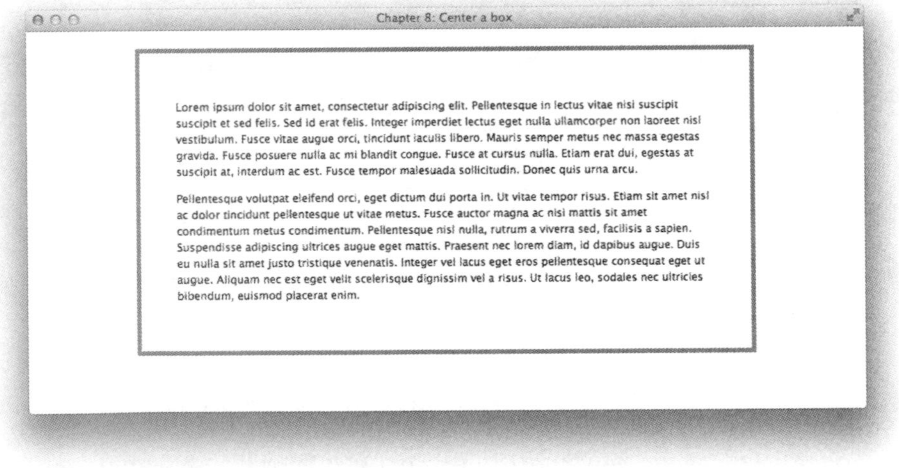

Figure 8.14. Centering a box

The stylesheet looks like this:

```
body {
  background-color: #fff;
  color: #000;
  margin: 0;
  padding: 0;
  font: 0.75em/1.5 "Lucida Grande", "Lucida Sans Unicode",
    "Lucida Sans", Verdana, Tahoma, sans-serif;
}

.wrapper {
  width: 600px;
  padding: 40px;
  margin: 20px auto 40px auto;
  border: 5px solid rgb(126,111,113);
}
```

Discussion

This technique allows you to center a box easily. When we set the left and right margins to auto, we're asking the browser to calculate equal values for each margin, thereby centering the box.

How do I create a thumbnail gallery?

This solution brings together several of the techniques we've looked at in this chapter by creating a neat gallery listing of thumbnail images.

Solution

The thumbnail listing can be seen in Figure 8.15.

Figure 8.15. Our thumbnail gallery

The gallery is created using the following markup:

chapter_08/gallery.html

```
<!DOCTYPE html>
<html>
<head>
  <meta charset="utf-8" />
  <title>Chapter 8: Gallery</title>
  <link rel="stylesheet" href="gallery.css" />
</head>
<body>
<div class="wrapper">
  <ul class="gallery">
    <li><img src="widget1.jpg" alt="Widget the cat" />
      <span>Widget the cat</span></li>
    <li><img src="widget2.jpg" alt="This is my tongue" />
      <span>This is my tongue</span></li>
    <li><img src="widget3.jpg" alt="Widget the cat is looking very
      serious today" />
      <span>Widget the cat is looking very serious today</span></li>
    <li><img src="widget4.jpg" alt="Widget and his very favorite
      person" />
      <span>Widget and his very favorite person</span></li>
    <li><img src="widget5.jpg" alt="Widget explores" />
      <span>Widget explores</span></li>
```

```
      <li><img src="widget6.jpg" alt="Widget is sleeping" />
        <span>Widget is sleeping</span></li>
    </ul>
  </div>
</body>
</html>
```

```
body {
  background-color: #fff;
  color: #000;
  margin: 0;
  padding: 0;
  font: 0.75em/1.5 "Lucida Grande", "Lucida Sans Unicode",
    "Lucida Sans", Verdana, Tahoma, sans-serif;
}

.wrapper {
  width: 80%;
  margin: 20px auto 40px auto;
}

ul.gallery {
  margin: 0;
  padding: 0;
  list-style: none;
}

ul.gallery li {
  display: inline-block;
  width: 240px;
  margin: 0 20px 20px 0;
  border: 1px solid #000;
  position: relative;
  -webkit-box-shadow: 1px 2px 5px 2px rgba(0, 0, 0, 0.3);
  -moz-box-shadow: 1px 2px 5px 2px rgba(0, 0, 0, 0.3);
  box-shadow: 1px 2px 5px 2px rgba(0, 0, 0, 0.3);
}

ul.gallery img {
  display: block;
}

ul.gallery span {
```

```
  position: absolute;
  bottom: 0;
  left: 0;
  background-color: rgba(0,0,0,0.7);
  color: rgb(255,255,255);
  width: 220px;
  padding: 10px;
}

ul.gallery span {
  margin-left: -9999px;
}

ul.gallery li:hover span {
  margin-left: 0;
}
```

The final effect for the gallery is shown in Figure 8.16—when a user hovers over an image, a styled caption will appear.

Figure 8.16. Hovering over an image brings up a caption

Discussion

The gallery items have been marked up as an unordered list of images. Without any CSS at all, this would display as in Figure 8.17.

Figure 8.17. The gallery before adding any CSS

The first task is to remove the margins, padding, and bullets that the browser applies by default to lists. If you're using a reset stylesheet (refer to the section called "How can I remove browsers' default padding and margins from all elements?" in Chapter 2), you might have already removed these for all lists, so you could skip this step.

Next we need to deal with the list items and make them display next to each other. I'm doing this by setting their `display` property to `inline-block`. You may remember when we discussed block and inline elements earlier in this chapter that `inline-block` makes an item act like a block element, but not drop onto a new line. We can use this to our advantage here:

```
ul.gallery li {
  display: inline-block;
  width: 240px;
  margin: 0 20px 20px 0;
  border: 1px solid #000;
}
```

After adding this, we can see that our gallery starts to display as in Figure 8.18.

Figure 8.18. The gallery after setting list items to display: `inline-block`

You might have seen techniques to address this problem that use `float`. I find that `display: inline-block` is often a better solution for this purpose. I can demonstrate why by removing `display: inline-block` and adding `float: left`:

```
ul.gallery li {
  float: left;
  width: 240px;
```

```
    margin: 0 20px 20px 0;
    border: 1px solid #000;
}
```

In Figure 8.18, you can see that the third image has a large caption and so is taller than the other boxes. I've reduced the size of the browser window shown in Figure 8.19 to better show the issue as the images flow into two columns. As you can see, the different heights of the boxes cause the items to display untidily. If we were to use `inline-block` instead, this issue would disappear.

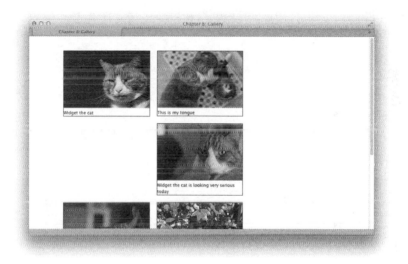

Figure 8.19. The same display using the `float` method

A good reason to use float would be when you need to accommodate browsers without support for `inline-block`, such as Internet Explorer 6 and 7. A way around this problem would be to use `inline-block` for supporting browsers, and in a stylesheet included with conditional comments use the float method to support these older browsers. If you're using float, you'll also want to ensure that items have the same height, if possible, to avoid the problem just shown.

A drop shadow completes the look of the list items. Next, I want to set the caption to display on top of the images.

Now we're going to use absolute positioning to move the captions to the bottom of the boxes. First, set `position: relative` on the list items. This makes the list item the positioning context for each caption:

```
ul.gallery li {
  display: inline-block;
  width: 240px;
  margin: 0 20px 20px 0;
  border: 1px solid #000;
  position: relative;
  -webkit-box-shadow: 1px 2px 5px 2px rgba(0, 0, 0, 0.3);
  -moz-box-shadow: 1px 2px 5px 2px rgba(0, 0, 0, 0.3);
  box-shadow: 1px 2px 5px 2px rgba(0, 0, 0, 0.3);
}
```

We can then position the caption to the bottom-left and style it. I'm using `rgba` to make it semitransparent:

```
ul.gallery div {
  position: absolute;
  bottom: 0;
  left: 0;
  background-color: rgba(0,0,0,0.7);
  color: rgb(255,255,255);
  width: 220px;
  padding: 10px;
}
```

You can see the result in Figure 8.20.

Figure 8.20. The gallery with styled captions

As a final touch, I'm only showing my captions when users hovers their mouse cursor over an image. To do this without JavaScript, I can simply set a large left margin on each caption:

```
ul.gallery div {
  margin-left: -9999px;
}
```

On the hover state of the `li` element, I set the `margin` back to `0`, which makes the caption appear:

```
ul.gallery li:hover div {
  margin-left: 0;
}
```

Positioned: Absolutely

This chapter has introduced some of the necessary concepts to grasp in order to use CSS to lay out entire pages and components of pages. We finished with a small example of how we can pull these techniques together to complete a layout element.

Even the most complex of CSS layouts use the same few techniques. A solid understanding of them will help you to break down any CSS task and work out the best way to build it. We'll see some further examples of this in the next chapter.

CSS for Layout

While writing the fourth edition of this book, it's apparent how practical and usable CSS has become since the previous edition. In just under two years, we've gone from CSS3 being an attractive but hard-to-implement concept, to being able to put much of what it offers into practice. We now have improved ways to create many design effects, from shadows to rounded corners. We're able to precisely target elements in our pages with CSS3 selectors, and can eliminate clutter to our markup when styling page elements.

When using CSS for layout purposes, however, there's been less progress. Our basic tools are those we discussed in Chapter 8: floating, positioning, and clearing elements to create layout. This chapter will show you how to use those building blocks in practical ways.

One area that has rapidly evolved recently is in providing support for smartphones, tablets, and other mobile devices—in a myriad of screen sizes—to access the Web. We'll spend much of this chapter exploring the area of responsive design, and how we can use traditional layout techniques to create designs that display neatly across a range of devices. Modern web design simply must heed the rising popularity of mobile browsing.

How do I create a two-column layout?

If you're new to using CSS for layout purposes, the first trick you might want to know is how to organize your content into two columns, as in Figure 9.1.

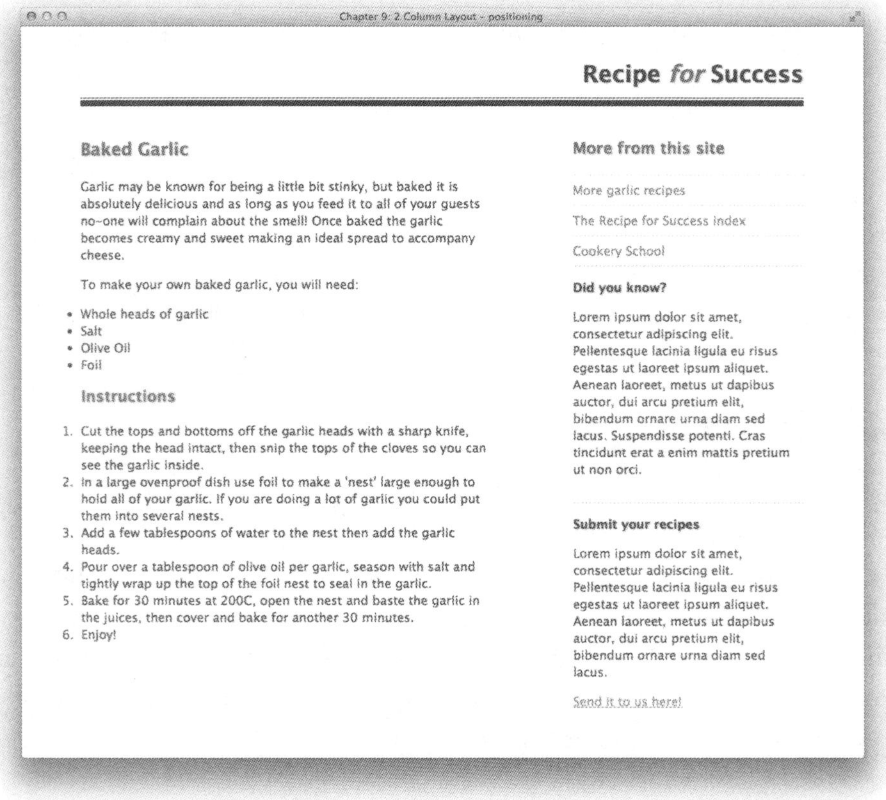

Figure 9.1. A simple two-column layout

Solution

The markup and CSS that follows will create a simple fixed-width layout using positioning to control how the columns display in a browser:

```
chapter_09/2col-positioning.html

<!DOCTYPE html>
<html>
<head>
```

```
  <meta charset="utf-8" />
  <title>Chapter 9: 2 Column Layout - positioning</title>
  <link rel="stylesheet" href="2col-positioning.css" />
</head>
<body>
  <div class="wrapper">
    <div class="header">
      <h1>Recipe <span>for</span> Success</h1>
    </div>
    <div class="main">
      <div class="article">
        <h1>Baked Garlic</h1>

        <p>Garlic may be known for being a little bit stinky, but
           baked it is absolutely delicious and as long as you feed
           it to all of your guests no-one will complain about the
           smell! Once baked the garlic becomes creamy and sweet
           making an ideal spread to accompany cheese.</p>
        <p>To make your own baked garlic, you will need:</p>

        <ul class="ingredients">
        <li>Whole heads of garlic</li>
        <li>Salt</li>
        <li>Olive Oil</li>
        <li>Foil</li>
        </ul>

        <h2>Instructions</h2>

        <ol>
          <li>Cut the tops and bottoms off the garlic heads with a
             sharp knife, keeping the head intact, then snip the
             tops of the cloves so you can see the garlic inside.
             </li>
          <li>In a large ovenproof dish use foil to make a 'nest'
             large enough to hold all of your garlic. If you are
             doing a lot of garlic you could put them into several
             nests.</li>
          <li>Add a few tablespoons of water to the nest then add
             the garlic heads.</li>
          <li>Pour over a tablespoon of olive oil per garlic,
             season with salt and tightly wrap up the top of the
             foil nest to seal in the garlic.</li>
          <li>Bake for 30 minutes at 200C, open the nest and baste
             the garlic in the juices, then cover and bake for
```

```
              another 30 minutes.</li>
          <li>Enjoy!</li>
        </ol>
      </div>


      <div class="aside">
        <h2>More from this site</h2>
        <ul class="nav">
          <li><a href="">More garlic recipes</a></li>
          <li><a href="">The Recipe for Success index</a></li>
          <li><a href="">Cookery School</a></li>
        </ul>

        <div class="box">
          <h3>Did you know?</h3>
          <p>Lorem ipsum dolor sit amet, consectetur adipiscing
            elit. Pellentesque lacinia ligula eu risus egestas ut
            laoreet ipsum aliquet. Aenean laoreet, metus ut dapibus
            auctor, dui arcu pretium elit, bibendum ornare urna diam
            sed lacus. Suspendisse potenti. Cras tincidunt erat a
            enim mattis pretium ut non orci.</p>
        </div>

        <div class="box">
          <h3>Submit your recipes</h3>
          <p>Lorem ipsum dolor sit amet, consectetur adipiscing
            elit. Pellentesque lacinia ligula eu risus egestas ut
            laoreet ipsum aliquet. Aenean laoreet, metus ut dapibus
            auctor, dui arcu pretium elit, bibendum ornare urna diam
            sed lacus. </p>
          <p><a href="">Send it to us here!</a></p>
        </div>
      </div>
    </div>
  </div>
</body>
</html>
```

chapter_09/2col-positioning.css

```
body {
  background-color: rgb(255,255,255);
  color: rgb(59,67,68);
  margin: 0;
  padding: 0;
```

```css
    font: 1em/1.4 "Lucida Grande", "Lucida Sans Unicode",
      "Lucida Sans", Verdana, Tahoma, sans-serif;
}

h1, h2, h3 {
  margin: 0;
  padding: 0 0 1em 0;
  text-shadow: 1px 1px 2px rgba(0,0,0,0.3);
}

ul, ol, p {
  margin:0;
  padding: 0 0 1em 0;
}


h1 {
  font-size: 137.5%;
  color: rgb(241,47,93);
}

h2 {
  font-size: 125%;
  color: rgb(241,47,93);
}

h3 {
  font-size: 100%;
}

a:link, a:visited {
  color: rgba(241,47,93,0.8);
}

a:hover {
  color: rgb(241,47,93);
  text-decoration: none;
}

.nav {
  list-style-type: none;
  padding: 0;
}

.nav a:link, .nav a:visited {
```

```css
  text-decoration: none;
  display: block;
  border-top: 1px solid rgb(232,243,248);
  padding: 0.5em 0 0.5em 0;
  color: rgb(66,148,182);
}

.nav a:hover {
  background-color: rgba(232,243,248,0.3);
}

.box {
  border-top: 1px solid rgb(219,230,236);
  padding: 1em 0 1em 0;
}

.wrapper {
  width: 940px;
  margin: 0 auto 0 auto;
}

.header {
  text-align: right;
  padding: 40px 0 0 0;
  border-bottom: 8px solid rgb(59,67,68);
  margin-bottom: 40px;
}

.header h1 {
  font-size: 187.5%;
  border-bottom: 1px solid rgb(59,67,68);
  margin-bottom: 2px;
  padding-bottom: 10px;
  color: rgb(59,67,68);
}

.header h1 span {
  font-style: italic;
  color: rgb(241,47,93);
}

.main {
  position: relative;
}
```

```
.article {
  position: absolute;
  top: 0;
  left: 0;
  width: 540px;
}

.aside {
  width: 300px;
  position: absolute;
  top: 0;
  right: 0;
}
```

Discussion

Our design starts out, as always, as a marked-up HTML document. We then add some CSS to style the text in the document. After doing so, the page displays in a linear fashion as in Figure 9.2.

Figure 9.2. Adding CSS to style the document text

Our first task is to fix the width of the layout area and center it within the browser viewport:

chapter_09/2col-positioning.css *(excerpt)*

```
.wrapper {
  width: 940px;
  margin: 0 auto 0 auto;
}
```

The layout is now centered, as seen in Figure 9.3.

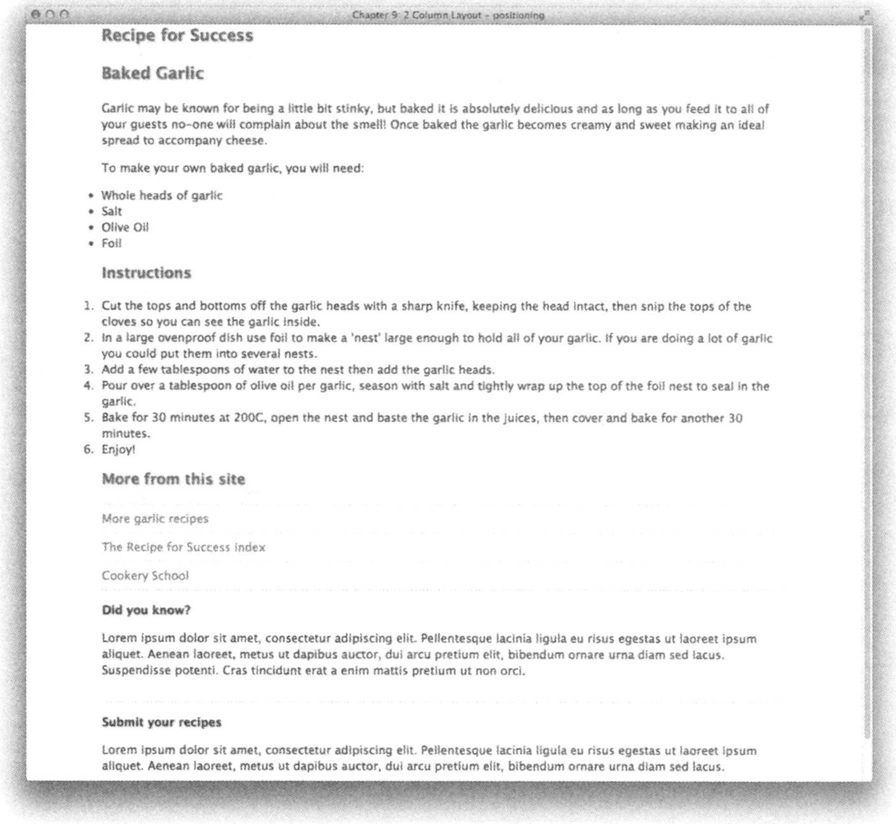

Figure 9.3. A fixed-width, centered layout

We can now have a look at the header, where the CSS is very simple. We just align the text right and then add padding to the header and the h1 within it, along with some simple rules to style the text. The CSS follows, and you can see the result in Figure 9.4:

```
chapter_09/2col-positioning.css (excerpt)

.header {
  text-align: right;
  padding: 40px 0 0 0;
  border-bottom: 8px solid rgb(59,67,68);
  margin-bottom: 40px;
}

.header h1 {
  font-size: 187.5%;
  border-bottom: 1px solid rgb(59,67,68);
  margin-bottom: 2px;
  padding-bottom: 10px;
  color: rgb(59,67,68);
}
```

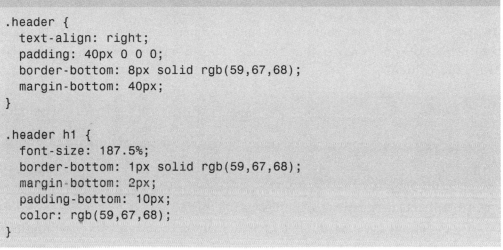

Figure 9.4. The header after adding CSS

To arrange the two columns using absolute positioning, I first need to create a positioning context for them. If I use `position: absolute`, they'll position themselves against the viewport; I actually want to place them within the main area of my document, below the header.

My markup has a `div` that wraps both columns; it has a `class` of `main`. I set `position: relative` on the `div` so that it creates a positioning context—the container for my two columns:

chapter_09/2col-positioning.css *(excerpt)*

```css
.main {
  position: relative;
}
```

Now I simply position my two columns within this container. I set `article` and `aside` to `position: absolute`. Then I position `article` top and `left` within this container, and `aside` top and `right`:

chapter_09/2col-positioning.css *(excerpt)*

```css
.article {
  position: absolute;
  top: 0;
  left: 0;
  width: 540px;
}

.aside {
  width: 300px;
  position: absolute;
  top: 0;
  right: 0;
}
```

Our simple two-column layout is complete. This technique can be used anywhere in a layout—from major columns of content to small elements within a container. We'll discover some weaknesses with positioning in the next section, but you should still find it useful in some contexts.

How do I create a two-column layout with a footer?

Our simple positioned layout has a weakness, and we can discover what it is by adding a footer to the layout. As our items are positioned, they're removed from the document flow, so the footer acts as if they're not there at all, displaying across the content rather than below the two columns. You can see this rather unpleasant effect in Figure 9.5.

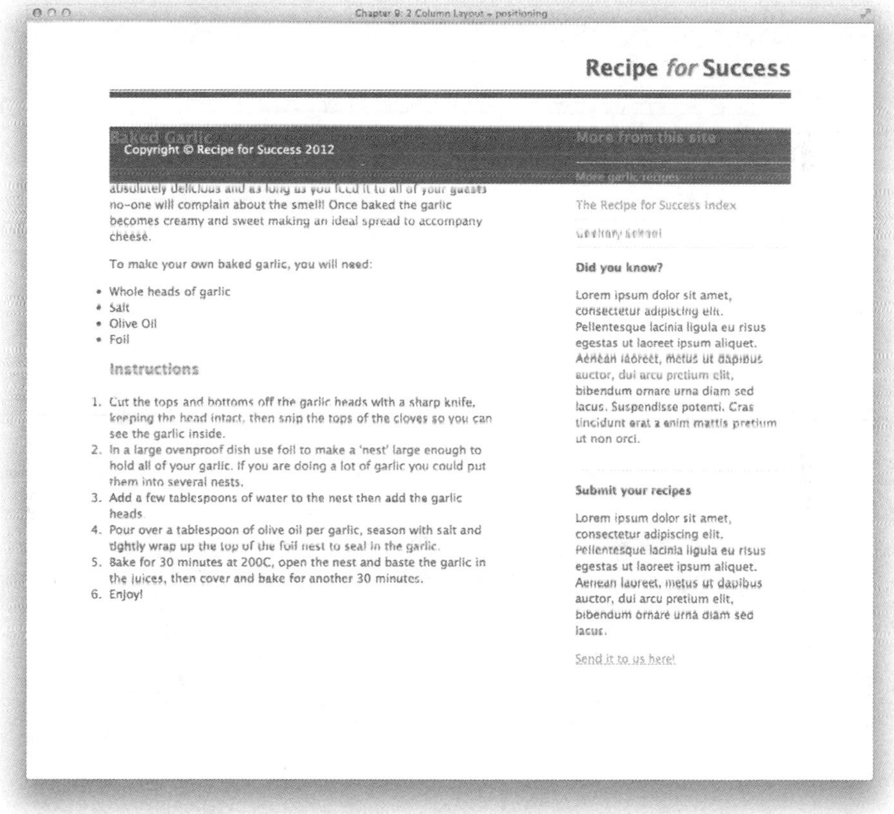

Figure 9.5. We have a footer—just not where we'd like it

Solution

To allow for a footer that will sit below the columns, we need a different approach to our layout. One of the more popular and cross-browser-friendly approaches is to use floats. Figure 9.6 shows how floats can be used to position two columns.

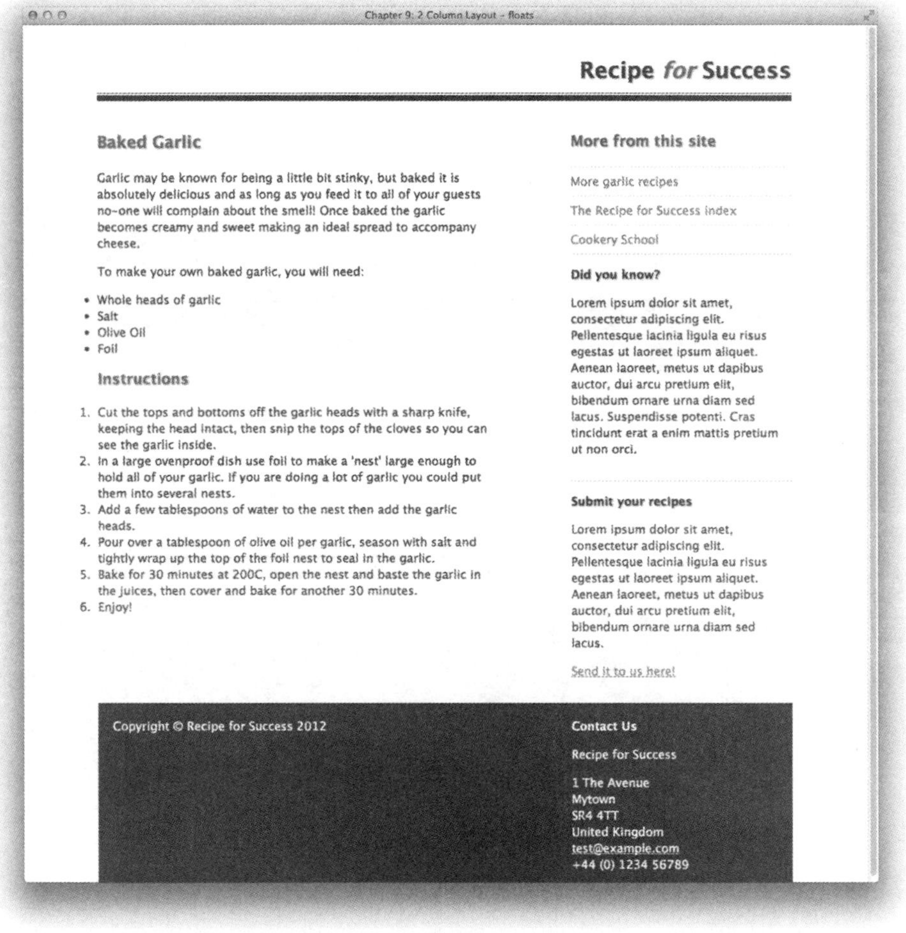

Figure 9.6. A two-column layout using floats, with our footer at the bottom

The markup we'll use is more or less the same as in the section called "How do I create a two-column layout?" The containing div `main` is unnecessary, so there's no need to create a new positioning context when using floats, and we've added the `footer` div within the wrapper:

```
<!DOCTYPE html>
<html>
<head>
  <meta charset="utf-8" />
  <title>Chapter 9: 2 Column Layout - floats</title>
  <link rel="stylesheet" href="2col-float.css" />
</head>
<body>
  <div class="wrapper">
    <div class="header">
      <h1>Recipe <span>for</span> Success</h1>
    </div>

    <div class="article">
      <h1>Baked Garlic</h1>

      <p>Garlic may be known for being a little bit stinky, but
        baked it is absolutely delicious and as long as you feed
        it to all of your guests no-one will complain about the
        smell! Once baked the garlic becomes creamy and sweet
        making an ideal spread to accompany cheese.</p>
      <p>To make your own baked garlic, you will need:</p>

      <ul class="ingredients">
        <li>Whole heads of garlic</li>
        <li>Salt</li>
        <li>Olive Oil</li>
        <li>Foil</li>
      </ul>

      <h2>Instructions</h2>

      <ol>
        <li>Cut the tops and bottoms off the garlic heads with a
          sharp knife, keeping the head intact, then snip the tops
          of the cloves so you can see the garlic inside.</li>
        <li>In a large ovenproof dish use foil to make a 'nest'
          large enough to hold all of your garlic. If you are doing
          a lot of garlic you could put them into several nests.
          </li>
        <li>Add a few tablespoons of water to the nest then add the
          garlic heads.</li>
        <li>Pour over a tablespoon of olive oil per garlic, season
```

```
          with salt and tightly wrap up the top of the foil nest to
          seal in the garlic.</li>
        <li>Bake for 30 minutes at 200C, open the nest and baste the
          garlic in the juices, then cover and bake for another
          30 minutes.</li>
        <li>Enjoy!</li>
      </ol>

  </div>

  <div class="aside">
    <h2>More from this site</h2>
    <ul class="nav">
      <li><a href="">More garlic recipes</a></li>
      <li><a href="">The Recipe for Success index</a></li>
      <li><a href="">Cookery School</a></li>
    </ul>
    <div class="box">
      <h3>Did you know?</h3>
      <p>Lorem ipsum dolor sit amet, consectetur adipiscing
        elit. Pellentesque lacinia ligula eu risus egestas ut
        laoreet ipsum aliquet. Aenean laoreet, metus ut dapibus
        auctor, dui arcu pretium elit, bibendum ornare urna diam
        sed lacus. Suspendisse potenti. Cras tincidunt erat a
        enim mattis pretium ut non orci.</p>
    </div>

    <div class="box">
      <h3>Submit your recipes</h3>
      <p>Lorem ipsum dolor sit amet, consectetur adipiscing
        elit. Pellentesque lacinia ligula eu risus egestas ut
        laoreet ipsum aliquet. Aenean laoreet, metus ut dapibus
        auctor, dui arcu pretium elit, bibendum ornare urna diam
        sed lacus. </p>
      <p><a href="">Send it to us here!</a></p>
    </div>
  </div>
  <div class="footer cf">
    <p class="copy">Copyright &copy; Recipe for Success 2012</p>

    <div class="vcard">
      <h3>Contact Us</h3>
      <p class="fn org">Recipe for Success</p>
      <div class="adr">
        <div class="street-address">1 The Avenue</div>
```

```
            <div class="Locality">Mytown</div>
            <div class="postal-code">SR4 4TT</div>
            <div class="country-name">United Kingdom</div>
            <div><a class="email" href="mailto:test@example.com">
              test@example.com</a></div>
            <div class="tel value">+44 (0) 1234 56789</div>
          </div>
        </div>
      </div>
    </div>
  </body>
</html>
```

chapter_09/2col-float.css *(excerpt)*

```css
.article {
  float: left;
  width: 540px;
}

.aside {
  width: 300px;
  float: right;
}

.footer {
  clear: both;
  background-color: rgb(59,67,68);
  color: rgb(255,255,255);
  padding: 20px;
  overflow:auto;
}

.footer .copy {
  float: left;
  width: 520px;
}

.footer .vcard {
  float: right;
  width: 280px;
}
```

```
.footer a:link, .footer a:visited {
  color: rgb(255,255,255);
}
```

Discussion

While the `float` property takes elements out of the normal document flow and changes the way they relate to other elements, it also enables them to be cleared. So an element—the footer in this instance—can be set to `clear: both` and then display below the floated elements.

To display our columns using `float` rather than `position` simply involves removing the `position`, `top`, `left`, and `right` properties; instead, we use `float` set to `left` and `right`, respectively:

chapter_09/2col-float.css *(excerpt)*

```
.article {
  float: left;
  width: 540px;
}

.aside {
  width: 300px;
  float: right;
}
```

We can then set the `clear` property on our footer:

chapter_09/2col-float.css *(excerpt)*

```
.footer {
  clear: both;
  background-color: rgb(59,67,68);
  color: rgb(255,255,255);
  padding: 20px;
}
```

We're going to use `float` again on elements within our footer, and this will give us a chance to look at some of the potential issues you might encounter when using `float` and `clear`.

I've set a background color and some padding on my footer, which now displays as in Figure 9.7.

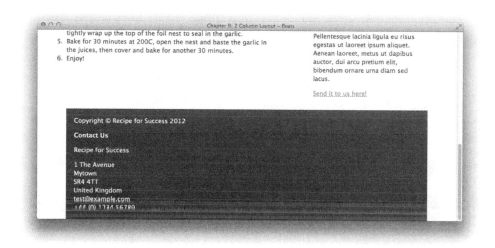

Figure 9.7. The page once the footer element has been styled

I want my copyright content to display in the left column, matching the article div above it, and the contact information to display in the right column, lining up underneath the aside div. Once again, we float these left and right—the width of each being 10 pixels narrower than the columns above to account for the padding on the footer:

chapter_09/2col-float.css *(excerpt)*

```
.footer .copy {
  float: left;
  width: 520px;
}

.footer .vcard {
  float: right;
  width: 280px;
}
```

Now try refreshing the browser: most of the footer has disappeared! What on earth has happened?

If you highlight the text as in Figure 9.8, you can see that the footer element is still there. What's happened is that the background color of the footer has collapsed to the same height as the padding on the top and bottom of the `footer` div: ten pixels. The copyright statement and contact text have their `color` set to `white`, so they disappear against the white page background.

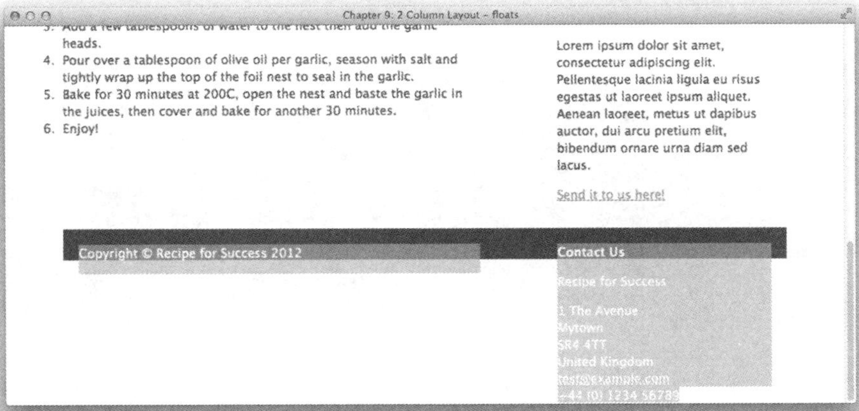

Figure 9.8. The amazing disappearing footer

The reason why the footer background has disappeared is that the two columns of content have been taken out of the normal flow using `float`. The solution is to set a `clear` below these two columns—just as the footer itself clears the main two columns on the page.

Clearing Inside Containers

You are now encountering one of the most-discussed and troubling issues of layout using floats: how to self-clear a page element.

There's no markup below our two footer columns to which we can add a `clear` property. A very basic solution would be to add a bit of redundant markup in the form of a `div` with a `class` of `clear`:

```
<div class="footer">
  <p class="copy">Copyright &copy; Recipe for Success 2012</p>
    <div class="vcard">
      <h3>Contact Us</h3>
```

```
  <p class="fn org">Recipe for Success</p>
  <div class="adr">
    <div class="street-address">1 The Avenue</div>
    <div class="Locality">Mytown</div>
    <div class="postal-code">SR4 4TT</div>
    <div class="country-name">United Kingdom</div>
    <div><a class="email" href="mailto:test@example.com">
      test@example.com</a></div>
    <div class="tel value">+44 (0) 1234 56789</div>
  </div>
</div>
<div class="clear"></div>
</div>
```

Now set the class .clear to clear: both:

```
.clear {
  clear: both;
}
```

This will clear the footer; however, it's a relatively inelegant approach! I'm going to show you some other solutions, all of which are valid ways to clear floats. Knowing a few methods is handy, as floats can trigger odd layout bugs (especially in older versions of Internet Explorer). Having a few tricks up your sleeve means if one technique is giving you problems, you can try another.

Floating the Outer Container

If you float an element or elements within a wrapping element that is itself floated, that wrapping element will then safely contain the inner floated elements, and all your floated elements will display according to plan. So, in our example, if we float .footer left, it will contain our inner, floated elements, and the footer will display in full:

```
.footer {
  clear: both;
  background-color: rgb(59,67,68);
  color: rgb(255,255,255);
  padding: 20px;
  float: left;
  width: 900px;
}
```

The main problem with floating a containing element in this manner is that, when floating an element, you need to give it an explicit width, and this may not always be preferable or possible. Even in situations where it is, declaring widths on internal elements of your pages makes them less flexible if they're used elsewhere across your site (for instance, the width may be incorrect for the dimensions of another page). You also need to calculate margins and padding carefully. In our example, we'd need to set a width of 900 pixels, taking into account the 20 pixels on each side of the footer.

Setting `overflow: auto` or `overflow: hidden`

Another trick that will cause a wrapper to neatly contain floated elements is to set `overflow: auto` or `overflow: hidden` on the container. Watch out for any content that might extend beyond the container (for example, a long URL that does not wrap), as it will either generate a scrollbar if the `overflow` is set to `auto`, or will fail to show if the `overflow` is set to `hidden`:

```css
.footer {
  clear: both;
  background-color: rgb(59,67,68);
  color: rgb(255,255,255);
  padding: 20px;
  overflow: auto;
}
```

Those warnings aside, this is a very simple technique that you can use in many situations.

Clearfix Hack

Another technique you may come across is known as the clearfix hack. I tend to avoid using it in my work, though, as the previous two methods suffice in most situations. There are a few versions of the clearfix hack, but they use generated content to add markup that clears the container. The example we've used in this case is explained on Nicolas Gallagher's site:[1]

---

[1] http://nicolasgallagher.com/micro-clearfix-hack/

chapter_09/2col-float.css *(excerpt)*

```css
/* For modern browsers */
.cf:before,
.cf:after {
    content:"";
    display: table;
}

.cf:after {
    clear: both;
}

/* For IE 6/7 (trigger hasLayout) */
.cf {
    zoom:1;
}
```

In our layout, we'd add the class cf to the footer, like this:

chapter_09/2col-float.html *(excerpt)*

```html
<div class="footer cf">
```

The float would then self-clear.

How do I create a three-column layout?

We've explored a basic two-column page set-up, but how easy is it to add a third column to our fixed width layout, perhaps to add some subnavigation?

Solution

Adding a third column to take care of subnavigation is actually quite simple. We can just add our subnavigation element structure to the existing markup, float it left, and then adjust our other columns to give it some space. The markup and CSS follow, and the result can be seen in Figure 9.9:

chapter_09/3col-float.html *(excerpt)*

```html
<!DOCTYPE html>
<html>
<head>
```

```
  <meta charset="utf-8" />
  <title>Chapter 9: 3 Column Layout - floats</title>
  <link rel="stylesheet" href="3col-float.css" />
</head>
<body>
  <div class="wrapper">
    <div class="header">
      <h1>Recipe <span>for</span> Success</h1>
    </div>

    <div class="subnav">
      <h2>Recipes for...</h2>
      <ul class="nav">
        <li><a href="">Breakfast</a></li>
        <li><a href="">Lunch</a></li>
        <li><a href="">Dinner</a></li>
        <li><a href="">Entertaining</a></li>
        <li><a href="">Cakes &amp; Biscuits</a></li>
        <li><a href="">Bread</a></li>
        <li><a href="">Gluten Free</a></li>
      </ul>
    </div>

    <div class="article">
      <h1>Baked Garlic</h1>
      <p>
      ⋮
      </p>
    </div>
    <div class="aside">
      ⋮
    </div>
    <div class="footer">
      <p>
      ⋮
      </p>

    </div>

  </div>

</body>
</html>
```

chapter_09/3col-float.css *(excerpt)*

```
.subnav {
  width: 220px;
  float: left;
  margin-right: 20px;
}

.article {
  float: left;
  width: 440px;
}

.aside {
  width: 220px;
  float: right;
}
```

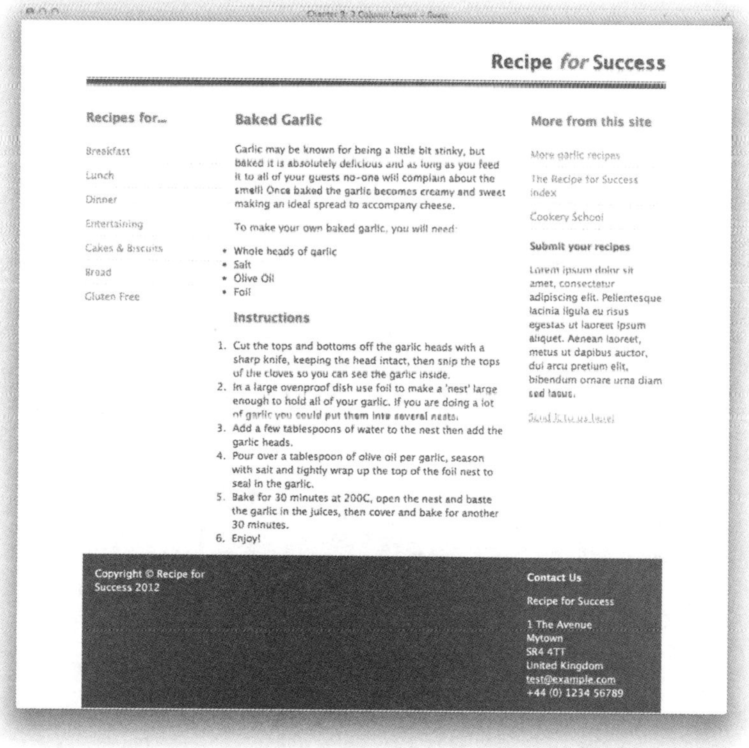

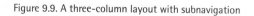

Figure 9.9. A three-column layout with subnavigation

Discussion

When you add an extra column to your layout, you need to ensure that all your width calculations are correct. In our two-column layout, we could just float our .article and .aside elements left and right; because the total width of the two combined was less than the 940-pixel total width of the wrapper, a natural gap was left between them.

With a three-column layout, we float both .subnav and .article left. If there was no right-hand margin on .subnav, there would be no space between the two elements, but adding a 20-pixel right margin to .subnav creates a gutter between them, ensuring the text in each column does not abut.

How do I create a fixed-width layout with a full-width header and footer?

The layout that we have been working on so far is completely contained within a 940-pixel wrapper. This means that the dark-gray header and footer bars stop at 940 pixels wide. A common site design structure involves a fixed central content area that allows the background color on some or all of the containers to bleed out to the edges of the viewport, as seen in Figure 9.10. So how is this achieved?

Solution

We need to make a few changes to our markup to enable a wide footer:

chapter_09/3col-wide-footer.html *(excerpt)*

```
<!DOCTYPE html>
<html>
<head>
  <meta charset="utf-8" />
  <title>Chapter 9: 3 Column Layout - floats, wide footer</title>
  <link rel="stylesheet" href="3col-wide-footer.css" />
</head>
<body>
  <div class="header">
    <div class="inner">
      <div class="wrapper">
        <h1>Recipe <span>for</span> Success</h1>
```

```
        </div>
      </div>
    </div>
    <div class="wrapper">
      <div class="subnav">
        <h2>Recipes for...</h2>
        ⋮
      </div>
      <div class="article">
        <h1>Baked Garlic</h1>
      </div>
      <div class="aside">
        <h2>More from this site</h2>
        ⋮
      </div>
    </div>
    <div class="footer">
    <div class="wrapper">
      <p class="copy">Copyright &copy; Recipe for Success 2012</p>
      <div class="vcard">
        ⋮
      </div>
    </div>
    </div>
  </div>

</body>
</html>
```

chapter_09/3col-wide-footer.css *(excerpt)*

```
/* remove the bottom border from the h1 and add to the new .inner */

.header h1 {
  font-size: 187.5%;
  padding-bottom: 10px;
  color: rgb(59,67,68);
}
.header .inner {
  border-bottom: 1px solid rgb(59,67,68);
  margin-bottom: 2px;
}

/* remove the left and right padding on footer and add back to
   internal columns */
```

```
.footer {
  clear: both;
  background-color: rgb(59,67,68);
  color: rgb(255,255,255);
  overflow: auto;
  padding: 20px 0 20px 0;
}

.footer .copy {
  float: left;
  width: 220px;
}

.footer .vcard {
  float: right;
  width: 220px;
}
```

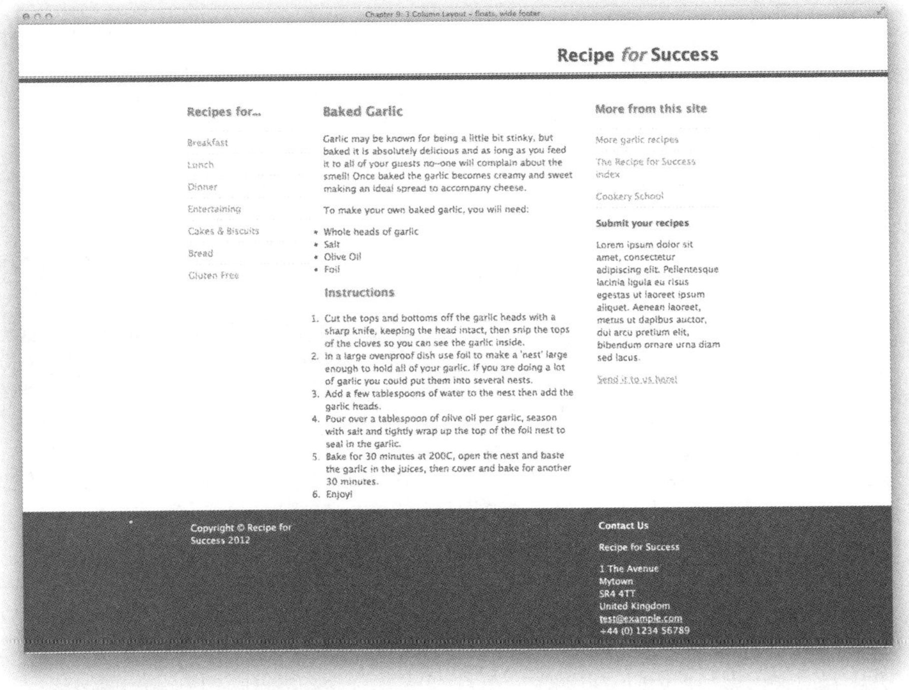

Figure 9.10. The fixed-width, centered layout with full-width header and footer bars

Discussion

To create this effect, we simply reuse our wrapper `div`. This is the element that creates our centered layout. The CSS applied to it looks as follows:

chapter_09/3col-wide-footer.css *(excerpt)*

```css
.wrapper {
  width: 940px;
  margin: 0 auto 0 auto;
}
```

In our earlier layouts, the `wrapper div` was wrapped around the entire layout. To create the full-width header and footer effect, we need to reuse this `wrapper div` inside the header and footer, in addition to wrapping the main content with it.

First, remove the wrapper from the markup completely. This will cause the columns to spread out across the full width of the viewport, as in Figure 9.11.

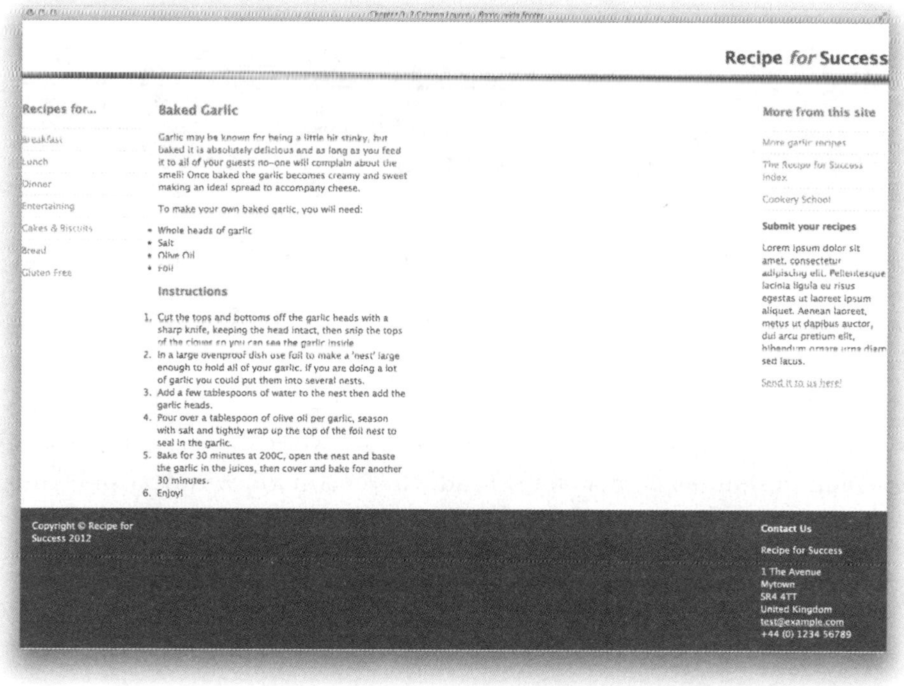

Figure 9.11. Removing the wrapper causes the columns to widen

We then put the wrapper back in after the closing `header div` end tag, so that it starts to wrap content from before the `subnav div`, and close it above the start of the `footer div`. This will pull the main content back into place on the page, leaving the header and footer spread out full width, as shown in Figure 9.12.

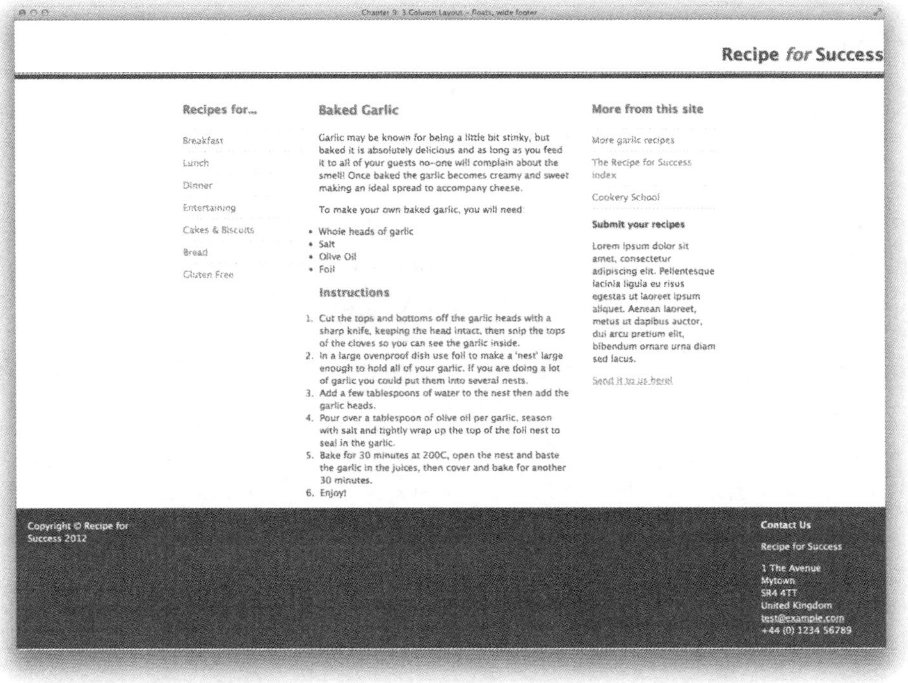

Figure 9.12. Wrapping the main content, with the header and footer spread out

Now use the wrapper class again to wrap `divs` around the contents of the header and footer, adding them directly after the opening `header` and `footer div` tags, and closing them before the corresponding end tags. This will bring the contents of the header and footer back into the centered position, while allowing the footer background and the bottom border on the header to remain full width, as in Figure 9.13.

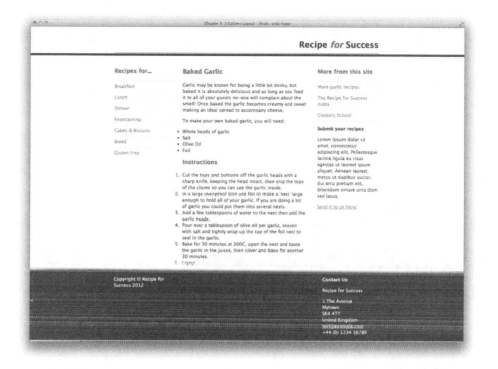

Figure 9.13. Header and footer contents have a background, and bottom border remains full width

We need to do a little bit of tidying up, removing the left and right padding on the footer and adding it back to the internal columns of content (on their width values). We want these columns to line up with the columns above them, as was shown earlier in Figure 9.10:

```
                          chapter_09/3col-wide-footer.css (excerpt)

/* remove the bottom border from the h1 and add to the new .inner */

.header h1 {
  font-size: 187.5%;
  padding-bottom: 10px;
  color: rgb(59,67,68);
}
.header .inner {
  border-bottom: 1px solid rgb(59,67,68);
  margin-bottom: 2px;
}

/* remove the left and right padding on footer and add back to
```

```
    internal columns */

.footer {
  clear: both;
  background-color: rgb(59,67,68);
  color: rgb(255,255,255);
  overflow: auto;
  padding: 20px 0 20px 0;
}

.footer .copy {
  float: left;
  width: 220px;
}

.footer .vcard {
  float: right;
  width: 220px;
}
```

In addition, because the thin border on the header was applied to the h1 nested inside it, that border is now contained within our wrapper div and won't run full width. To fix this, we can add an extra div with a class of inner just outside the header wrapper, and apply the border values to that in the stylesheet.

How do I create a design that works well on mobile devices?

Fixed-width layouts work well for desktop and are fairly easy to implement. We can calculate our widths in units of measurement that are easy to understand, work out our gutter widths, and achieve a pleasing design aesthetic. Increasingly, though, people aren't viewing the sites that we design on a desktop browser; instead, they're viewing content on smartphones or tablets, and these devices have a range of screen sizes and viewing formats.

Up until recently, the big debate was whether you should use a fixed-width layout—like the one we've been building in this chapter—or a **liquid layout**. A liquid layout stretches out to fit the browser window, and uses percentages for column measurements. Liquid layouts worked well when most people were using a fairly limited range of screen resolutions. Not so long ago, you'd mostly be dealing with resolutions between 800 by 600 pixels to 1,600 by 1,200 pixels. Creating a design that would look reasonable if stretched to 1,600 pixels but still worked at 800 was possible, although it did require compromise.

The problem with liquid layouts becomes obvious at large screen resolutions with the browser maximized: lines become very long and text hard to read. These layouts also struggle when viewed on mobile devices, as the columns then become tiny, often with a single word on each line.

Many website owners, developers, and designers have attempted to remedy this issue by maintaining completely separate, independent mobile sites. The problem with this technique is that modern mobile devices are very flexible when it comes to web page display, and users don't necessarily want to view a bare-bones, pared-down version of a site. They want to see *all* of the content, but want it displayed in a way that makes it easy to read on their device.

Solution

The best solution to supporting a wide range of devices with differing viewport widths is to use **responsive design**. Responsive design is quite a broad topic, but in a nutshell it involves flexible design methods that respond to a user's behavior and preferences when viewing websites. We're going to learn how to transform your fixed-width layout into a mobile-first responsive design.

There are no changes to the markup of the wide footer example in the section called "How do I create a fixed-width layout with a full-width header and footer?" apart from some stylesheet links, which we'll explore shortly; however, changes need to be made to the CSS. You can see the results of our responsive layouts in various browser sizes in Figure 9.14, Figure 9.15, and Figure 9.16. The rules for laying out text remain the same as our previous example:

chapter_09/3col-responsive.css *(excerpt)*

```
.wrapper {
  width: 90%;
  margin: 0 auto 0 auto;
}

@media only screen and (min-width: 768px) {
  .subnav {
```

```
    width: 31.42857%; /* 220/700 */
    float: left;
  }

  .article {
    float: right;
    width: 65.71428%; /* 460/700 */
  }

  .aside {
    width: 100%;
    clear: both;
  }

  .footer .copy {
    float: left;
    width: 31.42857%; /* 220/700 */
  }

  .footer .vcard {
    float: right;
    width: 31.42857%; /* 220/700 */
  }
}

@media only screen and (min-width: 992px) {
  .wrapper {
    max-width: 1180px;
  }

  .subnav {
    width: 23.404255%; /* 220/940 */
    margin-right: 2.1276596%; /* 20/940 */
  }

  .article {
    float: left;
    width: 46.808511%; /* 440/940 */
  }

  .aside {
    width: 23.404255%; /* 220/940 */
    float: right;
    clear: none; /* to counteract the clearing of the previous
      breakpoint */
```

```
    }

    .footer .copy {
      width: 23.404255%; /* 220/940 */
    }

    .footer .vcard {
      width: 23.404255%; /* 220/940 */
    }
}
```

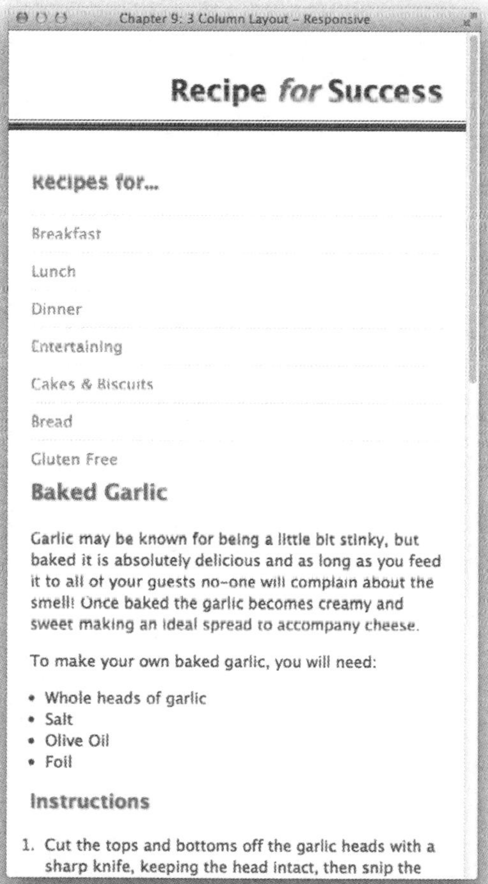

Figure 9.14. The layout as seen on a small device such as a smartphone

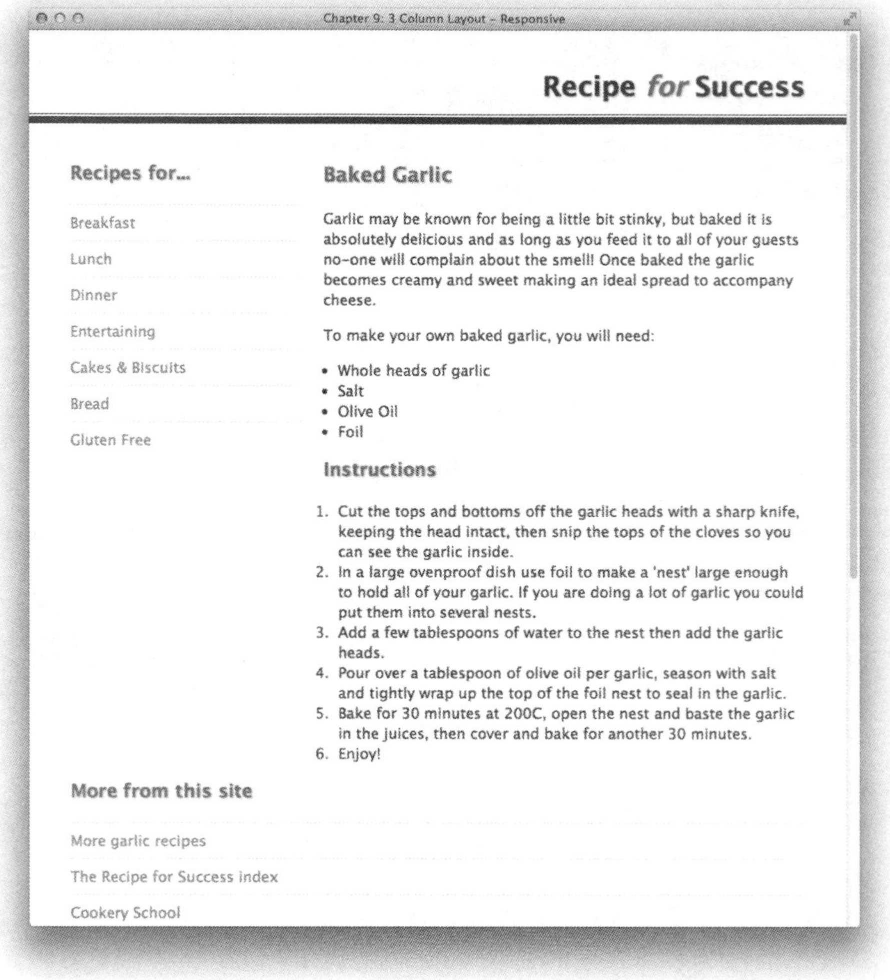

Figure 9.15. The layout as it would display on a tablet or midsized screen

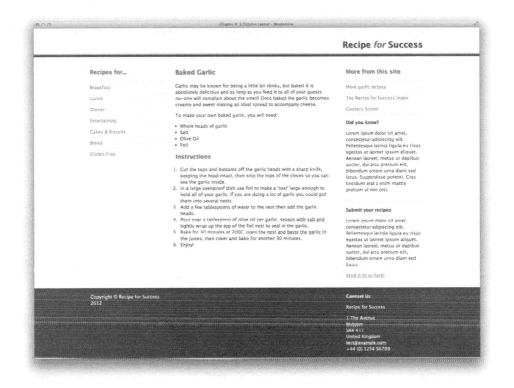

Figure 9.16. A regular desktop layout

Discussion

The majority of our stylesheet remains the same as in the section called "How do I create a fixed-width layout with a full-width header and footer?"; we want to display all our text styling in the top part of the document to all users, whether they're using a smartphone, a tablet, or a desktop browser.

We change the rule for `.wrapper`, removing the fixed 940-pixel width and replacing it with a value of 90%:

chapter_09/3col-responsive.css (excerpt)

```
.wrapper {
  width: 90%;
  margin: 0 auto 0 auto;
}
```

Our layout will now display as in Figure 9.17.

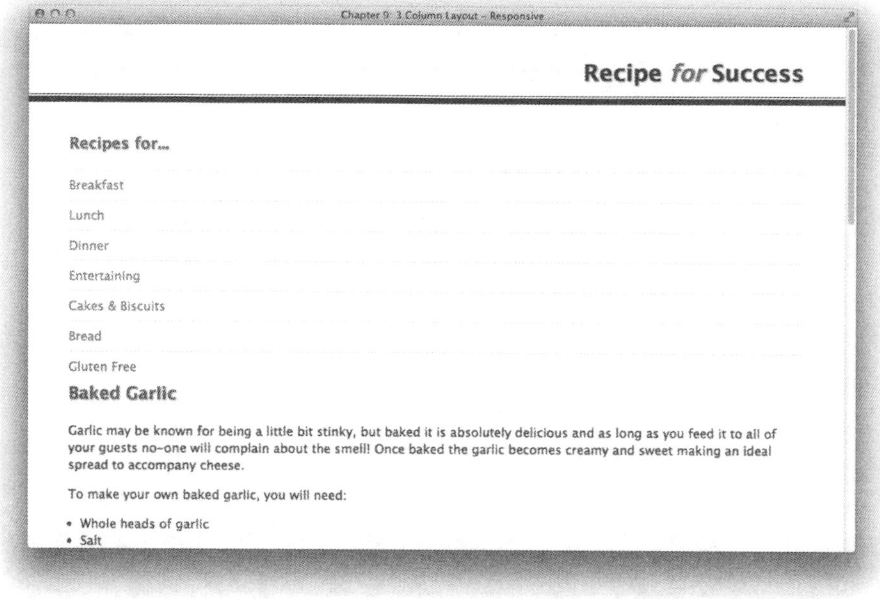

Figure 9.17. The default style for all devices

We now need to create our set of **media queries**, which you can see in our stylesheet. Media queries are part of the CSS3 specification and enable us to target devices by certain properties, such as their screen width. You can use media queries within a stylesheet as we have here, or in your HTML document, as we will do in a later example.

For this simple site, we're going to target three width-related breakpoints. First, we'll have a default stylesheet that will be used by all devices. Then we'll use a media query to check if the browser window is wider than 768 pixels. If it is, we'll arrange the content into two columns. Finally, we're also going to check for desktop widths by looking for screens wider than 992 pixels, in which the layout will display over three columns. The media queries we'll need are as follows:

```
@media only screen and (min-width: 768px) {
    /* css for 768 pixel width devices and wider goes here */
}

@media only screen and (min-width: 992px) {
    /* css for 992 pixel width devices and wider goes here */
}
```

Inside the section for `min-width: 768px`, we need to add code that will arrange our site into two columns. As we have a three-column layout—consisting of our `subnav`, `article`, and `aside`—we're going to drop the `aside div` below the other two columns at this width.

We need to be able to calculate the new widths of our columns, but as we've set the width of `.wrapper` to a percentage (90%), we're unsure what its *exact* width will be at this point. The actual viewport could be anywhere from 768 pixels to 991 pixels, and with the width of the wrapper set to 90%, that makes its potential exact width anywhere between 691 pixels and 892 pixels. This means we can't use pixels to size our individual columns; we need to calculate percentages.

First, we decide on an arbitrary width for `.wrapper` at this breakpoint that's between these two values; let's go with 700 pixels. The calculation that we need to remember is this: target / container = percentage.

So, our wrapper is 700 pixels wide and our `.subnav` is 220 pixels wide. We also want to leave a 20-pixel gutter between `.subnav` and `.article`; therefore, `.article` will be 460 pixels wide if we float these columns left and right respectively. We calculate the percentage width of `.subnav` as follows: 220/700 = 31.42857%.

We then calculate `.article`: 460/700 = 65.71428%. We can now enter these values as the column widths into our CSS. We also need to set our `.aside` to a width of 100%, and give it a rule of `clear: both` so that it drops underneath these first two columns:

chapter_09/3col-responsive.css *(excerpt)*

```css
@media only screen and (min-width: 768px) {
  .subnav {
    width: 31.42857%; /* 220/700 */
    float: left;
  }

  .article {
    float: right;
    width: 65.71428%; /* 460/700 */
  }

  .aside {
    width: 100%;
```

```
      clear: both;
   }
}
```

Okay, let's test it. Load the site in your browser, and pull your window down to a narrow view, so that the content displays as one column. Now stretch it out wider to see it rearrange itself into two columns. Your first fluid grid!

To tidy up this screen width, we can use the same width calculations to arrange the two chunks of footer content into two columns as we have had in previous examples. Our final media query for min-width: 768px is as follows:

chapter_09/3col-responsive.css (excerpt)

```css
@media only screen and (min-width: 768px) {
  .subnav {
    width: 31.42857%; /* 220/700 */
    float: left;
  }

  .article {
    float: right;
    width: 65.71428%; /* 460/700 */
  }

  .aside {
    width: 100%;
    clear: both;
  }

  .footer .copy {
    float: left;
    width: 31.42857%; /* 220/700 */
  }

  .footer .vcard {
    float: right;
    width: 31.42857%; /* 220/700 */
  }
}
```

Now let's create the three-column version, which will provide desktop-browser users with the same experience they had when they viewed the fixed-width version of our site.

Our completed `min-width: 992px` section follows. It should be fairly familiar to you from the previous width calculations, with a couple of exceptions:

chapter_09/3col-responsive.css *(excerpt)*

```
@media only screen and (min-width: 992px) {
  .wrapper {
    max-width: 1180px;
  }

  .subnav {
    width: 23.404255%; /* 220/940 */
    margin-right: 2.1276596%; /* 20/940 */
  }

  .article {
    float: left;
    width: 46.808511%; /* 440/940 */
  }

  .aside {
    width: 23.404255%; /* 220/940 */
    float: right;
    clear: none; /* to counteract the clearing of the previous
      breakpoint */
  }

  .footer .copy {
    width: 23.404255%; /* 220/940 */
  }

  .footer .vcard {
    width: 23.404255%; /* 220/940 */
  }
}
```

Our first task is to set `.wrapper` to have a maximum width of 1,180 pixels. What this does is stop the layout from being any wider than 1,180 pixels, so that users avoid the problem of content being laid out too widely to be readable.

Let's set our target container at 940 pixels wide in this version, and then use that to calculate our percentages. This time round, of course, we have three columns to calculate widths for.

With the first two columns both floated left, we need to add a `margin-right` to `.subnav` to stop `.article` colliding against it. We calculate the 20-pixel margin in exactly the same way as we calculate the column widths: 20 / 940 = 2.1276596%.

The final addition to this media query is to our `.aside`. In our previous media query, we gave it a rule of `clear: both`. Here, though, we need to unset this rule so that the other two columns aren't cleared, and the `.aside` floats up into its place on the far right of the layout.

Adding Some Device-specific Fixes

There are a couple of lines you will want to add to your HTML document if you're creating a responsive design. The first is a `meta` tag:

```
<meta name="viewport" content="width=device-width,
  target-densitydpi=160dpi, initial-scale=1.0" />
```

This `meta` tag means that mobile browsers will set the width of the browser viewport equal to the width of the device. If you've browsed the Web using a mobile device, you'll have noticed that your first view of a website is usually zoomed out. In the case of our earlier fixed-width, three-column layout, the first view you would be presented with on a smartphone is all three columns on the page; you'd need to zoom in to read the content you wanted to isolate.

As we've gone to the effort of creating a customized smartphone version of our layout, we want mobile browsers to display it zoomed in, and this `meta` tag will ensure this happens.

The second line we want to add to our HTML is a link—just above the closing `body` tag at the bottom of the page—to a JavaScript file:

```
<script src="ios-orientationchange-fix.js"></script>
```

I have included the file in the code archive, or you can download it from GitHub.[2]

---

[2] https://github.com/scottjehl/iOS-Orientationchange-Fix

This file fixes an orientation problem (at the time of writing),[3] where iOS devices may display a layout incorrectly when a user switches from landscape to portrait. At some point, Apple will no doubt fix this bug, and it will eventually only be an issue for older iOS devices still in circulation; hence, check that this is still a requirement when implementing your layouts.

Enquiries May Be Ignored

Versions of Internet Explorer earlier than IE9 offer no support for media queries, so they'll ignore all media query declarations within your CSS, thus serving only the mobile version of the site. See the section called "What about older browsers and responsive design?" for some suggestions as to how to accommodate visitors using these browsers.

So, that's it—we've created a simple responsive layout. Despite this being a basic project, the principles we've investigated remain the same for more complex responsive layouts, and we'll have a look at a slightly different example in the section called "How can I use responsive-design techniques when my site is image-heavy?"

How do I create a print stylesheet?

While we are ensuring that users on a range of mobile or desktop devices have a rewarding experience viewing our site, there's another group we should consider: those who wish to print content displayed on our site.

Solution

Fortunately, we can create a print-specific stylesheet for our site, as illustrated in Figure 9.18. We'll also need to add a `link` tag in the `head` of our HTML document that points to this standalone stylesheet:

```
chapter_09/3col-responsive.html (excerpt)

<link rel="stylesheet" href="3col-responsive.css" media="screen" />
  ⋮
<link rel="stylesheet" href="3col-responsive-print.css"
  media="print" />
```

---

[3] http://filamentgroup.com/lab/a_fix_for_the_ios_orientationchange_zoom_bug/

```css
body {
  background-color: rgb(255,255,255);
  color: rgb(0,0,0);
  padding: 20px;
  font: 1em/1.4 "Lucida Grande", "Lucida Sans Unicode",
    "Lucida Sans", Verdana, Tahoma, sans-serif;
}

h1, h2, h3 {
  margin: 0;
  padding: 0 0 1em 0;
}

p {
  margin:0;
  padding: 0 0 1em 0;
}

ul, ol {
  margin:0;
  padding: 0 0 1em 1em;
}


h1 {
  font-size: 137.5%;
}

h2 {
  font-size: 125%;
}

h3 {
  font-size: 100%;
}

a:link, a:visited {
  color: rgb(0,0,0);
}

.header {
  text-align: right;
  padding: 20px 0 0 0;
```

```css
  border-bottom: 8px solid rgb(0,0,0);
  margin-bottom: 40px;
}

.header h1 {
  font-size: 187.5%;
  padding-bottom: 10px;
}

.header .inner {
  border-bottom: 1px solid rgb(0,0,0);
  margin-bottom: 2px;
}

.header h1 span {
  font-style: italic;
}

.footer {
  border-top: 1px solid rgb(0,0,0);
  padding: 20px 0 20px 0;
  overflow: auto;
}

.wrapper {
  width: 90%;
  margin: 0 auto 0 auto;
}

.subnav {
  display: none;
}

.aside {
  display: none;
}

.footer .vcard {
  display: none;
}
```

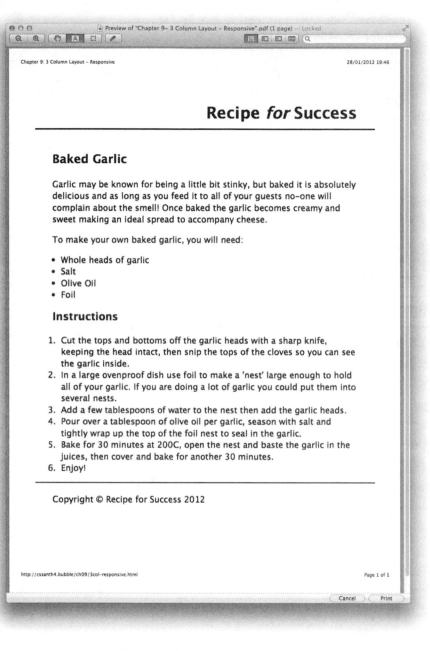

Figure 9.18. Our layout in a print preview

Discussion

Our example site is a recipe site, so it's highly likely that people will want to print out the recipes to refer to them in the kitchen. We can customize a separate print stylesheet to ensure that users only print out the recipe itself, and not the navigation area or other elements on the site that are unnecessary for their purpose.

The first action is to set the media attribute on the link to our original stylesheet to screen. The means that the main stylesheet (**3col-responsive.css**) will only be used when the site is displayed onscreen. We then add a second link tag pointing to our print-specific stylesheet; this has a media attribute of print. Browsers will use this stylesheet to render the document ready to be printed out.

We can now set some basic CSS for the print-view text. Our first task is to go through the stylesheet and set any element on the page that we don't want users to print to display: none:

```
chapter_09/3col-responsive-print.css (excerpt)
.subnav {
  display: none;
}

.aside {
  display: none;
}

.footer .vcard {
  display: none;
}
```

We can then go and tweak other styles to suit a printed copy of our web page; for instance, eliminating the color and text-shadow properties on our h1s, h2s, and h3s, and deleting our a:hover selector altogether. We'll test in our browser's print preview facility until we're happy with the result.

Think of the Ink

When creating a print stylesheet, think about how the content to be printed will be used. The Automobile Association (AA) website in the UK allows you to print out driving directions, for example, and the print stylesheet for the site prints out map directions using a large font size, which is useful when you're trying to navigate while driving. Many browsers won't print out background colors and images, so make sure everything remains legible.

Furthermore, unless you're creating a multicolumn layout for print, either avoid setting widths on containers or set them to **100%**; that way the content will fit the page nicely, whatever size the paper is used for printing.

If your content has a lot of inline links, you can use generated content to display a URL after its corresponding link in the printed document by adding the following CSS:

```
a:link:after {
   content: " (" attr(href) ") ";
}
```

Finally, be considerate of your user's ink supply: set large images to `display: none` and hide advertising banners.

How can I use responsive-design techniques when my site is image-heavy?

Our responsive layout has behaved nicely, but so far it's only comprised text—an unlikely scenario for most modern websites. How can we use images in responsive design without them breaking out of their bounding boxes?

Solution

The design shown in Figure 9.19, Figure 9.20, Figure 9.21, Figure 9.22, and Figure 9.23 is a photography portfolio design containing a number of images. It also complies to a strict grid layout, no matter what screen width you view it at. Here's our foundation HTML markup, followed by a series of specific stylesheets applying to each grid layout:

```
                                        chapter_09/responsive.html
<!DOCTYPE html>
<html>
<head>
  <meta charset="utf-8" />
```

```
    <title>Chapter 9: Responsive images</title>

    <meta name="viewport" content="width=device-width,
      target-densitydpi=160dpi, initial-scale=1.0" />

    <link rel="stylesheet" href="responsive-basic.css" />
    <link rel="stylesheet" media="only screen and (min-width: 460px)"
      href="responsive-410.css" />
    <link rel="stylesheet" media="only screen and (min-width: 768px)"
      href="responsive-700.css" />
    <link rel="stylesheet" media="only screen and (min-width: 992px)"
      href="responsive-940.css" />
    <link rel="stylesheet" media="only screen and (min-width: 1280px)"
      href="responsive-1180.css" />

    <!--[if (lt IE 9) & (!IEMobile)]>
      <script src="selectivizr-min.js"></script>
      <link rel="stylesheet" href="responsive-ie-old.css" />
    <![endif]-->

</head>
<body>
  <div class="header">
    <div class="wrapper">
      <h1>My Portfolio</h1>

      <ul class="nav">
        <li><a href="">About</a></li>
        <li><a href="">Photos</a></li>
        <li><a href="">Contact</a></li>
      </ul>
    </div>
  </div>

  <div class="wrapper">
    <div class="feature">
      <img src="gallery/main.jpg" alt="path from the coast to
        Dunstanburgh Castle, Northumberland" />
      <div class="caption">Dunstanburgh Castle, Northumberland</div>
    </div>

    <div class="intro">
      <h2>A trip to Northumberland</h2>
      <p>The photos in this gallery were taken on a recent trip to
        Northumberland in the North East of the United Kingdom.</p>
```

```
      <p>The North-East coast is my favourite place in the world.
        It can get very cold and windy but you are rewarded for
        braving the elements by an amazing coastline, castles and
        the opportunity to see puffins and terns on the Farne
        Islands.</p>
  </div>

  <div class="gallery">
    <ul>
      <li><img src="gallery/one.jpg" alt="Dunstanburgh Castle"
        width="280" />
        <span class="caption">Dunstanburgh Castle</span>
      </li>
      <li><img src="gallery/two.jpg" alt="Dunstanburgh Castle"
        width="280" />
        <span class="caption">Dunstanburgh Castle</span>
      </li>
      <li><img src="gallery/three.jpg" alt="Lindisfarne Abbey
        ruins" width="280" />
        <span class="caption">Lindisfarne Abbey ruins</span>
      </li>
      <li><img src="gallery/four.jpg" alt="Dunstanburgh Castle"
        width="280" />
        <span class="caption">Dunstanburgh Castle</span>
      </li>
      <li><img src="gallery/five.jpg" alt="Lindisfarne Abbey
        ruins" width="280" />
        <span class="caption">Lindisfarne Abbey ruins</span>
      </li>
      <li><img src="gallery/six.jpg" alt="Lindisfarne Abbey ruins"
        width="280" />
        <span class="caption">Lindisfarne Abbey ruins</span>
      </li>
      <li><img src="gallery/seven.jpg" alt="Lily" width="280" />
        <span class="caption">Lily</span>
      </li>
      <li><img src="gallery/eight.jpg" alt="Lily" width="280" />
        <span class="caption">Lily</span>
      </li>
      <li><img src="gallery/nine.jpg" alt="Glasshouses"
        width="280" />
        <span class="caption">Glasshouses</span>
      </li>
      <li><img src="gallery/ten.jpg" alt="Beach at Craster"
        width="280" />
```

```
        <span class="caption">Beach at Craster</span>
      </li>
    </ul>
  </div>
</div>

<div class="footer">
  <div class="wrapper">
    <p>All photos &copy; Rachel Andrew | Find me on
      <a href="http://www.flickr.com/photos/rachelandrew/">
      Flickr</a></p>
  </div>
</div>

<script src="ios-orientationchange-fix.js"></script>
</body>
</html>
```

chapter_09/responsive-basic.css

```css
body {
  margin: 0;
  padding: 0;
  font: 1em/1.4 "Lucida Grande", "Lucida Sans Unicode",
    "Lucida Sans", Verdana, Tahoma, sans-serif;
  background-color: rgb(255,255,255);
  color: rgb(59,67,68);
}

.wrapper {
  width: 90%;
  margin: 0 auto 0 auto;
}

img {
  max-width: 100%;
  display: block;
}

h1,h2,h3 {
  margin: 0;
  padding: 0;
}

h2 {
```

```
    font-size: 125%;
    padding: 0 0 1em 0;
}

p {
    margin: 0;
    padding: 0 0 1em 0;
}

ul {
    margin: 0;
    padding: 0;
}

a:link, a:visited {
    color: rgb(122,106,83);
}

.header {
    background-color: rgb(59,67,68);
    color: rgb(255,255,255);
    border-bottom: 1px solid rgb(0,0,0);
    margin-bottom: 1em;
}

.header .wrapper {
    position: relative;
}

.header h1 {
    display: inline-block;
    padding: 1em 0 0.3em 0;
    font-size: 125%;
    font-weight: normal;
    text-shadow: 1px 1px 2px rgba(0,0,0,0.7);
}

.header .nav  {
    padding-bottom: 1em;
}

.header .nav li {
    display: inline;
    font-size: 125%;
    color: rgb(255,255,255);
```

```
    padding: 0 0.5em 0 0;
    text-shadow: 1px 1px 2px rgba(0,0,0,0.7);
}

.header .nav a:link, .header .nav a:visited {
    text-decoration: none;
    color: rgb(255,255,255);
}

.feature  {
    background-color: rgb(59,67,68);
    color: rgb(255,255,255);
    margin: 0 0 1em 0;
}

.caption {
    padding: 0.3em;
    font-size: 87.5%;
    text-shadow: 1px 1px 2px rgba(0,0,0,0.7);
}

.gallery ul {
    list-style-type: none;
    margin: 0 0 1em 0;
    padding: 0;
}

.footer {
    border-top: 1px solid rgb(59,67,68);
    font-size: 87.5%;
    padding: 1em 0 1em 0;
}
```

Figure 9.19. The mobile layout uses just the **responsive-basic.css** stylesheet

chapter_09/responsive-410.css *(excerpt)*

```
.gallery {
  overflow: hidden;
  clear: both;
}

.gallery li {
  float: left;
  width: 48.78048%;
  margin: 0 0 2.43902% 2.43902%;
}

.gallery li:nth-child(2n+1) {
  margin-left: 0;
}
```

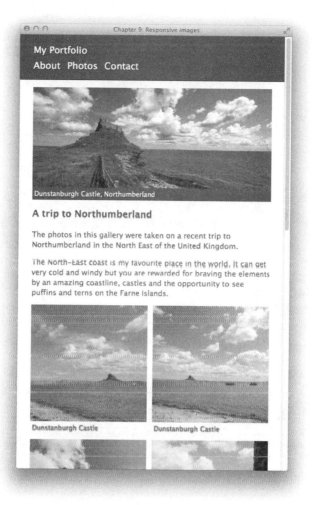

Figure 9.20. A slightly wider display arranges the images into a two-column grid

chapter_09/responsive-700.css *(excerpt)*

```css
.header .nav {
  position: absolute;
  top: 20px;
  right: 0;
  list-style-type: none;
}

.header h1 {
  padding: 20px 0 20px 0;
  font-size: 175%;
```

```
}

.header .nav li {
  font-size: 175%;
}

.gallery li:nth-child(n) {
  width: 31.42857%;
  margin: 0 0 2.85714% 2.85714%;
}

.gallery li:nth-child(3n+1) {
  margin-left: 0;
}
```

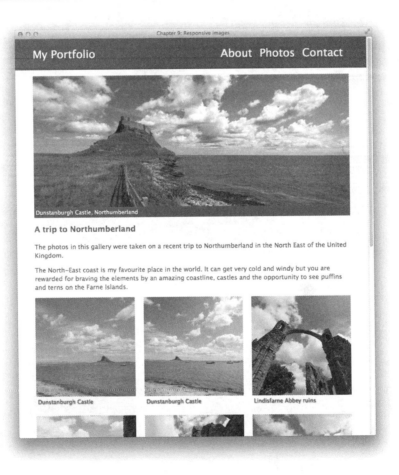

Figure 9.21. On a tablet we see the images across three columns

chapter_09/responsive-940.css *(excerpt)*

```css
.gallery {
  overflow: hidden;
  clear: both;
}

.gallery li:nth-child(n) {
  width: 23.40425%;
  margin: 0 0 2.12765% 2.12765%;
}

.gallery li:nth-child(4n+1) {
  margin-left: 0;
}
```

Figure 9.22. The small desktop view shows images across four columns

```css
.wrapper {
  max-width: 1180px;
}

.feature {
  float: left;
  width: 79.66101%;
}

.intro {
  float: right;
  width: 18.64406%;
}

.gallery li:nth-child(n) {
  width: 18.64406%;
  margin: 0 0 1.69491% 1.69491%;
}

.gallery li:nth-child(5n+1) {
  margin-left: 0;
}
```

Figure 9.23. On a very wide screen, we move the introductory text next to the large image

Discussion

If you look at this design in a browser, you'll discover that not only does the grid scale between width breakpoints, the images do as well. To facilitate this, we need to add a very simple rule in our CSS:

chapter_09/responsive-basic.css (excerpt)

```css
img {
  max-width: 100%;
}
```

When we set this rule, all images' maximum widths will be, at most, equal to the width of the image itself; they'll display smaller as their containers shrink when the browser is resized.

We can see this behavior by looking at the large feature image, **main.jpg**. We use the same image on all screen sizes, but it scales right down to neatly fit our mobile layout, or up to its full size on a desktop layout.

 Size Matters

If you're thinking that it's not ideal having mobile users download images with large footprints, you'd be right. At the time of writing, however, this problem doesn't have an easy solution. Responsive design is a new field, and serving responsive images at appropriate sizes for various viewport dimensions is something that is being discussed at length within the web community. Searching for the phrase "responsive images" should bring up the latest thinking on the issue, and there are helpful tools[4] and articles[5] popping up on the Web all the time.

If you are just using a single image, optimize the image as much as possible, and make sure it is no larger than it needs to be for the largest width it will display at. Don't let the fact that you are using responsive images make you avoid resizing and optimizing your images before uploading them to your site!

Now we can look at the rest of our layout.

As with our recipe website, we'll use a **mobile-first strategy**, but this time we're going to employ separate stylesheets. Mobile-first means that we only load the stylesheets that the device being used can actually utilize. Our **responsive-basic.css** stylesheet is the file that we expect all devices to download and use, so it contains all our basic formatting. It's linked into our HTML document with a regular `link` element:

```
<link rel="stylesheet" href="responsive-basic.css" />
```

With this stylesheet in play, our image gallery will display in a linear fashion, one image below another.

Next, let's add a stylesheet that will be used by a browser viewport wider than or equal to 460 pixels:

---

[4] http://adaptive-images.com/
[5] http://www.cloudfour.com/responsive-imgs-part-2/

```
<link rel="stylesheet" media="only screen and (min-width: 460px)"
  href="responsive-410.css" />
```

The media attribute used here is just like the media query we used within our CSS for the recipe website. In this stylesheet, we're using a grid that is 410 pixels wide with six columns of 60 pixels, each with a ten-pixel gutter. The dimensions of this grid will help us work out the calculations for the percentage widths we need:

```
gutter = 10px | 2.43902%
1 = 60px  | 14.63414%
2 = 130px | 31.70731%
3 = 200px | 48.78048%
4 = 270px | 65.85365%
5 = 340px | 82.92682%
6 = 410px | 100%
```

In this stylesheet, we'll set .gallery to overflow: hidden so that it contains the floated elements inside. We can then float our gallery list items left, and give each a percentage width of 48.78048%. We obtain this value from the three-column width calculation.

 Spacing Issues

In Chapter 8, we looked at a gallery example that used display: inline-block for layout purposes. Ideally, we would use that here, but inline-block preserves whitespace and creates gaps between elements, unfortunately. Counteracting this can be problematic; spacing can be inconsistent between browsers, so where the calculations are vital (as in this layout), I've reverted to using floats.

If you can remove all the whitespace between the li elements—for example, if you're generating your content from a server-side script and can ensure the script outputs no whitespace—you would be safe to replace the float here with inline-block.

As you'll discover, CSS development tends to involve a range of compromises, and it pays to have a few tricks up your sleeve when deciding what works best in each circumstance.

We also add a left and bottom margin of 2.43902%, the calculation we arrived at in evaluating gutters of 10 pixels:

```
                                chapter_09/responsive-410.css (excerpt)

.gallery {
  overflow: hidden;
  clear: both;
}

.gallery li {
  float: left;
  width: 48.78048%;
  margin: 0 0 2.43902% 2.43902%;
}
```

Finally, we need to remove the left-hand margin on the *first* and *every other* li using the nth-child selector:

```
                                chapter_09/responsive-410.css (excerpt)

.gallery li:nth-child(2n+1) {
  margin-left: 0;
}
```

This creates the layout shown in Figure 9.20.

We can now move on to our tablet layout. We'll link to this stylesheet once again using a media query:

```
<link rel="stylesheet" media="only screen and (min-width: 768px)"
  href="responsive-700.css" />
```

This stylesheet is working from a width of 700 pixels; that's nine columns of 60 pixels, with gutters in between that are 20 pixels wide. Here are our calculations:

```
gutter = 20px | 2.85714%
1 = 60px  | 8.57142%
2 = 140px | 20%
3 = 220px | 31.42857%
4 = 300px | 42.85714%
5 = 380px | 54.28571%
6 = 460px | 65.71428%
7 = 540px | 77.14285%
8 = 620px | 88.57142%
9 = 700px | 100%
```

The stylesheet that we need to use follows. At this breakpoint, we have enough room in the header to move the navigation menu onto the same line as the h1 element (**My Portfolio**), as well as increase the size of this text:

chapter_09/responsive-700.css *(excerpt)*

```
.header .nav {
  position: absolute;
  top: 20px;
  right: 0;
  list-style-type: none;
}

.header h1 {
  padding: 20px 0 20px 0;
  font-size: 175%;
}

.header .nav li {
  font-size: 175%;
}
```

We then recalculate our column widths so that we end up with three images on each row of the grid, each being three columns in width:

```
.gallery li {
  width: 31.42857%;
  margin: 0 0 2.85714% 2.85714%;
}
```

Finally, we need to change the .gallery li selector so that the first and every *third* list item thereafter (:nth-child(3n+1)) has no left margin. However, in addition to implementing its own rules, this stylesheet will also inherit the CSS rules from the stylesheet before it; in particular, **responsive-410.css**. Here we removed the left margin on the first and every *second* list item thereafter. This isn't what we want in our new stylesheet and corresponding screen size; we need to update the margin-left property for our .gallery li:nth-child(2n+1) selector with our new gutter width:

```
.gallery li:nth-child(2n+1) {
  margin-left: 2.85714%;
}

.gallery li:nth-child(3n+1) {
  margin-left: 0;
}
```

Of course, we could refine this markup by writing a rule for all `.gallery` `li`s as well as our `:nth-child(2n+1)` items using `:nth-child(n)`:

chapter_09/responsive-700.css *(excerpt)*

```
.gallery li:nth-child(n) {
  width: 31.42857%;
  margin-left: 2.85714%;
}

.gallery li:nth-child(3n+1) {
  margin-left: 0;
}
```

Now all items will have a correct column width, but because we have placed our `:nth-child(3n+1)` selector at the end, specificity determines that each first, fourth, seventh (etc) item will have its `margin-left` value overridden with a value of 0.

Keep Checking Your Stylesheets

As you move up through layouts of different widths, check whether you need to update anything done in an earlier stylesheet.

Now let's deal with our desktop layouts, inserting another `link` into our HTML document's `head`:

```
<link rel="stylesheet" media="only screen and (min-width: 992px)"
  href="responsive-940.css" />
```

This layout still uses an overall 940-pixel width grid of 12 columns of 60 pixels each, separated by 20-pixel gutters:

```
gutter = 20px | 2.12765%
1 = 60px  | 6.38297%
2 = 140px | 14.89361%
3 = 220px | 23.40425%
4 = 300px | 31.91489%
5 = 380px | 40.42553%
6 = 460px | 48.93617%
7 = 540px | 57.4468%
8 = 620px | 65.95744%
9 = 700px | 74.46808%
10 = 780px | 82.97872%
11 = 860px | 91.48936%
12 = 940px | 100%
```

We display four images to each row, and thus add a margin-left: 0 value to our first item and every *fourth* thereafter (:nth-child(4n+1)). As we did in our **responsive-700.css** stylesheet, we need to remember to update :nth-child selectors from previous stylesheets to our recalculated gutter widths:

chapter_09/responsive-940.css *(excerpt)*

```
.gallery li:nth-child(n) {
  width: 23.40425%;
  margin: 0 0 2.12765% 2.12765%;
}


.gallery li:nth-child(4n+1) {
  margin-left: 0;
}
```

Nearly there! Last of all, we can add the link to our wide desktop stylesheet:

```
<link rel="stylesheet" media="only screen and (min-width: 1280px)"
  href="responsive-1180.css" />
```

To prevent our layout from becoming too wide, we set .wrapper to a maximum width of 1180 pixels:

chapter_09/responsive-1180.css *(excerpt)*

```
.wrapper {
  max-width: 1180px;
}
```

We can also calculate our grid from that width: 15 columns, 60 pixels wide, with 20-pixel gutters:

```
gutter = 20px | 1.69491%
1 = 60px | 5.08474%
2 = 140px | 11.8644%
3 = 220px | 18.64406%
4 = 300px | 25.42372%
5 = 380px | 32.20338%
6 = 460px | 38.98305%
7 = 540px | 45.76271%
8 = 620px | 52.54237%
9 = 700px | 59.32203%
10 = 780px | 66.10169%
11 = 860px | 72.88135%
12 = 940px | 79.66101%
13 = 1020 | 86.44067%
14 = 1100 | 93.22033%
15 = 1180 | 100%
```

We can capitalize on the space afforded to us by this screen width by changing the layout of the feature and intro divs, floating the first element left and the second right. Let's have feature take up 12 columns, and intro three columns:

chapter_09/responsive-1180.css *(excerpt)*

```
.feature {
  float: left;
  width: 79.66101%;
}

.intro {
  float: right;
  width: 18.64406%;
}
```

Now we can recalculate the widths of our list items and the margins on the first and every *fifth* element thereafter. Our gallery images each take up three columns, and this means that the image in the `feature` `div` will line up with the first four images in the gallery below it—with `intro` sitting in a column that lines up with the fifth image below it:

chapter_09/responsive-1180.css *(excerpt)*

```
.gallery li:nth-child(n) {
  width: 18.64406%;
  margin: 0 0 1.69491% 1.69491%;
}

.gallery li:nth-child(5n+1) {
  margin-left: 0;
}
```

That's it! You have a responsive, image-heavy layout that complies with a strict grid.

When creating these layouts, I tend to calculate my column widths and gutters just as we did at the start of each stylesheet here. It certainly pays to insert the calculations in a block comment at the start of your stylesheet. There are also a number of grid frameworks available that use this same basic technique, which you may find useful.

What about older browsers and responsive design?

It's impossible to discuss responsive design without considering older browser support. In the section called "How do I create a design that works well on mobile devices?", we added a JavaScript file to provide a fix for a bug in iOS devices, but what can we use to accommodate older browsers that don't deal so well with modern responsive design techniques?

Solution

As already mentioned, Internet Explorer below IE9 doesn't support media queries. If a user is viewing our previous example sites in Internet Explorer 6, 7, or 8, they'll be presented with the view rendered by our basic, mobile-specific stylesheet. These browsers will completely ignore the media queries we inserted into our CSS, as well as the separate stylesheets we created and linked to in our HTML document.

There are two possible solutions to this issue. The first is to use a JavaScript polyfill called Respond.js that causes these older browsers to load the CSS rules within the media queries. A polyfill is simply a piece of code or plugin that takes care of functionality you'd expect a browser to perform natively.

You can download the Respond.js project from GitHub.[6] Remember to read the attached notes to ensure that your stylesheets can be parsed by the script.

The second solution is what I tend to do in production, and that is *not* to try to serve media queries to old versions of Internet Explorer at all. Instead, I add a separate stylesheet (or stylesheets) that sets Internet Explorer to display the site at a fixed width as in the CSS below. The result can be seen in Figure 9.24:

chapter_09/responsive.html (excerpt)

```html
<!--[if (lt IE 9) & (!IEMobile)]>
  <link rel="stylesheet" href="responsive-ie-old.css" />
<![endif]-->
```

chapter_09/responsive-ie-old.css

```css
.wrapper {
  width: 940px;
}

.header .nav {
  position: absolute;
  top: 20px;
  right: 0;
  list-style-type: none;
}

.header h1 {
  padding: 20px 0 20px 0;
  font-size: 175%;
}
```

---

[6] https://github.com/scottjehl/Respond

```
.header .nav li {
  font-size: 175%;
}

.feature img {
  width: 940px;
}

.gallery {
  overflow: hidden;
  clear: both;
  width: 960px;
  margin-left: -20px;
}

.gallery li {
  float: left;
  width: 220px;
  margin: 0 0 20px 20px;
}

.gallery li img {
  display: block;
  height: 220px;
  width: 220px;
}
```

Figure 9.24. Our fixed-width layout in Internet Explorer 8

Discussion

The CSS for this solution should look fairly straightforward. Remember that Internet Explorer versions lower than IE9 receive no positioning information from your media query-linked stylesheets, so you need to add all the rules that you want applied in your IE-only stylesheet.

Here, we've fixed the width of `.wrapper` to 940 pixels, and then set the widths of other elements in pixels too—just as we would have done had we been creating a fixed-width layout from the outset.

Another issue we can take care of in this stylesheet is to compensate for Internet Explorer not supporting the `nth-child` selector prior to IE9. Instead of using `nth-child` to remove the left margin on list elements as they wrap around each row with the browser's resizing, we can use an old trick: setting a negative left margin on

`.gallery`, and then ignoring the extra left margin on each `.gallery li`. These left margins will be counteracted by the negative margin set on the gallery itself:

chapter_09/responsive-ie-old.css *(excerpt)*

```css
.gallery {
  overflow: hidden;
  clear: both;
  width: 960px;
  margin-left: -20px;
}

.gallery li {
  float: left;
  width: 220px;
  margin: 0 0 20px 20px;
}
```

We've also set widths and heights on images, as there's no need for them to respond to changing column widths anymore. If you go back as far as IE6, you'll find that `max-width` has no support, so the images will display at their largest size.

If you're going to polyfill Internet Explorer's lack of support for media queries, you'd do well to read Ethan Marcotte's article on fluid images,[7] which includes some tips for working with old versions of IE.

 Leave IE till Last

> I usually create my old-IE stylesheet right at the end of development. That way, I can just copy in the rules that are needed from the other stylesheets, rather than having to constantly remember adding them throughout the development process.

Whether you try to polyfill media queries or just serve older browsers a fixed-width stylesheet is up to you. As always, check what browsers visitors to your site are using and formulate a browser support policy based on that.

---

[7] http://unstoppablerobotninja.com/entry/fluid-images/

What is the future of CSS layouts?

At the beginning of this chapter, I mentioned that there have been fewer practical, usable advances for CSS layouts than we've seen in other parts of the specification. However, this is about to change, and I hope that by the time a fifth edition of this book comes out, we'll have the browser support to really take advantage of these new features.

So, just as a quick glance into the future, and to give you some extras to play with in your own time to keep your skills up to date, let's have a look at the tools we hope to be able to use soon.

CSS3 Grid Layout

The CSS3 Grid Layout is currently a W3C Working Draft[8] and at the time of writing is implemented only in Internet Explorer 10 Developer Preview, with an –ms prefix. What's exciting about Grid Layout is that it will enable the sort of control you have when laying a site out using tables, but is not tied to **source-ordered content**—that is, placing your most important content at the beginning of your HTML document. This would be incredibly useful for responsive design.

Currently, when creating a complex responsive design we have to think very carefully about the order of the HTML source. We want it to be able to collapse to one column in a usable way if necessary, but still enable us to float the columns into the right position for multicolumn layouts.

There's an alternate proposal for Grid Layout in the CSS Template Layout Module.[9] This is also currently in Working Draft, but with no browser implementation at present.

Flexible Box Layout Module

Also in Working Draft is the Flexible Box Layout Module,[10] another potentially useful module when working with responsive designs.

---

[8] http://www.w3.org/TR/css3-grid-layout/
[9] http://www.w3.org/TR/css3-layout/
[10] http://www.w3.org/TR/2009/WD-css3-flexbox-20090723/

Currently, we have no good way of vertically centering elements, or placing a set of elements inside a box and using CSS to say "spread these items out evenly." These are problems that the Flexible Box Layout Module should solve. Where Grid Layout should solve our full-page layout problems, flexible boxes will solve many of the small issues we have with components in our layouts.

Support is reasonably good for flexible boxes; it's included in IE10 Preview, and Firefox and Chrome have implemented it in recent releases. There's also a polyfill called flexie.js,[11] which provides cross-browser support for the module, and the developers of **flexie.js** have created a Flexbox Playground[12] for you to experiment inside, as seen in Figure 9.25.

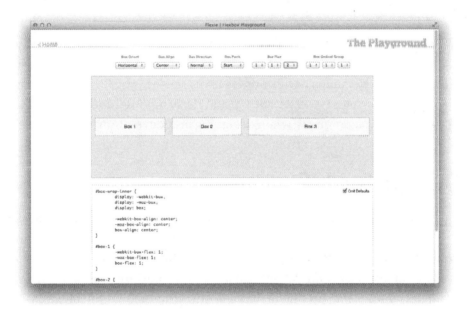

Figure 9.25. The Flexbox Playground

CSS Multicolumn Layout Module

Another module with reasonable cross-browser support is CSS3 Multicolumn Layout Module.[13] This module is at Candidate Recommendation stage, the next stage up from Working Draft. With the exception of Internet Explorer, it's implemented in

---

[11] http://flexiejs.com
[12] http://flexiejs.com/playground/
[13] http://www.w3.org/TR/css3-multicol/

current browsers, and is also part of IE10 Developer Preview, so we can assume it will make it into Internet Explorer 10.

Multicolumn layouts will enable us to create newspaper-style columns of equal measurements by adding a `column-count` property to the containing element:

```
.article {
  column-count: 3;
}
```

There are also properties for controlling the width of columns, setting points where you want content to break, and balancing columns so that they all end up the same length.

Once Internet Explorer 10 is released—which will mean that all current browsers provide support for much that's included in the above modules—I expect that we'll see more and more examples of developers using these new CSS layout properties. The future of CSS layouts is very exciting, and these modules mean that we'll have to make far fewer compromises when designing and developing CSS layouts than we do at present.

A Design for Life

In this chapter, we've seen how to use the fundamental building blocks of CSS layout to create responsive designs for all web users, regardless of what device they're using. More complex designs use the same techniques to structure the different components of a layout. When you come to tackle any design, try to break it down into its component parts—the main layout structure and the elements inside —and then approach their positioning in the simplest way possible.

You'll sometimes need to make compromises to deal with the thorny issues of browser support, but as we've seen, CSS for layout is improving all the time. Browsers now support the older tools of our trade more consistently—such as floats and positioning—with support arriving for new and exciting CSS3 modules.

This is an exciting time to be a web designer or developer! Whether you're reading this book as a newcomer to CSS, or as an old hand refreshing your skills, I hope you continue to experiment and build on the tips and tricks we've studied together.

Index

Symbols

(hash), 9
* (asterisk), 71, 256–258, 265
+ (plus sign), 11
. (period), 8
: (colon), 12, 15
:: (double colon), 15
> (greater-than), 10
{}, 6

A

absolute positioning, 320–324
absolute-size keywords, 29–30
accessibility issues
    AJAX, 266
    color, 115–116
    forms, 247–248, 264–266
    tables, 177–180
active pseudo-class, 36–37
adjacent selector, 11, 47–49
after pseudo-element, 17
AJAX, 266
ARIA (Accessible Rich Internet Applications), 265
asterisk (*), 71, 256–258, 265
attribute selectors, 17–18, 148–151
ayouts
    image-heavy, 382–401

B

background color
    accessibility issues, 115–116
    in headings, 43–44
    on page, 80–82
    removing, 221
background gradients, 93–97
background images
    adding, 80–82
    content images vs, 93, 116
    for elements, 90–93, 99–102
    fixing position, 88–90
    as gradients, 95
    multiple, 99–102
    order of, 100–102
    positioning, 85–88
    scaling to window size, 97–99
    tiling, 82, 83–85
background property, 89–90, 99
background-attachment property, 88–90
background-color property, 82
background-image property, 82, 93–95
background-position property, 85–88
background-repeat property, 83–85
Basic User Interface Module (BUI), 242, 266
before pseudo-element, 16–17
behavior property, 283
beveled effect, 232
blink effect, 34
block-level elements, 302–305, 306, 319
blockquote element, 55
border property, 80, 189
border-collapse property, 185–186
border-radius property, 110–112, 142, 280–282
borders
    image, 77–80

Congratulations on Finishing the Book

Are you ready to scale the heights of CSS?

Test yourself with our online quiz. With questions based on the content in the book, only true CSS warriors can achieve a perfect score.

Take the Quiz Here:

http://www.sitepoint.com/quiz-cssant

Hey ...

Thanks for buying this book. We really appreciate your support!

We'd like to think that you're now a "Friend of SitePoint," and so would like to invite you to our special "Friends of SitePoint" page.

Here you can SAVE up to 43% on a range of other super-cool SitePoint products.

Save over 40% with this link:

Link: 🌐 sitepoint.com/friends

Password: friends